P9-CBX-094

ARCO

PREPARATION FOR THE

PRAXIS II™

EXAM

18th Edition

ARCO

PREPARATION FOR THE
PRAXIS II™
EXAM

18ᵗʰ Edition

Joan U. Levy
Norman Levy

THOMSON
—★—
PETERSON'S

Australia • Canada • Mexico • Singapore • Spain • United Kingdom • United States

An ARCO Book

ARCO is a registered trademark of Thomson Learning, Inc., and is used herein under license by Thomson Peterson's.

About Thomson Peterson's

Thomson Peterson's (www.petersons.com) is a leading provider of education information and advice, with books and online resources focusing on education search, test preparation, and financial aid. Its Web site offers searchable databases and interactive tools for contacting educational institutions, online practice tests and instruction, and planning tools for securing financial aid. Peterson's serves 110 million education consumers annually.

For more information, contact Peterson's, 2000 Lenox Drive, Lawrenceville, NJ 08648; 800-338-3282; or find us on the World Wide Web at www.petersons.com/about

© 2005 Thomson Peterson's, a part of The Thomson Corporation
Thomson Learning™ is a trademark used herein under license.

Previous editions © 1990, 1994, 1996, 1998, 2001, 2002, 2003, 2004

Editor: Wallie Walker Hammond; Production Editor: Teresina Jonkoski;
Manufacturing Manager: Ivona Skibicki; Composition Manager: Melissa Ignatowski;
Cover Design: Chris Chattin

ALL RIGHTS RESERVED. No part of this work covered by the copyright herein may be reproduced or used in any form or by any means—graphic, electronic, or mechanical, including photocopying, recording, taping, Web distribution, or information storage and retrieval systems—without the prior written permission of the publisher.

For permission to use material from this text or product, submit a request online at www.thomsonrights.com

Any additional questions about permissions can be submitted by e-mail to thomsonrights@thomson.com

ISBN 13: 978-0-7689-1838-0
ISBN 10: 0-7689-1838-3

Printed in the United States of America

10 9 8 7 6 5 4 3   07 06

Eighteenth Edition

Petersons.com/publishing

Check out our Web site at www.petersons.com/publishing to see if there is any new information regarding the tests and any revisions or corrections to the content of this book. We've made sure the information in this book is accurate and up-to-date; however, the format or content of the tests may have changed since the time of publication.

Other Recommended Titles:

ARCO Preparation for the Praxis I: PPST Exam

ARCO Prepare for the NYSTCE: LAST and ATS-W

CONTENTS

Part IV: Multiple Subjects Assessment for Teachers (MSAT)

Part I:

The Praxis Series

INTRODUCTION

THE PRAXIS SERIES

The Praxis Series consists of standardized examinations designed to measure the academic proficiencies of students entering or completing teacher preparation programs and individuals seeking professional certification. Developed and administered by the Educational Testing Service, the Praxis Series assesses knowledge and skills at three levels of proficiency:

- Praxis I: Academic Skills Assessments measures basic proficiency in reading, mathematics, and writing.
- Praxis II: Subject Assessments measures content area knowledge.
- Praxis III: Classroom Performance Assessments provides a training and evaluation framework for classroom performance.

Praxis I: Academic Skills Assessments

The Praxis I: Academic Skills Assessments measures basic proficiency in reading, mathematics, and writing by means of the Academic Skills Assessments or the Computer-Based Academic Skills Assessments (CBT). It may be used as an entrance exam for teacher-training programs or as a preliminary licensing exam.

The Paper-Based Academic Skills Assessments

Note that there are two versions of the Pre-Professional Skills Test (PPST). The paper-and-pencil test contains standard multiple-choice questions and an essay question on a designated topic. It consists of three tests as follows:

Test 1: Reading. A 60-minute test consisting of 40 multiple-choice questions based on 100- to 200-word passages and shorter statements of a sentence or two. Questions fall into the following topic areas:

Literal Comprehension (approximately 55 percent of multiple-choice questions)
- Main idea questions
- Supporting idea questions
- Organization questions
- Vocabulary questions

Critical and Inferential Comprehension (approximately 45 percent of multiple-choice questions)
- Argument evaluation questions
- Inferential reasoning questions
- Generalization questions

Test 2: Mathematics. A 60-minute test consisting of 40 multiple-choice questions divided among the following topic areas:

Conceptual Knowledge (approximately 15 percent of multiple-choice questions)
- Number sense
- Operation sense

Procedural Knowledge (approximately 30 percent of multiple-choice questions)
- Computation
- Estimation
- Solving ratio, proportion, and percent problems
- Solving equations and inequalities
- Probability
- Algorithmic thinking

Representations of Quantitative Information (approximately 30 percent of multiple-choice questions)
- Interpretation of graphs, charts, and tables
- Identifying and recognizing patterns in data
- Predicting trends and making inferences from data
- Understanding relationships between values in a table or graph

Measurement and Informal Geometry (approximately 15 percent of multiple-choice questions)
- U.S. and metric systems
- Using geometric concepts to solve linear, area, and volume problems
- Recognizing and using geometric properties and relationships

Formal Mathematical Reasoning (approximately 10 percent of multiple-choice questions)
- Interpreting logical connectives and quantifiers
- Determining validity of arguments
- Identifying generalizations

Test 3: Writing. A 60-minute test divided into two 30-minute sections. One section consists of 38 multiple-choice questions, and the other section consists of a single essay question on an assigned topic. The multiple-choice questions are divided among the following topic areas:

Usage (approximately 55 percent of multiple-choice questions)
- Identifying errors in grammar
- Identifying errors in word choice or idiom
- Identifying errors in punctuation and capitalization
- Identifying sentences that have no errors

Sentence Correction (approximately 45 percent of multiple-choice questions)
- Selecting the correct and most effective rephrasing of a sentence
- Correcting errors of grammar, usage, and word choice

The Computerized PPST

The computer-based test (CBT) consists of questions that appear on the computer screen, and examinees must indicate their answers using the computer keyboard or a mouse. Examinees may be required to select single or multiple responses, to highlight or reorder information, or to provide their own answers. A special MARK tool allows examinees to proceed without answering a question. It also allows examinees to mark a question that has been answered and go back and review or change it. Students will be able to see what questions they have or have not answered and what questions they have marked on a special review screen.

Like the paper-and-pencil PPST, the computerized PPST consists of three tests. Candidates may take one, two, or all three tests at one time. Following is a brief description of each computer-based test.

READING	75 minutes, 46 multiple-choice questions
MATHEMATICS	75 minutes, 46 multiple-choice questions
WRITING	38 minutes, 44 multiple-choice questions 30 minutes, one essay question

Test 1: Reading. A 75-minute test consisting of 46 computer-generated multiple-choice questions based on 200- to 400-word passages—some accompanied by graphs, charts, or diagrams—from the areas of social science, science and nature, humanities, and education. Questions may require test-takers to highlight information, move information from one place to another, choose one or more answers, or check boxes in a table. Questions fall into the following topic areas:

Comprehension (approximately 60 percent of multiple-choice questions)

- Main idea and summary questions
- Supporting idea and detail questions
- Organization questions

Analysis and Application (approximately 40 percent of multiple-choice questions)

- Applying ideas presented to other situations
- Recognizing arguments and their logic
- Determining inferences and assumptions
- Defining words in context
- Distinguishing facts from opinions

Test 2: Mathematics. A 75-minute test consisting of 46 computer-delivered multiple-choice questions that may require test-takers to highlight an answer choice, arrange numbers in order, complete a graph or table, mark a point on a scale, or enter a numerical response. Questions are divided among the following topic areas:

Number Sense and Operation Sense (approximately 25 percent of multiple-choice questions)

- Understanding the order of numbers
- Recognizing equivalent forms of a number
- Performing computations in problem solving
- Selecting a sequence of operations
- Recognizing alternative ways to solve problems

Mathematical Relationships (approximately 20 percent of multiple-choice questions)

- Interpreting and applying ratios, proportions, and percents
- Determining probabilities
- Formulating equations
- Solving equations and inequalities

Data Interpretation (approximately 25 percent of multiple-choice questions)
- Reading and understanding data presented in various formats
- Recognizing relationships in data
- Constructing and completing tables, charts, and graphs
- Determining average, range, median, or mode of a set of data

Geometry and Measurement (approximately 20 percent of multiple-choice questions)
- Determining length, perimeter, area, and volume of two- and three-dimensional figures
- Using various systems of measurement and converting from one to another

Reasoning (approximately 10 percent of multiple-choice questions)
- Interpreting sentences containing logical connectives and quantifiers
- Drawing conclusions from given statements
- Determining validity of conclusions

Test 3: Writing. A 68-minute test presented in two sections: a 38-minute computer-adaptive section containing 44 multiple-choice questions and a 30-minute essay section consisting of a single essay. The writing test is divided among the following topic areas:

Error Recognition (50 percent of test score)
- Recognizing errors in structure
- Recognizing errors in word choice
- Recognizing errors in punctuation and capitalization

Essay Writing (50 percent of test score)
- Ability to formulate a thesis or state a position clearly
- Ability to organize ideas logically and support ideas with appropriate examples or details
- Ability to vary sentence structure and write clearly, correctly, and effectively

Praxis II

Praxis II includes the Principles of Learning and Teaching (PLT), the Multiple Subjects Assessment for Teachers (MSAT), and the Subject Assessments.

The Principles of Learning and Teaching (PLT)

The Principles of Learning and Teaching (PLT) is used to test the beginning teacher's knowledge of teaching standards. The test includes four case histories that represent different teaching situations. Each case history is followed by 3 short-answer questions related to the teaching situation. There are 12 short-answer questions covering required content areas, such as student motivation and students as diverse learners. The test also contains two sections of 12 multiple-choice questions based on the required content areas.

Multiple Subjects Assessment for Teachers (MSAT)

The Multiple Subjects Assessment for Teachers (MSAT) is used to test the knowledge and critical-thinking skills of prospective teachers. The MSAT consists of a multiple-choice test called the Content Knowledge Test and a short-answer test called Content Area Exercises. The MSAT is currently offered six times a year, in September, November, January, March, April, and June. The use of calculators without a QWERTY keypad *is* permitted on the MSAT exams.

The Content Knowledge Test is a 2-hour test consisting of 120 multiple-choice questions divided among the following subject areas:

- Literature and Language Studies — 24 questions
- Mathematics — 24 questions
- Visual and Performing Arts — 12 questions
- Physical Education — 8 questions
- Human Development — 8 questions
- History/Social Sciences — 22 questions
- Science — 22 questions

Content Area Exercises is a 3-hour test consisting of 18 short essay questions divided among the following subject areas:

- Literature and Language Studies — 3 questions
- Mathematics — 3 questions
- Visual and Performing Arts — 2 questions
- Physical Education — 2 questions
- Human Development — 2 questions
- History/Social Sciences — 3 questions
- Science — 3 questions

Note: Nonprogrammable calculators are allowed for the MSAT.

Subject Assessments

The chart on the following pages indicates test times and the number of multiple-choice or essay questions for the other specialty area tests and subject assessments that are part of Praxis II.

For Additional Information about the Praxis Series

Additional information about test dates and registration procedures can be found in the *Registration Bulletin* that is available at most college education offices or from the Educational Testing Service at the following address:

The Praxis Series
Educational Testing Service
P.O. Box 6051
Princeton, NJ 08541-6051
Phone: 800-772-9476 (toll-free)
Web site: www.ets.org/praxis

Specialty Area Tests and Subject Assessments

TEST CODE	TEST FEE	SUBJECT AREA	TEST TIME	NUMBER OF MULTIPLE–CHOICE QUESTIONS	NUMBER OF ESSAY QUESTIONS
		Arts			
20131	$75	Art Making	1 hr	–	2 + 2 exercises
20132	$75	Art: Content, Traditions, Criticism, and Aesthetics	1 hr	3	–
10133	$75	Art: Content Knowledge	2 hrs	120	–
10110	$75	Music Education	2 hrs	150	–
20112	$75	Music: Analysis	1 hr	–	1 + 2 exercises
30111	$75	Music: Concepts and Processes	1 hr	–	2
10113	$75	Music: Content Knowledge	2 hrs	135	–
10640	$75	Theater	2 hrs	108	–
		Biology and General Science			
20030	$75	Biology and General Science	2 hrs	160	–
30233	$75	Biology: Content Essays	1 hr	–	3
20231	$60	Biology: Content Knowledge, Part 1	1 hr	75	–
20232	$60	Biology: Content Knowledge, Part 2	1 hr	75	–
30433	$75	General Science: Content Essays	1 hr	–	3
10431	$60	General Science: Content Knowledge, Part 1	1 hr	60	–
10432	$60	General Science: Content Knowledge, Part 2	1 hr	60	–
30234	$75	Life Science: Pedagogy	1 hr	–	1
		Business and Technology			
10700	$75	Agriculture	2 hrs	140	–
10900	$75	Agriculture (CA)	2 hrs	148	–
10780	$75	Agriculture (PA)	2 hrs	140	–
10100	$75	Business Education	2 hrs	160	–
10791	$60	Business (PA): Accounting	1 hr	80	–
10810	$75	Cooperative Education	2 hrs	157	–
10560	$75	Marketing Education	2 hrs	120	–
10050	$75	Technology Education	2 hrs	150	–
10890	$75	Vocational General Knowledge	2 hrs	110	–
		Education			
10020	$75	Early Childhood Education	2 hrs	150	–
20010	$75	Education in the Elementary School	2 hrs	150	–
20021	$85	*NEW* Education of Young Children	2 hrs	60	6 constructed responses
10011	$75	Elementary Education: Curriculum, Instruction, and Assessment	2 hrs	110	–

Specialty Area Tests and Subject Assessments (cont'd)

TEST CODE	TEST FEE	SUBJECT AREA	TEST TIME	NUMBER OF MULTIPLE-CHOICE QUESTIONS	NUMBER OF ESSAY QUESTIONS
20012	$90	Elementary Education: Content Area Exercises	2 hrs	–	4
20550	$75	Health Education	2 hrs	120	–
10850	$75	Health and Physical Education	2 hrs	145	–
10091	$75	Physical Education: Content Knowledge	2 hrs	120	–
30092	$75	Physical Education: Movement Forms—Analysis and Design	1 hr	–	2
20093	$75	Physical Education: Movement Forms—Video Evaluation	1 hr	–	2
20530	$75	Pre–Kindergarten Education	2 hrs	103	–
10860	$75	Safety/Driver Education	2 hrs	125	–
10088	$115	Teaching Foundations: History–Social Science	4 hrs	50	2 constructed responses
10068	$115	Teaching Foundations: Mathematics	4 hrs	50	2 constructed responses
10528	$115	Teaching Foundations: Multiple Subjects	4 hrs	50	4 constructed responses
10048	$115	Teaching Foundations: Reading/Language Arts	4 hrs	50	2 constructed responses
10438	$115	Teaching Foundations: Science	4 hrs	50	2 constructed responses
		Education of Students with Disabilities			
10271	$85	Education of Deaf and Hard of Hearing Students	2 hrs	40	2 constructed responses
10382	$75	Education of Exceptional Students: Learning Disabilities	1 hr	30	3 constructed responses
10542	$75	Education of Exceptional Students: Mild to Moderate Disabilities	1 hr	–	5 constructed responses
10544	$75	Education of Exceptional Students: Severe to Profound Disabilities	1 hr	–	5 constructed responses
10352	$60	Special Education: Application of Core Principles across Categories of Disability	1 hr	50	–
20351	$60	Special Education: Knowledge–Based Core Principles	1 hr	60	–
10690	$75	Special Education: Preschool/Early Childhood	2 hrs	110	–
20371	$60	Special Education: Teaching Students with Behavioral Disorders/Emotional Disturbance	1 hr	50	–
20381	$60	Special Education: Teaching Students with Learning Disabilities	1 hr	50	–
20321	$60	Special Education: Teaching Students with Mental Retardation0	1 hr	50	–

Specialty Area Tests and Subject Assessments (cont'd)

TEST CODE	TEST FEE	SUBJECT AREA	TEST TIME	NUMBER OF MULTIPLE-CHOICE QUESTIONS	NUMBER OF ESSAY QUESTIONS
10880	$75	Teaching Speech to Students with Language Impairments	2 hrs	120	–
10370	$75	Teaching Students with Emotional Disturbance	2 hrs	120	–
10380	$75	Teaching Students with Learning Disabilities	2 hrs	120	–
10290	$75	Teaching Students with Orthopedic Impairments	2 hrs	130	–
10280	$75	Teaching Students with Visual Impairments	2 hrs	120	–
		English, Reading, and Communication			
20800	$75	Communication (PA)	2 hrs	150	–
10041	$75	English Language, Literature, and Composition: Content Knowledge	2 hrs	150	2
20042	$90	English Language, Literature, and Composition: Essays	2 hrs	–	2
30043	$75	English Language, Literature, and Composition: Pedagogy	1 hr	–	2
10300	$75	Reading Specialist	2 hrs	145	–
10220	$75	Speech Communication	2 hrs	150	–
20360	$75	English to Speakers of other Languages	2 hrs	120	–
10640	$75	Theater	2 hrs	–	–
		Guidance, Administration, and School Services			
10340	$75	Audiology	2 hrs	150	–
10410	$75	Educational Leadership: Administration and Supervision	2 hrs	145	–
10310	$75	Library Media Specialist	2 hrs	145	–
20420	$75	School Guidance and Counseling	2 hrs	140	–
10400	$75	School Psychologist	2 hrs	135	–
20211	$75	School Social Worker	2 hrs	100	–
20330	$75	Speech–Language Pathology	2 hrs	150	–
		Languages			
10840	$60	Foreign Language Pedagogy (PA)	1 hr	55	–
10170	$75	French (contains listening)	2 hrs	155–160	–
10171	$75	French: Productive Language Skills (contains speaking)	1 hr	–	9 exercises
20173	$75	French: Content Knowledge (contains listening)	2 hrs	140	–
30172	$75	French: Linguistic, Literary, and Cultural Analysis	1 hr	–	3 exercises
20180	$75	German (contains listening)	2 hrs	160	–
20181	$75	German: Content Knowledge (contains listening)	2 hrs	140	–
10600	$75	Latin	2 hrs	130	–

Specialty Area Tests and Subject Assessments (cont'd)

TEST CODE	TEST FEE	SUBJECT AREA	TEST TIME	NUMBER OF MULTIPLE-CHOICE QUESTIONS	NUMBER OF ESSAY QUESTIONS
10191	$75	Spanish: Content Knowledge (contains listening)	2 hrs	140	–
30193	$75	Spanish: Linguistic, Literary, and Cultural Analysis	1 hr	–	3 exercises
30194	$75	Spanish: Pedagogy	1 hr	–	3 exercises
20192	$75	Spanish: Productive Language Skills (contains speaking)	1 hr	–	9 exercises
		Mathematics			
10061	$75	Mathematics: Content Knowledge	2 hrs	50	–
20065	$75	Mathematics: Pedagogy	1 hr	–	3
20063	$75	Mathematics: Proofs, Models, and Problems, Part 1	1 hr	–	4 exercises
		Physical Science			
30242	$75	Chemistry: Content Essays	1 hr	–	3
20241	$60	Chemistry: Content Knowledge	1 hr	50	–
10070	$75	Chemistry, Physics, and General Science	2 hrs	140	–
20571	$75	Earth Science: Content Knowledge	2 hrs	100	–
20481	$60	Physical Science: Content Knowledge	1 hr	60	–
30483	$75	Physical Science: Pedagogy	1 hr	–	1
30260	$75	Physics	2 hrs	100	–
30262	$75	Physics: Content Essays	1 hr	–	3
10261	$60	Physics: Content Knowledge	1 hr	50	–
		Social Sciences			
10087	$75	Citizenship Education: Content Knowledge	2 hrs	115	–
10910	$75	Economics	2 hrs	105	–
10830	$75	Environmental Education	2 hrs	140	–
30920	$75	Geography	2 hrs	135	–
10930	$75	Government/Political Science	2 hrs	120	–
20390	$75	Psychology	2 hrs	120	–
10951	$75	Social Sciences: Content Knowledge	2 hrs	120	–
20082	$75	Social Studies: Analytical Essays	1 hr	–	2
10081	$75	Social Studies: Content Knowledge	2 hrs	130	–
20085	$90	Social Studies: Interpretation and Analysis	2 hrs	–	2 + 5 short answer
20083	$75	Social Studies: Interpretation of Materials	1 hr	–	5
30084	$75	Social Studies: Pedagogy	1 hr	–	2
20950	$75	Sociology	2 hrs	115	–
10940	$75	World and U.S. History	2 hrs	130	–
10941	$75	World and U.S. History: Content Knowledge	2 hrs	120	–

TEST PREPARATION

Registering for Praxis II

Test dates and registration procedures are listed in the free *Registration Bulletin,* which is available at most college education offices or from Educational Testing Service at the following address:

> The Praxis Series
> Educational Testing Service
> P.O. Box 6051
> Princeton, NJ 08541-6051
> Phone: 800-772-9476 (toll-free)

Information is also available at the ETS Web site: www.ets.org/praxis. In general, registration materials are due four to six weeks before the test date, and score reports are mailed four to six weeks after the test date.

What to Bring to the Test Center

On the day of the test, each candidate should bring the following items:

- Appropriate photo identification. A driver's license, a student ID card, a passport, or military identification will do.
- Admission ticket or letter of authorization
- Three sharpened No. 2 pencils with erasers
- A blue or black pen for the essay or constructed-response tests
- A watch. The tests are timed and you may not be able to see the clock in the examination room.

Test-Taking Tips

1. **Answer every question.** Specialty Area test scores are based on the number of questions you answer correctly. You are not penalized for incorrect answers, so it pays to guess! In fact, you should answer every question since a good guess can add to your score and a bad one has no ill effect.

2. **Watch your timing.** Each Praxis test is timed. Use the tests in this book to practice under timed conditions. Wear a watch or use a stopwatch and become comfortable with the time allowances given to you. Each question is worth the same number of points, so don't waste time on very difficult questions; instead, select your best educated guess for a hard question and continue with the rest of the test. Work as quickly as you can without getting careless. If you have time at the end of a subtest, check your work. You may not go on to the next test or go back to a previous test.

3. **Mark your answer sheet carefully.** Use only No. 2 pencils. Make sure you mark the answers in the correct row. Fill the answer bubbles completely, and if you change your mind about an answer, be sure to erase your first answer completely before you enter your new choice.

4. **Plan your essays.** First write an outline of the essay. Include an introductory paragraph stating the main idea and topic of your essay. Use details and examples in your essay to support your topic. Use an active voice; avoid using the passive voice. End your essay with a paragraph summarizing your main points.

Special Testing Arrangements

Candidates with a physical, emotional, learning, visual, or hearing disability who cannot take a Praxis test under standard conditions may request special test-taking arrangements. Candidates whose religious beliefs do not allow testing on Saturdays or members of the U.S. armed forces whose military duties preclude Saturday testing can request a Monday administration on the Monday immediately following the Saturday test.

Candidates requesting special arrangements can do so by writing to:

The Praxis Series
Test Administration Services
Educational Testing Service
P.O. Box 6054
Princeton, NJ 08541-6054

How Praxis II Is Scored

Specialty Area test scores range from 250 to 990, with intervals of 10 points. Scores are reported with two- or three-letter codes preceding the score to identify the examination. For example, Music Education would be ME and Physical Education would be PE. A candidate may receive scores as follows:

ME 560   (Music Education 560)
PE 780   (Physical Education 780)

The report for each Specialty Area test also gives the number and percent of questions answered correctly in each of the content categories measured by the test.

Each score report also compares the candidate to others who took the same edition of the test. About 25 percent of the candidates are in the low category, 25 percent are in the high category, and 50 percent fall in the average category.

For each test date, candidates receive one copy of their scores, and they can ask for up to three copies of their scores to be sent out to locations they request on the answer sheet. Only that particular test date scoring will be sent approximately four to six weeks after the test date. Scores are retained for five years only. After that time, they cannot be reported or sent. Candidates who want scores reported to places that were not listed on the answer sheet must send a letter to ETS or complete an Additional Score Report request form. The request together with the appropriate fee should be mailed to:

The Praxis Series
Educational Testing Service
P.O. Box 6052
Princeton, NJ 08541-6052

Canceling Your Score

Candidates cannot cancel previous scores from their permanent score record; however, they can cancel scores from a specific test if the request is received by ETS within seven days of that particular administration. Candidates who wish to cancel a score should fill out a Request for Score Cancellation form and send it immediately to ETS. Once scores have been canceled, they will not be reported to the candidate or to anyone else, and they cannot be reinstated on the record. There is no test refund for canceled scores.

Part II:

Principles of Learning and Teaching

OVERVIEW

The Principles of Learning and Teaching (PLT) assessment is designed to evaluate a beginning teacher's knowledge of job-related information, which should have been obtained in one's undergraduate education. The PLT is divided into four discrete grade-level sections as follows:

TEST NAME	TEST NUMBER
Early Childhood	0521
Grades K–6	0522
Grades 5–9	0523
Grades 7–12	0524

Each grade-level section above contains 4 case histories. Each case history presents a particular teaching situation followed by 3 short-answer questions dealing with an area of teaching within the case history. Short-answer questions require the examinee to write a brief response relating to a case history. You do not need to cite a specific theory or book in the answer, but responses will be graded according to professionally acceptable principles and practices of teaching. Make sure to answer all parts of the question. The allotted time for each short-answer question is 25 minutes. The questions are scored on a scale of 0–2. Remember, credit will not be issued for an off-topic response, so stay focused and read the directions carefully.

Twenty-four multiple-choice questions are also included in two sections of 12 questions. These multiple-choice questions are not associated with the case histories and are called *discrete multiple-choice questions*. Ten minutes are allotted for each multiple-choice section, so you must monitor your time carefully.

SHORT-ANSWER QUESTIONS

This section contains representative samples for the PLT assessment. You will find case histories with 2 short-answer questions, and following this are practice discrete multiple-choice questions and an Answer Key. By working through these case history scenarios and short-answer questions, as well as the multiple-choice questions, this book will help better prepare you for the Praxis II exam.

CASE HISTORY: EARLY CHILDHOOD

> *Directions:* The case history is followed by 2 short-answer questions.

Case History #1

Line Ms. Kaye is a first-grade teacher who just started teaching in the Brantree Elementary School, which is in located in a working-class neighborhood. During the second week of September, a staff de-
(5) veloper was assigned to the teacher to help assess her reading program. Mrs. Wilson just spent a morning observing Ms. Kaye's literacy period. She took detailed notes as to what she has observed.

Document 1:

(10) (teacher: Ms. Kaye, literacy period: 9:15 to 11 a.m)

The teacher had a read-aloud period in which she read to the class a repetitive story. Each student sat at his or her desk during this activity while the teacher stood in the front and read. This class
(15) is made up of 24 students seated at six tables containing 4 students. After she read the story, she gave the students other picture books containing similar vocabulary concepts to read on their own. The teacher walked around the room to have in-
(20) dividual students read to her. She noticed that one student, Diane, kept pronouncing blends as a single consonant when the pupil read to her. She then asked the student to answer a factual question about the story. However, after she asked the
(25) question, there was no response. As she worked with this student and several others, the other students became noisy. No one read consistently for more than 5 to 10 minutes. The teacher then went to the front of the room and then asked the stu-
(30) dents to write a response to what they were reading in their writing notebook. Some student began to write a few lines, while about 7 to 8 students were not even writing at all.

Document 2:

(teacher critique of her own lesson)
(35)   I feel the lesson was effective. I read aloud to the class picture books containing repetitive words to develop sight vocabulary. This motivated the students to read similar picture books on their own. When they read silently, I used the time to work
(40) individually with students. I helped students with their decoding skills. I tried to teach only those phonic skills that the student needed to decode at the moment. I tried to help other kids with comprehension by asking and then rephrasing some factual questions. Writing skills were also rein-
(45) forced during this period by having them write a response to the story. These responses are not being checked because my goal is just to get them to write at this early point in the term. On a 4-point rubric, I rate my lesson as a 3 because it
(50) met all goals of literacy instruction.

Directions: Questions 1 and 2 require you to write short answers. You are not expected to cite specific theories or texts in your answers; however, your responses to the questions will be evaluated with respect to professionally accepted principles and practices in teaching and learning. Be sure to answer all parts of the questions. Write your answers in the spaces indicated in the response book.

Question 1

After the staff developer received the teacher's self-evaluation, she had a mentoring conference with the teacher to decide on several ways the teacher can improve her effectiveness in teaching reading. However, before the conference, she had the teacher read several articles on literacy instruction. They had jointly come up with some recommendations. State THREE possible recommendations the teacher and staff developer could come up with and describe how each recommendation could be implemented.

Outline

Sample Answer

First, the teacher will choose picture books related to a particular genre. A possible genre would be school-content-related concepts, such as calendar words, shapes, or number words. In this way, the students would be learning sight words more closely aligned with the learning standards. Then, the teacher can either have the students choose to read on their own what the teacher read or books containing similar concepts. Then, instead of having the students read silently, sets of pupils will do paired reading after the teacher modeled appropriate fluency and inflection during her read aloud period. Similar readers should be paired with each other so that the task will not become a tutoring session. Instead it should be a session in which the students share similar skills. After the students read aloud to each other, time should be given for the pair to discuss what they just read using modeled phrases to reinforce appropriate book discussions. Finally, if the teacher goes around the room and sees decoding weaknesses during the shared reading activity, she should create a mini lesson. If the lesson is on blending, then the teacher should use words from the story either the teacher or they read. Only those phonic skills should be taught that the student needs to read effectively. Formal phonic instruction should be avoided so as to increase academic learning time.

Question 2

The staff developer wants to make sure that the teacher understands how to make a mini lesson. She asks the teacher to make up a sample mini lesson. Describe and discuss at least six elements that make up an effective mini lesson.

Outline

_____

_____

_____

_____

_____

_____

_____

_____

_____

_____

_____

_____

_____

_____

_____

_____

_____

_____

_____

_____

Sample Answer

A mini lesson should start off with a teaching point or objective based upon an observed weakness a majority of the class may have during the literacy block. If the teacher observes that students do not capitalize when writing, then a mini lesson on capitalization would be warranted. Next, the mini lesson should describe the method of instruction. The teacher could teach the lesson either as a demonstration, guided practice, or an inquiry, or he/she could explain and give examples. As part of the teaching method, the materials being used should also be described. Third, the teacher should make a connection during the lesson to what has been and will be learned. She could say, "I notice that you do not know which names should be capitalized." Next, the mini lesson should describe how the instructor should teach that lesson. After this direct instruction, the teacher has to then find a way to actively involve the student in learning the skill. If the teacher creates a chart of capitalized words during the teaching phase of the mini lesson, then the students will create their own chart from a list of uncapitalized words. Finally, the teacher has to link the mini lesson to previous instruction by rephrasing what has been learned.

CASE HISTORY: K–6

Directions: The case history is followed by 2 short-answer questions.

Case History #1

Line Mrs. Smith is a beginning third-grade teacher and is being mandated by her principal to teach social studies as a multidisciplinary unit. This teacher has never created such a unit before. Af-
(5) ter reviewing the state guidelines for social studies and looking at examples from more experienced teachers, she decides to create a unit on communities.

Before she starts teaching her unit, she gives
(10) the lesson to Mr. Vine, the school's principal, to review.

Objectives:
- People in the United States are often mobile and move from one place to another.
(15)
- Changes in communication have affected the lives of people in different parts of the country.
- Different immigrant groups have made many inventions.

Multisensory activities:
(20)
- Oregon trail DVD-ROM
- Globe of the world
- Video tape of "How the West was Won"
- Nineteenth-century photographs
- Colored markers to highlight different
(25) information

- Utilization of construction paper for three-dimensional presentation
- Map of pioneer trails in the United States
- Library book containing photographs
(30)
- Social studies textbook
- Book review about immigrant life

Academic concepts being taught as part of the lesson:

English
(35)
- Pretend you are immigrants and write letters back home describing America
- Describe different types of steamships found in the first half of the nineteenth century
- Draw an illustration of a tenement with cap-
(40) tions describing each part of the building

Group project:
- Work in cooperative groups containing four or five students
- Tell about different groups: Italians, Irish,
(45) Jewish
- Groups will build and present displays containing different information about immigrants
- Groups will present handouts to the class
- A rubric will be used to grade the project

Directions: Questions 1 and 2 require you to write short answers. You are not expected to cite specific theories or texts in your answers; however, your responses to the questions will be evaluated with respect to professionally accepted principles and practices in teaching and learning. Be sure to answer all parts of the questions. Write your answers in the spaces indicated in the response book.

Question 1

Mr. Vine has a conference with the teacher prior to Mrs. Smith's presentation of the lesson. He decides to use a mentoring strategy with Mrs. Smith. He asks her to edit the lesson. He wants improvements in the objectives, academic concepts, multidisciplinary activities, and group projects.

- *Describe ONE way Mrs. Smith can improve each part: objectives, academic concepts, multidisciplinary activities, and group project.*

- *Explain how each improvement will improve the coherence of the multidisciplinary unit. Base your response on principles of effective instructional strategies.*

<u>Outline</u>

Sample Answer

The last objective is irrelevant to the topic. A better objective would be that mass transportation and automobiles contributed to changes in communities. Secondary sources should be removed from the multisensory activities to be replaced possibly by artwork depicting urban advertisements from the early part of the twentieth century. Some English objectives are too broad. Instead of describing different steamships, this activity should be changed to researching different steamships in an encyclopedia or reference book. Finally, the directions for the group project are too broad and lack real directions to the student. The theme of the group project is how these immigrants adapted to the urban communities in the late nineteenth century. The steps to research this topic have to be broken down and task-analyzed so that different members of the group will know exactly what they have to do.

Question 2

The principal is concerned that Mrs. Smith's units lack a way to evaluate whether the students learned the objectives of the unit. Create a rubric describing how you would evaluate student mastery of the unit.

Outline

Sample Answer

The students will engage in 5 to 7 multisensory activities and document-relevant research for each. Each activity will be scored on a 4-point scale. The students will engage the unit using study/research skills from social studies and science. These skills will be stated as relevant objectives for each student. The students will utilize five performance standards. Different types of technology will be included in the group project using learned performance standards from math to science. Again, these will be measured on a 4-point scale.

CASE HISTORY: 7–12

Directions: The case history is followed by 2 short-answer questions.

Case History #1

Line Mr. Beneditine teaches a tenth-grade global studies class in Briarwood Central High School, which is within an upper-middle-class suburban school district. The class is studying Europe between
(5) 1815 and 1848. The teacher is dividing his class into cooperative learning groups. Each group has to research and report on the social, economic, and political changes within England, Prussia, France, and Austria-Hungary during this period.
(10) This is the first time that Mr. Beneditine is using a cooperative approach to do a social studies project. He has done some preliminary research within an in-service course on implementing cooperative learning within a secondary classroom.
(15) He has read Slavin, Johnson and Johnson, and Vygotsky. He has learned about various cooperative methods, such as TGT, Jigsaw, STAD, and Learning Together.

Document 1:

(letter from Mr. Toban)
(20) My son, Richard Toban, is in a group doing a global studies project. My son is a very bright boy and appears to be doing most of the work. The other children are doing little work because they are not motivated or lack the ability. I do
(25) not want him in the group. I want him to research the topic individually. Please let him do a traditional term-paper and get an individual mark. I do not want him to get a group mark because the other students may end up pulling down his
(30) grades.

Document 2:

(e-mail from Mrs. Nassam)
I read over my son's report about Prussian economic conditions between 1815 and 1848. I was surprised at the quality of the work and the high
(35) mark he received. My son has a long history of learning problems and is presently in a push-out resource room. I do not feel this paper is a reflection of my son's work. My son told me that in the group another boy wrote the whole report.
(40) I do not feel you are addressing my son's limitations. He needs to be directly taught the skills outlined on his IEP. He needs extensive writing and organization skills. I feel that my son will not learn the skills he needs and will fall through
(45) the cracks. He will not be able to pass an eleventh-grade social studies competency test. I look forward to hearing from you to resolve this matter.

Directions: Questions 1 and 2 require you to write short answers. You are not expected to cite specific theories or texts in your answers; however, your responses to the questions will be evaluated with respect to professionally accepted principles and practices in teaching and learning. Be sure to answer all parts of the questions. Write your answers in the spaces indicated in the response book.

Question 1

Mr. Beneditine has to write an outline of the cooperative approach to the chairperson of the social studies department of his high school. Describe an effective cooperative approach he could use and how it will be organized and evaluated.

<u>Outline</u>

Sample Answer

One approach he can have the students use for researching this topic is the jigsaw method of cooperative learning. In his classroom, he will divide his class into four groups. One group will research each country. Within each group, different students will research each issue. Finally, a fourth student will write an analysis of these developments as a conclusion to the paper. In doing the research, members of each group responsible for the same subpart will form expert groups that will gather the necessary information. Then, these experts will return to the original cooperative group and teach the information to their teammates. Once the teaching process is finished, one student will be chosen as a recorder to put together the information gathered by his peers. In this way, the group will synthesize the information into a cohesive paper. In evaluating the effectiveness of each cooperative group, the teacher will ask each group to reflect about what was learned, how it was learned, and the skills used to process and meet the goal. Then, a group grade will be given to each group. One part of a 4-point rubric will describe how each group worked together and the second part of the rubric will be whether they have met their cooperative learning goal.

Question 2

The teacher has to respond to the two parents that had concerns about his approach. How would he relay the information to the parents? And for each parent, the teacher has to describe three justifications for using this approach.

Outline

Sample Answer

The teacher would call each parent to arrange for them to come to school to discuss the matter. He would do this so he can show them concrete examples of the work the students were doing using this approach. He would state to Richard's father that (1) he set up the cooperative group with heterogeneous students, so that the burden would not be on any one student, (2) that he taught mini lessons along the way modeling how student can do research, gather information, and work together, and (3) he would cite research showing that this approach helped students develop higher-level thinking skills that should be facilitated in a brighter student.

For the parent of the handicapped child, he would state that (1) the approach helps students develop social skills, (2) that language and communication skills are often improved by students teaching and sharing with one another, and (3) by letting lower-achieving students help higher-achieving students, remedial instruction is often reinforced and applied within the classroom situation.

PRACTICE DISCRETE MULTIPLE-CHOICE QUESTIONS

ANSWER SHEET

Early Childhood

1. Ⓐ Ⓑ Ⓒ Ⓓ   7. Ⓐ Ⓑ Ⓒ Ⓓ   13. Ⓐ Ⓑ Ⓒ Ⓓ   19. Ⓐ Ⓑ Ⓒ Ⓓ

2. Ⓐ Ⓑ Ⓒ Ⓓ   8. Ⓐ Ⓑ Ⓒ Ⓓ   14. Ⓐ Ⓑ Ⓒ Ⓓ   20. Ⓐ Ⓑ Ⓒ Ⓓ

3. Ⓐ Ⓑ Ⓒ Ⓓ   9. Ⓐ Ⓑ Ⓒ Ⓓ   15. Ⓐ Ⓑ Ⓒ Ⓓ   21. Ⓐ Ⓑ Ⓒ Ⓓ

4. Ⓐ Ⓑ Ⓒ Ⓓ   10. Ⓐ Ⓑ Ⓒ Ⓓ   16. Ⓐ Ⓑ Ⓒ Ⓓ   22. Ⓐ Ⓑ Ⓒ Ⓓ

5. Ⓐ Ⓑ Ⓒ Ⓓ   11. Ⓐ Ⓑ Ⓒ Ⓓ   17. Ⓐ Ⓑ Ⓒ Ⓓ   23. Ⓐ Ⓑ Ⓒ Ⓓ

6. Ⓐ Ⓑ Ⓒ Ⓓ   12. Ⓐ Ⓑ Ⓒ Ⓓ   18. Ⓐ Ⓑ Ⓒ Ⓓ   24. Ⓐ Ⓑ Ⓒ Ⓓ

Grades K–6

1. Ⓐ Ⓑ Ⓒ Ⓓ   7. Ⓐ Ⓑ Ⓒ Ⓓ   13. Ⓐ Ⓑ Ⓒ Ⓓ   19. Ⓐ Ⓑ Ⓒ Ⓓ

2. Ⓐ Ⓑ Ⓒ Ⓓ   8. Ⓐ Ⓑ Ⓒ Ⓓ   14. Ⓐ Ⓑ Ⓒ Ⓓ   20. Ⓐ Ⓑ Ⓒ Ⓓ

3. Ⓐ Ⓑ Ⓒ Ⓓ   9. Ⓐ Ⓑ Ⓒ Ⓓ   15. Ⓐ Ⓑ Ⓒ Ⓓ   21. Ⓐ Ⓑ Ⓒ Ⓓ

4. Ⓐ Ⓑ Ⓒ Ⓓ   10. Ⓐ Ⓑ Ⓒ Ⓓ   16. Ⓐ Ⓑ Ⓒ Ⓓ   22. Ⓐ Ⓑ Ⓒ Ⓓ

5. Ⓐ Ⓑ Ⓒ Ⓓ   11. Ⓐ Ⓑ Ⓒ Ⓓ   17. Ⓐ Ⓑ Ⓒ Ⓓ   23. Ⓐ Ⓑ Ⓒ Ⓓ

6. Ⓐ Ⓑ Ⓒ Ⓓ   12. Ⓐ Ⓑ Ⓒ Ⓓ   18. Ⓐ Ⓑ Ⓒ Ⓓ   24. Ⓐ Ⓑ Ⓒ Ⓓ

Grades 5–9

1. Ⓐ Ⓑ Ⓒ Ⓓ   7. Ⓐ Ⓑ Ⓒ Ⓓ   13. Ⓐ Ⓑ Ⓒ Ⓓ   19. Ⓐ Ⓑ Ⓒ Ⓓ

2. Ⓐ Ⓑ Ⓒ Ⓓ   8. Ⓐ Ⓑ Ⓒ Ⓓ   14. Ⓐ Ⓑ Ⓒ Ⓓ   20. Ⓐ Ⓑ Ⓒ Ⓓ

3. Ⓐ Ⓑ Ⓒ Ⓓ   9. Ⓐ Ⓑ Ⓒ Ⓓ   15. Ⓐ Ⓑ Ⓒ Ⓓ   21. Ⓐ Ⓑ Ⓒ Ⓓ

4. Ⓐ Ⓑ Ⓒ Ⓓ   10. Ⓐ Ⓑ Ⓒ Ⓓ   16. Ⓐ Ⓑ Ⓒ Ⓓ   22. Ⓐ Ⓑ Ⓒ Ⓓ

5. Ⓐ Ⓑ Ⓒ Ⓓ   11. Ⓐ Ⓑ Ⓒ Ⓓ   17. Ⓐ Ⓑ Ⓒ Ⓓ   23. Ⓐ Ⓑ Ⓒ Ⓓ

6. Ⓐ Ⓑ Ⓒ Ⓓ   12. Ⓐ Ⓑ Ⓒ Ⓓ   18. Ⓐ Ⓑ Ⓒ Ⓓ   24. Ⓐ Ⓑ Ⓒ Ⓓ

Grades 7–12

1. Ⓐ Ⓑ Ⓒ Ⓓ   7. Ⓐ Ⓑ Ⓒ Ⓓ   13. Ⓐ Ⓑ Ⓒ Ⓓ   19. Ⓐ Ⓑ Ⓒ Ⓓ

2. Ⓐ Ⓑ Ⓒ Ⓓ   8. Ⓐ Ⓑ Ⓒ Ⓓ   14. Ⓐ Ⓑ Ⓒ Ⓓ   20. Ⓐ Ⓑ Ⓒ Ⓓ

3. Ⓐ Ⓑ Ⓒ Ⓓ   9. Ⓐ Ⓑ Ⓒ Ⓓ   15. Ⓐ Ⓑ Ⓒ Ⓓ   21. Ⓐ Ⓑ Ⓒ Ⓓ

4. Ⓐ Ⓑ Ⓒ Ⓓ   10. Ⓐ Ⓑ Ⓒ Ⓓ   16. Ⓐ Ⓑ Ⓒ Ⓓ   22. Ⓐ Ⓑ Ⓒ Ⓓ

5. Ⓐ Ⓑ Ⓒ Ⓓ   11. Ⓐ Ⓑ Ⓒ Ⓓ   17. Ⓐ Ⓑ Ⓒ Ⓓ   23. Ⓐ Ⓑ Ⓒ Ⓓ

6. Ⓐ Ⓑ Ⓒ Ⓓ   12. Ⓐ Ⓑ Ⓒ Ⓓ   18. Ⓐ Ⓑ Ⓒ Ⓓ   24. Ⓐ Ⓑ Ⓒ Ⓓ

EARLY CHILDHOOD

Directions: For each question, choose the best response and mark the corresponding circle on your answer sheet.

1. In developing a communication arts curriculum, a teacher must be aware of the logical order in which a child develops language skills. They are

   (A) listening, speaking, reading, and writing.
   (B) speaking, listening, reading, and writing.
   (C) listening, speaking, writing, and reading.
   (D) speaking, listening, writing, and reading.

2. In kindergarten, students acquire readiness skills needed for reading. Which are necessary prerequisites for reading?

   I.   Listening with interest to stories
   II. Rhyming words
   III. Learning a simple sight vocabulary
   IV. Interpreting pictures

   (A) I and IV only
   (B) III and IV only
   (C) III only
   (D) I, II and IV only

3. A school's principal feels that all teachers should act as role models, being fair, honest, and objective. This theory of moral development was stressed by

   (A) Kohlberg.
   (B) Piaget.
   (C) Maslow.
   (D) Bandura.

4. Operant conditioning is most closely associated with

   (A) Jung.
   (B) Pavlov.
   (C) Skinner.
   (D) Lovaas.

5. Visual-spatial organizational problems impair a child's ability to orient and discriminate objects and symbols. All of these are possible academic difficulties caused by this problem EXCEPT

   (A) consistent reversals of letters and words.
   (B) difficulties in drawing and tracing.
   (C) delays in reading comprehension.
   (D) immature manuscript letter formation.

6. All of the following statements concerning social relationships in the early school years are usually true EXCEPT

   (A) groups are small and shift rapidly.
   (B) friends are selected because of propinquity.
   (C) children play with others to satisfy personal rather than social desires.
   (D) friends are selected on the basis of same sex.

7. Which of the following cognitive skills would you NOT expect a four-year-old to develop in nursery school?

   (A) Knowing his/her street and town
   (B) Naming the letters and numbers
   (C) Describing the functional use of objects
   (D) Counting to five

8. According to the latest research, the primary purpose of preschool is to

   (A) stimulate language and learn concepts through play activities.
   (B) develop readiness skills for reading.
   (C) use workbooks to develop good study skills for elementary schools.
   (D) enrich a child's intellectual ability by learning a foreign language.

9. Which academic issue can be clarified by understanding Maslow's Needs Theory?

    (A) Delinquency in the public schools
    (B) The effects of different classroom structures
    (C) The effect of poverty on academic achievement
    (D) Sex education issues in the school

10. All of the following are correctly paired EXCEPT for

    (A) Silberman . . . Open Classroom.
    (B) Dewey . . . Progressive Education.
    (C) Ravitch . . . Multicultural Education.
    (D) Likert . . . Mastery Learning.

11. In the study of language development, pragmatics refer to the

    (A) study of sounds.
    (B) study of grammatical forms and their rules.
    (C) understanding of word meanings.
    (D) understanding of various rules and forms of language in a variety of contexts.

12. According to the latest research, multicultural education has been criticized for

    (A) not giving equal time to all of America's ethnic groups.
    (B) containing curriculum materials that may not be accurate.
    (C) giving a distorted view of minorities.
    (D) giving too much emphasis to Western culture.

13. Public education has become more of a federal issue in recent years. According to the U.S. constitution,

    (A) every student has a right to an education at public expense.
    (B) the federal government must fund education at an appropriate level.
    (C) public education is a discretionary power left to the states.
    (D) private and public schools must be funded by the federal government.

14. In the area of special education litigation, *PARC vs. Pennsylvania* is important because it

    (A) established that the handicapped cannot be denied a public education without due process of law.
    (B) established the precedent of appropriate versus optimal educational services.
    (C) denied educational services to students who are not teachable.
    (D) stated that the gifted have the right to special educational services at public expense.

15. Mr. Willliams has a first-grade student who has excellent visual memory but poor auditory processing skills. This student would best learn word recognition skills through

    (A) a linguistic learning approach.
    (B) phonic analysis.
    (C) a whole language approach.
    (D) a sight word approach.

16. The concepts of assimilation, accommodation, and equilibration are most closely associated with

    (A) Bruner.
    (B) Cruikshank.
    (C) Kirk.
    (D) Piaget.

17. All of the following have researched in the field of learning disabilities EXCEPT

    (A) Strauss and Lehtinen.
    (B) Hinshelwood.
    (C) Kephart.
    (D) Redl.

18. The federal government first got involved in funding public education with the passage of

    (A) the GI Bill of Rights.
    (B) Head Start.
    (C) the National Defense Education Act.
    (D) P.L. 94–142.

19. The quotation that education is the ". . . great equalizer of the condition of man. The balance wheel of the social machinery . . ." describes the position of

    (A) McGuffrey.
    (B) Mann.
    (C) Dewey.
    (D) Thorndike.

20. A preschool program designed to develop arithmetic readiness skills would focus on all of the following EXCEPT

   (A) classification.
   (B) seriation.
   (C) rote counting to twenty.
   (D) reversibility.

21. The concepts of *trust* vs. *maturity*, *autonomy* vs. *self-doubt*, and *initiative* vs. *guilt* are most closely associated with the work of

   (A) Jung.
   (B) Erikson.
   (C) Freud.
   (D) Bettelheim.

22. The theory of learning most resembling that of Piaget derives from the work of

   (A) Gagne.
   (B) Bruner.
   (C) Spock.
   (D) Bloom.

23. A theory of socialization viewed by Carl Rogers and Abraham Maslow emphasizes that

   (A) people grow toward the goal of self-actualization.
   (B) conflicts during different stages of development have to be resolved.
   (C) modeling plays a part in determining social skills.
   (D) genetics and disposition play a part in social development.

24. Telegraphic speech patterns would most likely be found in a

   (A) two-year-old.
   (B) three-year-old.
   (C) four-year-old.
   (D) five-year-old.

GRADES K–6

> *Directions:* For each question, choose the best response and mark the corresponding circle on your answer sheet.

1. A teacher gives her first-grade class a page that has a story in which pictures take the place of some words. The teacher is using which approach or method?

   (A) A whole-language approach
   (B) A language experience approach
   (C) The Spaulding method
   (D) The rebus method

2. A theory of socialization viewed by Carl Rogers and Abraham Maslow emphasizes that

   (A) people grow toward the goal of self-actualization.
   (B) conflicts during different stages of development have to be resolved.
   (C) modeling plays a part in determining social skills.
   (D) conditioning plays a part in creating social skills.

3. In setting up a behavior-modification program, a teacher observes Briana for three 1-hour sessions. The teacher randomly chooses another student in the class as a control. During this time, the teacher tallies the number of times Briana and the control student leave their seats during each 1-hour period. The teacher is recording baseline data using a

   (A) time interval.
   (B) variable interval.
   (C) frequency count.
   (D) fixed interval.

4. The principal of a middle school wishes to improve discipline. She sets up a committee of teachers, parents, and administrators to study this problem. After a series of meetings, they make ten recommendations. The principal then meets with the committee and tells them that although their recommendations have some merit, she has come up with her own strategy to deal with discipline and that she hopes the committee will help in its implementation. This principal could be described as being

   (A) egocentric.
   (B) democratic.
   (C) collegial.
   (D) discriminating.

5. It is important that a teacher adequately assess the cause of a behavior problem. If a student is constantly fighting during a group reading lesson, this behavior may be the result of all of the following EXCEPT

   (A) the reading material may be too difficult.
   (B) the reading material may be too easy.
   (C) the child may dislike reading because of a history of constant failure in this area.
   (D) the need for the child to be involved in psychotherapy.

6. Children with Attention Deficit Disorders are likely to exhibit which of the following characteristics?

   I. Hyperactivity
   II. Impulsivity
   III. Distractibility
   IV. Depression

   (A) II and III only
   (B) I only
   (C) III and IV only
   (D) I, II, and III only

7. Comparing performance on different versions of the same test is a measure of

   (A) alternate-form reliability.
   (B) split-half reliability.
   (C) test-retest reliability.
   (D) correlational reliability.

8. All of the following are examples of gross-motor skills EXCEPT

   (A) posture.
   (B) throwing.
   (C) balance.
   (D) fastening.

9. As a result of an accident, a fifth-grade teacher now has an orthopedic condition that prevents him from climbing stairs. His classroom was originally on the fourth floor of the school. The teacher requests that his class now be stationed on the first floor. The building administrator denies this request, saying that no classrooms are available. What resource does this teacher have?

   (A) The teacher should inform his union representative and file a grievance.
   (B) The teacher has to accept the judgment of his principal.
   (C) The teacher should retire on disability.
   (D) The teacher should inform the superintendent of his school district that the administrator's action is in violation of the ADA.

10. All of the following are characteristics of good spellers EXCEPT

    (A) they may substitute other words for those they cannot spell.
    (B) good knowledge of sequential probability.
    (C) good immediate memory for visual material.
    (D) high interest in reading.

11. A student who has difficulty following directions, playing board games, and beginning homework promptly most likely has a problem in

    (A) organization.
    (B) visual-motor skills.
    (C) study skills.
    (D) social development.

12. Students can better remember how to spell a word when

    (A) they have a good listening and reading vocabulary.
    (B) they can memorize all forty-five phonemes of the English language.
    (C) sequencing skills are developed.
    (D) they are given short lists to memorize.

13. Which of the following best describes the spelling errors of a sixth-grader who spells *manufacture* as *manfacture* and *happiness* as *happness*?

    (A) Substitutions of one sound for another
    (B) Omissions of a sound or syllable from a word
    (C) Adding a sound or syllable to the original
    (D) Putting sounds in the wrong order

14. A fourth-grade student has difficulty in motor planning. He does not know which way to form round manuscript letters and which way to form loops on small letters. He applies too much pressure, often breaking a pencil. The best strategy to deal with this problem is to

    (A) use a multisensory approach.
    (B) teach the child cursive to keep him in one direction.
    (C) use tracing and copying exercises.
    (D) teach the student how to use a spell checker on a word processor.

15. According to the latest research, one of the LEAST effective ways to teach reading is to

    (A) read Endicott Award-winning stories to a kindergarten class.
    (B) develop a sight vocabulary using the organic method.
    (C) sound out letters one at a time.
    (D) teach antonyms, synonyms, and roots.

16. A sixth-grade student receives a score of 93 on the verbal part and 91 on the performance part of the WISC III. On the Woodcock Johnson Psycho-educational Battery—Revised, the same student received a standard score of 91 on the word-identification subtest and a standard score of 97 on the passage-comprehension subtest. Based on this information, we can assume that

  (A) the student probably needs to be placed in a remedial reading program.
  (B) no decision can be made unless we find out grade-equivalent values.
  (C) the student does not need any services.
  (D) the student is probably functioning in the low-average range.

17. Many educators feel that standardized reading scores are not a valid measure for determining the progress of a local school district. It is felt that other factors contribute to an increase or a decline in a school's reading scores. All of the following are variables affecting reading EXCEPT

  (A) recent foreign immigration to the immediate area.
  (B) the special education population of a school.
  (C) whether school-based management has been successfully implemented.
  (D) the socioeconomic status of an area.

18. Which of the following is a valid criticism of public school choice?

  (A) It is less effective than private school choice.
  (B) Parents prefer to send their children to neighborhood schools.
  (C) Too many choices tend to confuse parents who may know little about different types of methodologies.
  (D) Public school choice is not supported by federal mandates.

19. When tests are used for program evaluation, they can be misinterpreted. Which of the following difficulties can arise when tests are used to assess the efficacy of various instructional techniques?

  I.   Schools may not be similar.
  II. Teachers can have different styles.
  III. There is no valid test measuring this concept.
  IV. The children being taught may be different.

  (A) I and III only
  (B) II and IV only
  (C) I only
  (D) I, II, and IV only

20. The best approach to use in teaching a student how to spell words such as *led*, *lead*, and *washed* would be to

  (A) develop the student's morphological skills.
  (B) teach the student to sound out the word.
  (C) teach phonological units.
  (D) develop visual-memory skills.

21. Which of the following are the primary goals of classroom tests?

  I.   To rank students in the class
  II. To practice what has been learned
  III. To find out what has been learned to guide further instruction
  IV. To determine eligibility for special pull-out programs

  (A) I only
  (B) III only
  (C) II and III only
  (D) III and IV only

22. Susan will learn this year to form declarative and interrogative sentences that will convey her thoughts, ideas, and feelings. She will begin to use capitals and end her sentences with a question mark, exclamation point, or period. Susan also will begin to use quotation marks. She will continue to learn how to spell those words most frequently used in her writing and reading. This student is probably in

  (A) second grade.
  (B) kindergarten.
  (C) sixth grade.
  (D) eighth grade.

23. Which of the following are examples of projective tests?

  I.   Thematic Apperception Test
  II. Minnesota Multiphasic Personality Inventory
  III. Rorshach
  IV. Kuder Preference Record

  (A) I, II, and III only
  (B) II and IV only
  (C) I and III only
  (D) II and III only

24. Most research demonstrates that the auditory function most related to reading is

  (A) memory.
  (B) sequencing.
  (C) discriminating.
  (D) closure.

GRADES 5–9

Directions: For each question, choose the best response and mark the corresponding circle on your answer sheet.

---

1. To maintain good student behavior, teachers must constantly monitor compliance with class procedures and student involvement in learning. All are effective monitoring techniques EXCEPT

   (A) scan the whole class and move about the room.
   (B) focus entirely on the students you are teaching when instructing small groups.
   (C) check the progress of each student when students are working on individual assignments and give verbal and nonverbal feedback.
   (D) avoid letting groups of students congregate around your desk to obstruct your view of the class.

2. Which author was NOT involved in the Progressive movement, which swept through elementary education in the early part of the twentieth century?

   (A) William White
   (B) Francis Parker
   (C) Edward L. Thorndike
   (D) William Wirt

3. A major problem in middle schools today is teacher burnout. Instructors have to learn to stay relaxed and to enjoy their jobs. All are good techniques to avoid burnout EXCEPT

   (A) learn to separate yourself from your students' problems at the end of the day.
   (B) take acting lessons to improve your stage presence.
   (C) do lesson plans and mark homework during lunch periods to avoid doing work at home.
   (D) learn to tolerate some things and ignore others.

4. Which of the following are effective techniques a sixth-grade teacher can use to teach about ecology and conservation?

   I.   Classify different trees, animals, and insects
   II. Study a garden and chart the food chains between one species and another
   III. Discuss interesting and motivating facts about different animals and plants
   IV. Place different chemicals on plants and observe; then describe the effects in a journal

   (A) II and IV only
   (B) I, III, and IV only
   (C) II and III only
   (D) I, II, and IV only

5. Which of the following are good examples of high-level pivotal questions that give history a human dimension that ten- or eleven-year-olds can grasp?

   I.   What was Martin Luther King's feeling when he spent a night in jail for going into a white restaurant?
   II. How did Cortés feel about taking the belongings of the Aztecs and keeping them?
   III. How did the Native Americans feel when the skills they always lived by could no longer be applied to the living conditions imposed upon them by their European conquerors?
   IV. How did the tools of medieval manor influence the living conditions of people at that time?

   (A) II, III, and IV only
   (B) I, II, and IV only
   (C) I, II, and III only
   (D) III and IV only

6. It has been concluded that children whose parents read to them show improved academic achievement. Recent research has shown that

   (A) most parents stop reading to their children after age nine.
   (B) children do not need constant reinforcement to become lifelong readers.
   (C) there is little correlation between being a good reader and watching television.
   (D) reading skill only slightly correlates with socioeconomic status.

7. Which is NOT an effective method to improve reading comprehension?

   (A) Have students predict what will happen next in a story
   (B) Teach the meaning of Greek and Latin prefixes to improve vocabulary comprehension
   (C) Visualize events within a story
   (D) Analyze information about a story aloud

8. All of the following describe the development of children age eleven to thirteen EXCEPT

   (A) they shift from impulsivity to the ability to grasp the meaning of social organization and adaptation.
   (B) sex differences in IQ scores become more evident.
   (C) there is an increased objectivity in thinking.
   (D) abstract thinking and judgment come into play.

9. Examining the history of education in the United States, one can conclude that

   (A) religion has played little role in shaping education in the United States.
   (B) school funding was adequate in the late eighteenth and early nineteenth century.
   (C) education is a right under the United States Constitution.
   (D) state-supported public education did not come into general existence until the middle of the nineteenth century.

10. Why should a middle-school study the Eskimos, Aztecs, and Native Americans in preference to the Greeks and Romans?

    (A) Roman and Greek society is more complexly structured, requiring abstract conceptualization of many broad social science concepts.
    (B) Eskimo, Aztec, and Native American cultures are better known to elementary school students and demonstrate complex social structures in a simpler fashion.
    (C) Roman and Greek cultures are too simplistic for this age level.
    (D) The teaching of Roman and Greek civilization is mandated by the state to be taught in secondary school only.

11. All are effective methods to handle students who chronically avoid work EXCEPT

    (A) safeguard the student's self-image by not lowering his or her grade.
    (B) give assistance or modify the assignment for students who cannot complete their work.
    (C) break the assignment into smaller parts.
    (D) call the parent in to create a plan of action.

12. During the middle school years, reading should

    (A) be taught as a separate subject.
    (B) focus on the development of phonic analysis.
    (C) be used as a way to gain information from various subject areas.
    (D) concentrate on basal stories to develop specific skills.

13. A twelve-year-old boy in sixth grade comes from a dysfunctional family and has been abused and neglected. He has been in six foster homes and has attended nine different elementary schools. The student is presently decoding on the second-grade level, but he can comprehend material orally at the fourth- or fifth-grade level. The most probable cause(s) of this student's reading problem is (are)

    I.   neurological factors.
    II. emotional factors.
    III. poor teaching.
    IV. immaturity.
    (A) I and III only
    (B) II only
    (C) III only
    (D) I and IV only

14. Which is NOT an effective lesson reinforcing the application of geographic concepts?

(A) Using a physical map to figure out which sites are practical as settlements in terms of food, shelter, and transportation

(B) Learning the capitals and topographical features of politically significant countries

(C) Comparing and contrasting ethnic and political maps to figure out the causes of both World Wars

(D) Having students inflate or deflate the size of countries based on their Gross Domestic Product

15. Progressing from the factual to comprehension to application to analysis to synthesis and finally to evaluation was developed by

(A) Hertzberg.

(B) Maslow.

(C) Bloom.

(D) Piaget.

16. The BEST way to develop math concepts is by

(A) solving problems by looking for correct answers.

(B) learning math as applied to actual situations, such as its being a tool of science.

(C) using a concrete approach to solving problems.

(D) showing students multiple approaches to solving math examples and problems.

17. A science teacher would conduct experiments using images and lenses to give students an understanding of

(A) laser beams.

(B) turbines.

(C) barometers.

(D) mirrors.

18. All are problems in meeting the needs of medically fragile students EXCEPT

(A) they are mandated to be in classes that contain only other health-impaired children.

(B) such children have the right to attend public school and be provided with medical assistance.

(C) paraprofessionals are asked to perform procedures that are not part of their job description.

(D) dealing with a child's medical needs takes time away from academics.

19. Critics of multicultural education as it is presently being taught at the middle-school level state that

(A) too few ethnic groups are being discussed.

(B) such a curriculum does not foster a national identity.

(C) there should no longer be any emphasis on Western Civilization.

(D) such a curriculum must have a bilingual component.

20. Which is an inappropriate way to manage off-task behavior?

(A) Redirect a student's attention to task and check his progress to make sure he is continuing work

(B) Make eye contact or move closer to the student

(C) Remind the student of the correct procedure to use, and ask him if he remembers it

(D) Stop an activity to correct a child who is no longer on task

21. A child who is in the resource room is placed in your class. He sometimes has difficulty understanding you or following directions. Effective methods to deal with such a youngster are described by all of the following EXCEPT

(A) seat him as close to you as possible.

(B) talk with the resource room teacher to find out what he can do.

(C) ask the child's previous year's teacher for suggestions.

(D) give the child less demanding work than the rest of the class.

22. On the first day of school, a student comes in 45 minutes late. Which of the following statements describes the best way to handle this situation?

(A) Do not allow the student in the room until you discuss with her the rules of punctuality

(B) Treat her as warmly as the other students, and tell her you will talk to her about what she missed as soon as you can

(C) Send her to an administrator to let her know your firm stand about punctuality

(D) Tell her she must come tomorrow with her parents

23. The LEAST effective procedure in the teaching of historical concepts would be to

    (A) look at pictures of buildings that existed fifty to one hundred years earlier on a particular neighborhood street.
    (B) read about important political leaders and heroes of their community.
    (C) have students interview old people for recollections of how they got around before cars were plentiful.
    (D) examine commonplace appliances used one hundred years ago.

24. Which are effective methods in teaching students critical reading skills?

    I.   Interpret editorials about a particular subject from different newspapers
    II. Read and interpret three different reviews on a movie
    III. Identify and categorize different propaganda techniques
    IV. Distinguish fiction from nonfiction materials

    (A) I and II only
    (B) III and IV only
    (C) III only
    (D) I, II, and III only

GRADES 7–12

Directions: For each question, choose the best response and mark the corresponding circle on your answer sheet.

1. Standardized tests contain different types of derived scores. All of these are derived scores EXCEPT

   (A) stanines.
   (B) percentiles.
   (C) criterion measures.
   (D) standard measures.

2. A student confides that she is being physically abused by her parents but begs you not to tell anyone. As an educator, what are you obliged to do?

   (A) Obey the wishes of the student
   (B) Call her parents to discuss the student's complaint
   (C) Call the police to get the student protection
   (D) You or a designee from the school should call the Department of Child Welfare so they can investigate the complaint

3. A principal believes that teachers must be role models, acting with fairness, honesty, and objectivity. This principal is following the theory of moral development stressed by

   (A) Kohlberg.
   (B) Freud.
   (C) Piaget.
   (D) Bandura.

4. *Operant conditioning* is most closely associated with

   (A) Jung.
   (B) Pavlov.
   (C) Skinner.
   (D) Lovaas.

5. Which of the following is NOT a provision of the Family Education Rights and Privacy Act, or "Buckley Amendment"?

   (A) School medical treatment records are confidential and cannot be released.
   (B) Parents have the right to inspect and review their child's education records.
   (C) Parents can challenge the contents of school records and request that such records be amended.
   (D) City, state, and federal agencies can request and receive school records without a parent's consent.

6. According to Bloom's Taxonomy, which of the following is a good example of a synthesis question?

   (A) What are the root causes of the Vietnam War?
   (B) Which is the most important battle of the Civil War?
   (C) Which are the names of three countries in the Middle East?
   (D) How are communism and fascism similar?

7. Which court case established the right of due process before a student is suspended for even a short period of time?

   (A) *Goss vs. Lopez*
   (B) *Mills vs. Washington, D.C.*
   (C) *Brown vs. Topeka*
   (D) *Lau vs. Nicholas*

8. Which of the following is (are) appropriate for a high school course in computer education?

   I.   How to create and work with files
   II. How to program in various computer languages
   III. How to use appropriate software to develop problem-solving and critical-thinking skills

   (A) I only
   (B) I and II only
   (C) II only
   (D) I, II, and III

9. In a psychology course, a teacher discusses awareness of society's expectations, negative vs. positive events, and observational learning. The teacher is trying to explain the concept of

    (A) impulse control.
    (B) operant conditioning.
    (C) socialization.
    (D) sublimation of inner needs.

10. All of the following are organizational skills EXCEPT

    (A) outlining information with subheadings.
    (B) taking notes.
    (C) summarizing information from another resource.
    (D) using an encyclopedia.

11. Public Law 94–142 includes all of the following handicapping conditions EXCEPT

    (A) learning disabled.
    (B) socially maladjusted.
    (C) emotionally disturbed.
    (D) blind.

12. Various public education advocacy groups feel which of the following poses the greatest threat to public education?

    (A) Using vouchers to pay for private school choice
    (B) Using vouchers to pay for public school choice
    (C) Increased funding of preschool programs
    (D) National standards for teacher certification

13. The average student is now watching about 24 hours of television a week. According to the latest research, how is learning affected by extensive television viewing?

    I. Shorter attention span
    II. Language problems
    III. Improved thinking ability

    (A) I only
    (B) II only
    (C) I, II and II
    (D) I and II only

14. According to the latest research, which is an important factor in successfully mainstreaming a learning disabled student?

    (A) Appropriate academic behavior such as attention and class participation
    (B) A history of good attendance in his/her special class
    (C) Doing homework consistently in the mainstream class
    (D) Achievement of IEP objectives

15. A social studies textbook written in 1936 probably would depict slavery

    (A) paternalistically.
    (B) positively.
    (C) as an unavoidable evil.
    (D) as an exploitative institution.

16. Which of the following is an example of *de jure segregation*?

    (A) A school board creating a separate school for minority students
    (B) An African-American school in an inner-city ghetto
    (C) A magnet school that selects students based on a qualifying exam
    (D) A separate school for extremely emotionally disturbed students

17. Bilingual instruction has been guided by research into second-language acquisition. According to this research,

    (A) academic language develops together with social language.
    (B) academic language is easier to learn than social language.
    (C) students are often frustrated when content area subjects are taught in the student's primary language.
    (D) academic language can take up to seven years to develop, even when a student has acquired fluent social language.

18. A Committee on Special Education has to decide where to place an adolescent with cerebral palsy. The student has a history of seizures that are controlled by medication. The pupil has average intellectual ability with only slight gaps in learning. The recommendation will probably be for a

(A) special class.
(B) day treatment center for adolescents with cerebral palsy.
(C) regular education class containing adaptive devices.
(D) regular education class with resource room.

19. A thorough analysis of whether private schools or public schools do a better job educating children reveals that

(A) the curriculum within most private schools is substandard.
(B) most private schools skew achievement by selecting only capable students.
(C) students who go to private schools have higher IQs.
(D) most private schools tend to segregate students by ability.

20. In recent years, most courts have ruled against cases of education negligence because

(A) state law holds that parents are responsible for whether or not a student learns.
(B) schools are not responsible for a student's ability.
(C) too many factors are involved in whether or not a student achieves in school.
(D) an education is not a constitutional right.

21. It is easiest to charge and eventually dismiss a tenured teacher if the teacher

(A) is proven to be incompetent.
(B) is absent excessively.
(C) is continually insubordinate.
(D) commits and is convicted of a criminal act.

22. A high school physics teacher lectures about quantum mechanics. He speaks for 45 minutes, asking only 5 questions during the lesson. When students ask for explanations, the teacher replies that the answers are in the textbook. The students seem bored and fidgety. The teacher writes no notes on the chalkboard except for a few simple diagrams. What are some valid criticisms of this lesson?

I.   There was little teacher-student interaction.
II. Terms and concepts should have been clarified by the teacher.
III. The teacher's presentation should have been better organized.

(A) I and III only
(B) II only
(C) I only
(D) I, II, and III

23. Education in the United States is primarily the responsibility of the

(A) local government.
(B) state government.
(C) federal government.
(D) parents.

24. In the early part of the twentieth century, the predominant educational philosophy was

(A) based on a factory model.
(B) greatly influenced by Dewey.
(C) based on humanistic ideals.
(D) based on a child-centered approach to learning.

ANSWER KEY

Early Childhood

1. A	7. B	13. C	19. B
2. D	8. A	14. A	20. C
3. D	9. C	15. D	21. B
4. C	10. D	16. D	22. B
5. C	11. D	17. D	23. A
6. D	12. B	18. C	24. A

Grades K–6

1. D	7. A	13. B	19. D
2. A	8. D	14. B	20. A
3. C	9. D	15. C	21. C
4. A	10. A	16. C	22. A
5. D	11. A	17. C	23. C
6. D	12. A	18. C	24. A

Grades 5–9

1. B	7. B	13. B	19. B
2. A	8. B	14. B	20. D
3. C	9. D	15. B	21. D
4. A	10. A	16. B	22. B
5. C	11. A	17. A	23. B
6. A	12. C	18. A	24. D

Grades 7–12

1. C	7. A	13. D	19. B
2. D	8. D	14. A	20. C
3. D	9. C	15. A	21. D
4. C	10. D	16. A	22. D
5. D	11. B	17. D	23. A
6. D	12. A	18. C	24. A

Part III

Praxis II:
Subject Assessments

ANSWER SHEETS

Biology and General Science

1	ⓐ	ⓑ	ⓒ	ⓓ	ⓔ
2	ⓐ	ⓑ	ⓒ	ⓓ	ⓔ
3	ⓐ	ⓑ	ⓒ	ⓓ	ⓔ
4	ⓐ	ⓑ	ⓒ	ⓓ	ⓔ
5	ⓐ	ⓑ	ⓒ	ⓓ	ⓔ
6	ⓐ	ⓑ	ⓒ	ⓓ	ⓔ
7	ⓐ	ⓑ	ⓒ	ⓓ	ⓔ
8	ⓐ	ⓑ	ⓒ	ⓓ	ⓔ
9	ⓐ	ⓑ	ⓒ	ⓓ	ⓔ
10	ⓐ	ⓑ	ⓒ	ⓓ	ⓔ
11	ⓐ	ⓑ	ⓒ	ⓓ	ⓔ
12	ⓐ	ⓑ	ⓒ	ⓓ	ⓔ
13	ⓐ	ⓑ	ⓒ	ⓓ	ⓔ
14	ⓐ	ⓑ	ⓒ	ⓓ	ⓔ
15	ⓐ	ⓑ	ⓒ	ⓓ	ⓔ
16	ⓐ	ⓑ	ⓒ	ⓓ	ⓔ
17	ⓐ	ⓑ	ⓒ	ⓓ	ⓔ
18	ⓐ	ⓑ	ⓒ	ⓓ	ⓔ
19	ⓐ	ⓑ	ⓒ	ⓓ	ⓔ
20	ⓐ	ⓑ	ⓒ	ⓓ	ⓔ
21	ⓐ	ⓑ	ⓒ	ⓓ	ⓔ
22	ⓐ	ⓑ	ⓒ	ⓓ	ⓔ
23	ⓐ	ⓑ	ⓒ	ⓓ	ⓔ
24	ⓐ	ⓑ	ⓒ	ⓓ	ⓔ
25	ⓐ	ⓑ	ⓒ	ⓓ	ⓔ

Business Education

1	ⓐ	ⓑ	ⓒ	ⓓ	ⓔ
2	ⓐ	ⓑ	ⓒ	ⓓ	ⓔ
3	ⓐ	ⓑ	ⓒ	ⓓ	ⓔ
4	ⓐ	ⓑ	ⓒ	ⓓ	ⓔ
5	ⓐ	ⓑ	ⓒ	ⓓ	ⓔ
6	ⓐ	ⓑ	ⓒ	ⓓ	ⓔ
7	ⓐ	ⓑ	ⓒ	ⓓ	ⓔ
8	ⓐ	ⓑ	ⓒ	ⓓ	ⓔ
9	ⓐ	ⓑ	ⓒ	ⓓ	ⓔ
10	ⓐ	ⓑ	ⓒ	ⓓ	ⓔ
11	ⓐ	ⓑ	ⓒ	ⓓ	ⓔ
12	ⓐ	ⓑ	ⓒ	ⓓ	ⓔ
13	ⓐ	ⓑ	ⓒ	ⓓ	ⓔ
14	ⓐ	ⓑ	ⓒ	ⓓ	ⓔ
15	ⓐ	ⓑ	ⓒ	ⓓ	ⓔ
16	ⓐ	ⓑ	ⓒ	ⓓ	ⓔ
17	ⓐ	ⓑ	ⓒ	ⓓ	ⓔ
18	ⓐ	ⓑ	ⓒ	ⓓ	ⓔ
19	ⓐ	ⓑ	ⓒ	ⓓ	ⓔ
20	ⓐ	ⓑ	ⓒ	ⓓ	ⓔ
21	ⓐ	ⓑ	ⓒ	ⓓ	ⓔ
22	ⓐ	ⓑ	ⓒ	ⓓ	ⓔ
23	ⓐ	ⓑ	ⓒ	ⓓ	ⓔ
24	ⓐ	ⓑ	ⓒ	ⓓ	ⓔ
25	ⓐ	ⓑ	ⓒ	ⓓ	ⓔ

Chemistry

1	ⓐ	ⓑ	ⓒ	ⓓ	ⓔ
2	ⓐ	ⓑ	ⓒ	ⓓ	ⓔ
3	ⓐ	ⓑ	ⓒ	ⓓ	ⓔ
4	ⓐ	ⓑ	ⓒ	ⓓ	ⓔ
5	ⓐ	ⓑ	ⓒ	ⓓ	ⓔ
6	ⓐ	ⓑ	ⓒ	ⓓ	ⓔ
7	ⓐ	ⓑ	ⓒ	ⓓ	ⓔ
8	ⓐ	ⓑ	ⓒ	ⓓ	ⓔ
9	ⓐ	ⓑ	ⓒ	ⓓ	ⓔ
10	ⓐ	ⓑ	ⓒ	ⓓ	ⓔ
11	ⓐ	ⓑ	ⓒ	ⓓ	ⓔ
12	ⓐ	ⓑ	ⓒ	ⓓ	ⓔ
13	ⓐ	ⓑ	ⓒ	ⓓ	ⓔ
14	ⓐ	ⓑ	ⓒ	ⓓ	ⓔ
15	ⓐ	ⓑ	ⓒ	ⓓ	ⓔ
16	ⓐ	ⓑ	ⓒ	ⓓ	ⓔ
17	ⓐ	ⓑ	ⓒ	ⓓ	ⓔ
18	ⓐ	ⓑ	ⓒ	ⓓ	ⓔ
19	ⓐ	ⓑ	ⓒ	ⓓ	ⓔ
20	ⓐ	ⓑ	ⓒ	ⓓ	ⓔ
21	ⓐ	ⓑ	ⓒ	ⓓ	ⓔ
22	ⓐ	ⓑ	ⓒ	ⓓ	ⓔ
23	ⓐ	ⓑ	ⓒ	ⓓ	ⓔ
24	ⓐ	ⓑ	ⓒ	ⓓ	ⓔ
25	ⓐ	ⓑ	ⓒ	ⓓ	ⓔ

Early Childhood Education

1	ⓐ	ⓑ	ⓒ	ⓓ	ⓔ
2	ⓐ	ⓑ	ⓒ	ⓓ	ⓔ
3	ⓐ	ⓑ	ⓒ	ⓓ	ⓔ
4	ⓐ	ⓑ	ⓒ	ⓓ	ⓔ
5	ⓐ	ⓑ	ⓒ	ⓓ	ⓔ
6	ⓐ	ⓑ	ⓒ	ⓓ	ⓔ
7	ⓐ	ⓑ	ⓒ	ⓓ	ⓔ
8	ⓐ	ⓑ	ⓒ	ⓓ	ⓔ
9	ⓐ	ⓑ	ⓒ	ⓓ	ⓔ
10	ⓐ	ⓑ	ⓒ	ⓓ	ⓔ
11	ⓐ	ⓑ	ⓒ	ⓓ	ⓔ
12	ⓐ	ⓑ	ⓒ	ⓓ	ⓔ
13	ⓐ	ⓑ	ⓒ	ⓓ	ⓔ
14	ⓐ	ⓑ	ⓒ	ⓓ	ⓔ
15	ⓐ	ⓑ	ⓒ	ⓓ	ⓔ
16	ⓐ	ⓑ	ⓒ	ⓓ	ⓔ
17	ⓐ	ⓑ	ⓒ	ⓓ	ⓔ
18	ⓐ	ⓑ	ⓒ	ⓓ	ⓔ
19	ⓐ	ⓑ	ⓒ	ⓓ	ⓔ
20	ⓐ	ⓑ	ⓒ	ⓓ	ⓔ
21	ⓐ	ⓑ	ⓒ	ⓓ	ⓔ
22	ⓐ	ⓑ	ⓒ	ⓓ	ⓔ
23	ⓐ	ⓑ	ⓒ	ⓓ	ⓔ
24	ⓐ	ⓑ	ⓒ	ⓓ	ⓔ
25	ⓐ	ⓑ	ⓒ	ⓓ	ⓔ

Educational Leadership: Administration and Supervision

1	ⓐ	ⓑ	ⓒ	ⓓ	ⓔ
2	ⓐ	ⓑ	ⓒ	ⓓ	ⓔ
3	ⓐ	ⓑ	ⓒ	ⓓ	ⓔ
4	ⓐ	ⓑ	ⓒ	ⓓ	ⓔ
5	ⓐ	ⓑ	ⓒ	ⓓ	ⓔ
6	ⓐ	ⓑ	ⓒ	ⓓ	ⓔ
7	ⓐ	ⓑ	ⓒ	ⓓ	ⓔ
8	ⓐ	ⓑ	ⓒ	ⓓ	ⓔ
9	ⓐ	ⓑ	ⓒ	ⓓ	ⓔ
10	ⓐ	ⓑ	ⓒ	ⓓ	ⓔ
11	ⓐ	ⓑ	ⓒ	ⓓ	ⓔ
12	ⓐ	ⓑ	ⓒ	ⓓ	ⓔ
13	ⓐ	ⓑ	ⓒ	ⓓ	ⓔ
14	ⓐ	ⓑ	ⓒ	ⓓ	ⓔ
15	ⓐ	ⓑ	ⓒ	ⓓ	ⓔ
16	ⓐ	ⓑ	ⓒ	ⓓ	ⓔ
17	ⓐ	ⓑ	ⓒ	ⓓ	ⓔ
18	ⓐ	ⓑ	ⓒ	ⓓ	ⓔ
19	ⓐ	ⓑ	ⓒ	ⓓ	ⓔ
20	ⓐ	ⓑ	ⓒ	ⓓ	ⓔ
21	ⓐ	ⓑ	ⓒ	ⓓ	ⓔ
22	ⓐ	ⓑ	ⓒ	ⓓ	ⓔ
23	ⓐ	ⓑ	ⓒ	ⓓ	ⓔ
24	ⓐ	ⓑ	ⓒ	ⓓ	ⓔ
25	ⓐ	ⓑ	ⓒ	ⓓ	ⓔ

Elementary Education: Content Knowledge

1	ⓐ	ⓑ	ⓒ	ⓓ	ⓔ
2	ⓐ	ⓑ	ⓒ	ⓓ	ⓔ
3	ⓐ	ⓑ	ⓒ	ⓓ	ⓔ
4	ⓐ	ⓑ	ⓒ	ⓓ	ⓔ
5	ⓐ	ⓑ	ⓒ	ⓓ	ⓔ
6	ⓐ	ⓑ	ⓒ	ⓓ	ⓔ
7	ⓐ	ⓑ	ⓒ	ⓓ	ⓔ
8	ⓐ	ⓑ	ⓒ	ⓓ	ⓔ
9	ⓐ	ⓑ	ⓒ	ⓓ	ⓔ
10	ⓐ	ⓑ	ⓒ	ⓓ	ⓔ
11	ⓐ	ⓑ	ⓒ	ⓓ	ⓔ
12	ⓐ	ⓑ	ⓒ	ⓓ	ⓔ
13	ⓐ	ⓑ	ⓒ	ⓓ	ⓔ
14	ⓐ	ⓑ	ⓒ	ⓓ	ⓔ
15	ⓐ	ⓑ	ⓒ	ⓓ	ⓔ
16	ⓐ	ⓑ	ⓒ	ⓓ	ⓔ
17	ⓐ	ⓑ	ⓒ	ⓓ	ⓔ
18	ⓐ	ⓑ	ⓒ	ⓓ	ⓔ
19	ⓐ	ⓑ	ⓒ	ⓓ	ⓔ
20	ⓐ	ⓑ	ⓒ	ⓓ	ⓔ
21	ⓐ	ⓑ	ⓒ	ⓓ	ⓔ
22	ⓐ	ⓑ	ⓒ	ⓓ	ⓔ
23	ⓐ	ⓑ	ⓒ	ⓓ	ⓔ
24	ⓐ	ⓑ	ⓒ	ⓓ	ⓔ
25	ⓐ	ⓑ	ⓒ	ⓓ	ⓔ

Elementary Education: Curriculum, Instruction, and Assessment

1	ⓐ	ⓑ	ⓒ	ⓓ	ⓔ
2	ⓐ	ⓑ	ⓒ	ⓓ	ⓔ
3	ⓐ	ⓑ	ⓒ	ⓓ	ⓔ
4	ⓐ	ⓑ	ⓒ	ⓓ	ⓔ
5	ⓐ	ⓑ	ⓒ	ⓓ	ⓔ
6	ⓐ	ⓑ	ⓒ	ⓓ	ⓔ
7	ⓐ	ⓑ	ⓒ	ⓓ	ⓔ
8	ⓐ	ⓑ	ⓒ	ⓓ	ⓔ
9	ⓐ	ⓑ	ⓒ	ⓓ	ⓔ
10	ⓐ	ⓑ	ⓒ	ⓓ	ⓔ
11	ⓐ	ⓑ	ⓒ	ⓓ	ⓔ
12	ⓐ	ⓑ	ⓒ	ⓓ	ⓔ
13	ⓐ	ⓑ	ⓒ	ⓓ	ⓔ
14	ⓐ	ⓑ	ⓒ	ⓓ	ⓔ
15	ⓐ	ⓑ	ⓒ	ⓓ	ⓔ
16	ⓐ	ⓑ	ⓒ	ⓓ	ⓔ
17	ⓐ	ⓑ	ⓒ	ⓓ	ⓔ
18	ⓐ	ⓑ	ⓒ	ⓓ	ⓔ
19	ⓐ	ⓑ	ⓒ	ⓓ	ⓔ
20	ⓐ	ⓑ	ⓒ	ⓓ	ⓔ
21	ⓐ	ⓑ	ⓒ	ⓓ	ⓔ
22	ⓐ	ⓑ	ⓒ	ⓓ	ⓔ
23	ⓐ	ⓑ	ⓒ	ⓓ	ⓔ
24	ⓐ	ⓑ	ⓒ	ⓓ	ⓔ
25	ⓐ	ⓑ	ⓒ	ⓓ	ⓔ

Family and Consumer Sciences

1 Ⓐ Ⓑ Ⓒ Ⓓ Ⓔ
2 Ⓐ Ⓑ Ⓒ Ⓓ Ⓔ
3 Ⓐ Ⓑ Ⓒ Ⓓ Ⓔ
4 Ⓐ Ⓑ Ⓒ Ⓓ Ⓔ
5 Ⓐ Ⓑ Ⓒ Ⓓ Ⓔ
6 Ⓐ Ⓑ Ⓒ Ⓓ Ⓔ
7 Ⓐ Ⓑ Ⓒ Ⓓ Ⓔ
8 Ⓐ Ⓑ Ⓒ Ⓓ Ⓔ
9 Ⓐ Ⓑ Ⓒ Ⓓ Ⓔ
10 Ⓐ Ⓑ Ⓒ Ⓓ Ⓔ
11 Ⓐ Ⓑ Ⓒ Ⓓ Ⓔ
12 Ⓐ Ⓑ Ⓒ Ⓓ Ⓔ
13 Ⓐ Ⓑ Ⓒ Ⓓ Ⓔ
14 Ⓐ Ⓑ Ⓒ Ⓓ Ⓔ
15 Ⓐ Ⓑ Ⓒ Ⓓ Ⓔ
16 Ⓐ Ⓑ Ⓒ Ⓓ Ⓔ
17 Ⓐ Ⓑ Ⓒ Ⓓ Ⓔ
18 Ⓐ Ⓑ Ⓒ Ⓓ Ⓔ
19 Ⓐ Ⓑ Ⓒ Ⓓ Ⓔ
20 Ⓐ Ⓑ Ⓒ Ⓓ Ⓔ
21 Ⓐ Ⓑ Ⓒ Ⓓ Ⓔ
22 Ⓐ Ⓑ Ⓒ Ⓓ Ⓔ
23 Ⓐ Ⓑ Ⓒ Ⓓ Ⓔ
24 Ⓐ Ⓑ Ⓒ Ⓓ Ⓔ
25 Ⓐ Ⓑ Ⓒ Ⓓ Ⓔ

Introduction to the Teaching of Reading

1 Ⓐ Ⓑ Ⓒ Ⓓ Ⓔ
2 Ⓐ Ⓑ Ⓒ Ⓓ Ⓔ
3 Ⓐ Ⓑ Ⓒ Ⓓ Ⓔ
4 Ⓐ Ⓑ Ⓒ Ⓓ Ⓔ
5 Ⓐ Ⓑ Ⓒ Ⓓ Ⓔ
6 Ⓐ Ⓑ Ⓒ Ⓓ Ⓔ
7 Ⓐ Ⓑ Ⓒ Ⓓ Ⓔ
8 Ⓐ Ⓑ Ⓒ Ⓓ Ⓔ
9 Ⓐ Ⓑ Ⓒ Ⓓ Ⓔ
10 Ⓐ Ⓑ Ⓒ Ⓓ Ⓔ
11 Ⓐ Ⓑ Ⓒ Ⓓ Ⓔ
12 Ⓐ Ⓑ Ⓒ Ⓓ Ⓔ
13 Ⓐ Ⓑ Ⓒ Ⓓ Ⓔ
14 Ⓐ Ⓑ Ⓒ Ⓓ Ⓔ
15 Ⓐ Ⓑ Ⓒ Ⓓ Ⓔ
16 Ⓐ Ⓑ Ⓒ Ⓓ Ⓔ
17 Ⓐ Ⓑ Ⓒ Ⓓ Ⓔ
18 Ⓐ Ⓑ Ⓒ Ⓓ Ⓔ
19 Ⓐ Ⓑ Ⓒ Ⓓ Ⓔ
20 Ⓐ Ⓑ Ⓒ Ⓓ Ⓔ
21 Ⓐ Ⓑ Ⓒ Ⓓ Ⓔ
22 Ⓐ Ⓑ Ⓒ Ⓓ Ⓔ
23 Ⓐ Ⓑ Ⓒ Ⓓ Ⓔ
24 Ⓐ Ⓑ Ⓒ Ⓓ Ⓔ
25 Ⓐ Ⓑ Ⓒ Ⓓ Ⓔ

Mathematics: Content Knowledge

1 Ⓐ Ⓑ Ⓒ Ⓓ Ⓔ
2 Ⓐ Ⓑ Ⓒ Ⓓ Ⓔ
3 Ⓐ Ⓑ Ⓒ Ⓓ Ⓔ
4 Ⓐ Ⓑ Ⓒ Ⓓ Ⓔ
5 Ⓐ Ⓑ Ⓒ Ⓓ Ⓔ
6 Ⓐ Ⓑ Ⓒ Ⓓ Ⓔ
7 Ⓐ Ⓑ Ⓒ Ⓓ Ⓔ
8 Ⓐ Ⓑ Ⓒ Ⓓ Ⓔ
9 Ⓐ Ⓑ Ⓒ Ⓓ Ⓔ
10 Ⓐ Ⓑ Ⓒ Ⓓ Ⓔ
11 Ⓐ Ⓑ Ⓒ Ⓓ Ⓔ
12 Ⓐ Ⓑ Ⓒ Ⓓ Ⓔ
13 Ⓐ Ⓑ Ⓒ Ⓓ Ⓔ
14 Ⓐ Ⓑ Ⓒ Ⓓ Ⓔ
15 Ⓐ Ⓑ Ⓒ Ⓓ Ⓔ
16 Ⓐ Ⓑ Ⓒ Ⓓ Ⓔ
17 Ⓐ Ⓑ Ⓒ Ⓓ Ⓔ
18 Ⓐ Ⓑ Ⓒ Ⓓ Ⓔ
19 Ⓐ Ⓑ Ⓒ Ⓓ Ⓔ
20 Ⓐ Ⓑ Ⓒ Ⓓ Ⓔ
21 Ⓐ Ⓑ Ⓒ Ⓓ Ⓔ
22 Ⓐ Ⓑ Ⓒ Ⓓ Ⓔ
23 Ⓐ Ⓑ Ⓒ Ⓓ Ⓔ
24 Ⓐ Ⓑ Ⓒ Ⓓ Ⓔ
25 Ⓐ Ⓑ Ⓒ Ⓓ Ⓔ

Music Education

1 Ⓐ Ⓑ Ⓒ Ⓓ Ⓔ
2 Ⓐ Ⓑ Ⓒ Ⓓ Ⓔ
3 Ⓐ Ⓑ Ⓒ Ⓓ Ⓔ
4 Ⓐ Ⓑ Ⓒ Ⓓ Ⓔ
5 Ⓐ Ⓑ Ⓒ Ⓓ Ⓔ
6 Ⓐ Ⓑ Ⓒ Ⓓ Ⓔ
7 Ⓐ Ⓑ Ⓒ Ⓓ Ⓔ
8 Ⓐ Ⓑ Ⓒ Ⓓ Ⓔ
9 Ⓐ Ⓑ Ⓒ Ⓓ Ⓔ
10 Ⓐ Ⓑ Ⓒ Ⓓ Ⓔ
11 Ⓐ Ⓑ Ⓒ Ⓓ Ⓔ
12 Ⓐ Ⓑ Ⓒ Ⓓ Ⓔ
13 Ⓐ Ⓑ Ⓒ Ⓓ Ⓔ
14 Ⓐ Ⓑ Ⓒ Ⓓ Ⓔ
15 Ⓐ Ⓑ Ⓒ Ⓓ Ⓔ
16 Ⓐ Ⓑ Ⓒ Ⓓ Ⓔ
17 Ⓐ Ⓑ Ⓒ Ⓓ Ⓔ
18 Ⓐ Ⓑ Ⓒ Ⓓ Ⓔ
19 Ⓐ Ⓑ Ⓒ Ⓓ Ⓔ
20 Ⓐ Ⓑ Ⓒ Ⓓ Ⓔ
21 Ⓐ Ⓑ Ⓒ Ⓓ Ⓔ
22 Ⓐ Ⓑ Ⓒ Ⓓ Ⓔ
23 Ⓐ Ⓑ Ⓒ Ⓓ Ⓔ
24 Ⓐ Ⓑ Ⓒ Ⓓ Ⓔ
25 Ⓐ Ⓑ Ⓒ Ⓓ Ⓔ

Physics

1 Ⓐ Ⓑ Ⓒ Ⓓ Ⓔ
2 Ⓐ Ⓑ Ⓒ Ⓓ Ⓔ
3 Ⓐ Ⓑ Ⓒ Ⓓ Ⓔ
4 Ⓐ Ⓑ Ⓒ Ⓓ Ⓔ
5 Ⓐ Ⓑ Ⓒ Ⓓ Ⓔ
6 Ⓐ Ⓑ Ⓒ Ⓓ Ⓔ
7 Ⓐ Ⓑ Ⓒ Ⓓ Ⓔ
8 Ⓐ Ⓑ Ⓒ Ⓓ Ⓔ
9 Ⓐ Ⓑ Ⓒ Ⓓ Ⓔ
10 Ⓐ Ⓑ Ⓒ Ⓓ Ⓔ
11 Ⓐ Ⓑ Ⓒ Ⓓ Ⓔ
12 Ⓐ Ⓑ Ⓒ Ⓓ Ⓔ
13 Ⓐ Ⓑ Ⓒ Ⓓ Ⓔ
14 Ⓐ Ⓑ Ⓒ Ⓓ Ⓔ
15 Ⓐ Ⓑ Ⓒ Ⓓ Ⓔ
16 Ⓐ Ⓑ Ⓒ Ⓓ Ⓔ
17 Ⓐ Ⓑ Ⓒ Ⓓ Ⓔ
18 Ⓐ Ⓑ Ⓒ Ⓓ Ⓔ
19 Ⓐ Ⓑ Ⓒ Ⓓ Ⓔ
20 Ⓐ Ⓑ Ⓒ Ⓓ Ⓔ
21 Ⓐ Ⓑ Ⓒ Ⓓ Ⓔ
22 Ⓐ Ⓑ Ⓒ Ⓓ Ⓔ
23 Ⓐ Ⓑ Ⓒ Ⓓ Ⓔ
24 Ⓐ Ⓑ Ⓒ Ⓓ Ⓔ
25 Ⓐ Ⓑ Ⓒ Ⓓ Ⓔ

Reading Specialist

1 Ⓐ Ⓑ Ⓒ Ⓓ Ⓔ
2 Ⓐ Ⓑ Ⓒ Ⓓ Ⓔ
3 Ⓐ Ⓑ Ⓒ Ⓓ Ⓔ
4 Ⓐ Ⓑ Ⓒ Ⓓ Ⓔ
5 Ⓐ Ⓑ Ⓒ Ⓓ Ⓔ
6 Ⓐ Ⓑ Ⓒ Ⓓ Ⓔ
7 Ⓐ Ⓑ Ⓒ Ⓓ Ⓔ
8 Ⓐ Ⓑ Ⓒ Ⓓ Ⓔ
9 Ⓐ Ⓑ Ⓒ Ⓓ Ⓔ
10 Ⓐ Ⓑ Ⓒ Ⓓ Ⓔ
11 Ⓐ Ⓑ Ⓒ Ⓓ Ⓔ
12 Ⓐ Ⓑ Ⓒ Ⓓ Ⓔ
13 Ⓐ Ⓑ Ⓒ Ⓓ Ⓔ
14 Ⓐ Ⓑ Ⓒ Ⓓ Ⓔ
15 Ⓐ Ⓑ Ⓒ Ⓓ Ⓔ
16 Ⓐ Ⓑ Ⓒ Ⓓ Ⓔ
17 Ⓐ Ⓑ Ⓒ Ⓓ Ⓔ
18 Ⓐ Ⓑ Ⓒ Ⓓ Ⓔ
19 Ⓐ Ⓑ Ⓒ Ⓓ Ⓔ
20 Ⓐ Ⓑ Ⓒ Ⓓ Ⓔ
21 Ⓐ Ⓑ Ⓒ Ⓓ Ⓔ
22 Ⓐ Ⓑ Ⓒ Ⓓ Ⓔ
23 Ⓐ Ⓑ Ⓒ Ⓓ Ⓔ
24 Ⓐ Ⓑ Ⓒ Ⓓ Ⓔ
25 Ⓐ Ⓑ Ⓒ Ⓓ Ⓔ

School Guidance and Counseling

1 Ⓐ Ⓑ Ⓒ Ⓓ Ⓔ
2 Ⓐ Ⓑ Ⓒ Ⓓ Ⓔ
3 Ⓐ Ⓑ Ⓒ Ⓓ Ⓔ
4 Ⓐ Ⓑ Ⓒ Ⓓ Ⓔ
5 Ⓐ Ⓑ Ⓒ Ⓓ Ⓔ
6 Ⓐ Ⓑ Ⓒ Ⓓ Ⓔ
7 Ⓐ Ⓑ Ⓒ Ⓓ Ⓔ
8 Ⓐ Ⓑ Ⓒ Ⓓ Ⓔ
9 Ⓐ Ⓑ Ⓒ Ⓓ Ⓔ
10 Ⓐ Ⓑ Ⓒ Ⓓ Ⓔ
11 Ⓐ Ⓑ Ⓒ Ⓓ Ⓔ
12 Ⓐ Ⓑ Ⓒ Ⓓ Ⓔ
13 Ⓐ Ⓑ Ⓒ Ⓓ Ⓔ
14 Ⓐ Ⓑ Ⓒ Ⓓ Ⓔ
15 Ⓐ Ⓑ Ⓒ Ⓓ Ⓔ
16 Ⓐ Ⓑ Ⓒ Ⓓ Ⓔ
17 Ⓐ Ⓑ Ⓒ Ⓓ Ⓔ
18 Ⓐ Ⓑ Ⓒ Ⓓ Ⓔ
19 Ⓐ Ⓑ Ⓒ Ⓓ Ⓔ
20 Ⓐ Ⓑ Ⓒ Ⓓ Ⓔ
21 Ⓐ Ⓑ Ⓒ Ⓓ Ⓔ
22 Ⓐ Ⓑ Ⓒ Ⓓ Ⓔ
23 Ⓐ Ⓑ Ⓒ Ⓓ Ⓔ
24 Ⓐ Ⓑ Ⓒ Ⓓ Ⓔ
25 Ⓐ Ⓑ Ⓒ Ⓓ Ⓔ

School Psychologist

1. Ⓐ Ⓑ Ⓒ Ⓓ Ⓔ
2. Ⓐ Ⓑ Ⓒ Ⓓ Ⓔ
3. Ⓐ Ⓑ Ⓒ Ⓓ Ⓔ
4. Ⓐ Ⓑ Ⓒ Ⓓ Ⓔ
5. Ⓐ Ⓑ Ⓒ Ⓓ Ⓔ
6. Ⓐ Ⓑ Ⓒ Ⓓ Ⓔ
7. Ⓐ Ⓑ Ⓒ Ⓓ Ⓔ
8. Ⓐ Ⓑ Ⓒ Ⓓ Ⓔ
9. Ⓐ Ⓑ Ⓒ Ⓓ Ⓔ
10. Ⓐ Ⓑ Ⓒ Ⓓ Ⓔ
11. Ⓐ Ⓑ Ⓒ Ⓓ Ⓔ
12. Ⓐ Ⓑ Ⓒ Ⓓ Ⓔ
13. Ⓐ Ⓑ Ⓒ Ⓓ Ⓔ
14. Ⓐ Ⓑ Ⓒ Ⓓ Ⓔ
15. Ⓐ Ⓑ Ⓒ Ⓓ Ⓔ
16. Ⓐ Ⓑ Ⓒ Ⓓ Ⓔ
17. Ⓐ Ⓑ Ⓒ Ⓓ Ⓔ
18. Ⓐ Ⓑ Ⓒ Ⓓ Ⓔ
19. Ⓐ Ⓑ Ⓒ Ⓓ Ⓔ
20. Ⓐ Ⓑ Ⓒ Ⓓ Ⓔ
21. Ⓐ Ⓑ Ⓒ Ⓓ Ⓔ
22. Ⓐ Ⓑ Ⓒ Ⓓ Ⓔ
23. Ⓐ Ⓑ Ⓒ Ⓓ Ⓔ
24. Ⓐ Ⓑ Ⓒ Ⓓ Ⓔ
25. Ⓐ Ⓑ Ⓒ Ⓓ Ⓔ

Special Education: Knowledge-Based Core Principles

1. Ⓐ Ⓑ Ⓒ Ⓓ Ⓔ
2. Ⓐ Ⓑ Ⓒ Ⓓ Ⓔ
3. Ⓐ Ⓑ Ⓒ Ⓓ Ⓔ
4. Ⓐ Ⓑ Ⓒ Ⓓ Ⓔ
5. Ⓐ Ⓑ Ⓒ Ⓓ Ⓔ
6. Ⓐ Ⓑ Ⓒ Ⓓ Ⓔ
7. Ⓐ Ⓑ Ⓒ Ⓓ Ⓔ
8. Ⓐ Ⓑ Ⓒ Ⓓ Ⓔ
9. Ⓐ Ⓑ Ⓒ Ⓓ Ⓔ
10. Ⓐ Ⓑ Ⓒ Ⓓ Ⓔ
11. Ⓐ Ⓑ Ⓒ Ⓓ Ⓔ
12. Ⓐ Ⓑ Ⓒ Ⓓ Ⓔ
13. Ⓐ Ⓑ Ⓒ Ⓓ Ⓔ
14. Ⓐ Ⓑ Ⓒ Ⓓ Ⓔ
15. Ⓐ Ⓑ Ⓒ Ⓓ Ⓔ
16. Ⓐ Ⓑ Ⓒ Ⓓ Ⓔ
17. Ⓐ Ⓑ Ⓒ Ⓓ Ⓔ
18. Ⓐ Ⓑ Ⓒ Ⓓ Ⓔ
19. Ⓐ Ⓑ Ⓒ Ⓓ Ⓔ
20. Ⓐ Ⓑ Ⓒ Ⓓ Ⓔ
21. Ⓐ Ⓑ Ⓒ Ⓓ Ⓔ
22. Ⓐ Ⓑ Ⓒ Ⓓ Ⓔ
23. Ⓐ Ⓑ Ⓒ Ⓓ Ⓔ
24. Ⓐ Ⓑ Ⓒ Ⓓ Ⓔ
25. Ⓐ Ⓑ Ⓒ Ⓓ Ⓔ

Special Education: Teaching Students with Mental Retardation

1. Ⓐ Ⓑ Ⓒ Ⓓ Ⓔ
2. Ⓐ Ⓑ Ⓒ Ⓓ Ⓔ
3. Ⓐ Ⓑ Ⓒ Ⓓ Ⓔ
4. Ⓐ Ⓑ Ⓒ Ⓓ Ⓔ
5. Ⓐ Ⓑ Ⓒ Ⓓ Ⓔ
6. Ⓐ Ⓑ Ⓒ Ⓓ Ⓔ
7. Ⓐ Ⓑ Ⓒ Ⓓ Ⓔ
8. Ⓐ Ⓑ Ⓒ Ⓓ Ⓔ
9. Ⓐ Ⓑ Ⓒ Ⓓ Ⓔ
10. Ⓐ Ⓑ Ⓒ Ⓓ Ⓔ
11. Ⓐ Ⓑ Ⓒ Ⓓ Ⓔ
12. Ⓐ Ⓑ Ⓒ Ⓓ Ⓔ
13. Ⓐ Ⓑ Ⓒ Ⓓ Ⓔ
14. Ⓐ Ⓑ Ⓒ Ⓓ Ⓔ
15. Ⓐ Ⓑ Ⓒ Ⓓ Ⓔ
16. Ⓐ Ⓑ Ⓒ Ⓓ Ⓔ
17. Ⓐ Ⓑ Ⓒ Ⓓ Ⓔ
18. Ⓐ Ⓑ Ⓒ Ⓓ Ⓔ
19. Ⓐ Ⓑ Ⓒ Ⓓ Ⓔ
20. Ⓐ Ⓑ Ⓒ Ⓓ Ⓔ
21. Ⓐ Ⓑ Ⓒ Ⓓ Ⓔ
22. Ⓐ Ⓑ Ⓒ Ⓓ Ⓔ
23. Ⓐ Ⓑ Ⓒ Ⓓ Ⓔ
24. Ⓐ Ⓑ Ⓒ Ⓓ Ⓔ
25. Ⓐ Ⓑ Ⓒ Ⓓ Ⓔ

Speech Communication

1. Ⓐ Ⓑ Ⓒ Ⓓ Ⓔ
2. Ⓐ Ⓑ Ⓒ Ⓓ Ⓔ
3. Ⓐ Ⓑ Ⓒ Ⓓ Ⓔ
4. Ⓐ Ⓑ Ⓒ Ⓓ Ⓔ
5. Ⓐ Ⓑ Ⓒ Ⓓ Ⓔ
6. Ⓐ Ⓑ Ⓒ Ⓓ Ⓔ
7. Ⓐ Ⓑ Ⓒ Ⓓ Ⓔ
8. Ⓐ Ⓑ Ⓒ Ⓓ Ⓔ
9. Ⓐ Ⓑ Ⓒ Ⓓ Ⓔ
10. Ⓐ Ⓑ Ⓒ Ⓓ Ⓔ
11. Ⓐ Ⓑ Ⓒ Ⓓ Ⓔ
12. Ⓐ Ⓑ Ⓒ Ⓓ Ⓔ
13. Ⓐ Ⓑ Ⓒ Ⓓ Ⓔ
14. Ⓐ Ⓑ Ⓒ Ⓓ Ⓔ
15. Ⓐ Ⓑ Ⓒ Ⓓ Ⓔ
16. Ⓐ Ⓑ Ⓒ Ⓓ Ⓔ
17. Ⓐ Ⓑ Ⓒ Ⓓ Ⓔ
18. Ⓐ Ⓑ Ⓒ Ⓓ Ⓔ
19. Ⓐ Ⓑ Ⓒ Ⓓ Ⓔ
20. Ⓐ Ⓑ Ⓒ Ⓓ Ⓔ
21. Ⓐ Ⓑ Ⓒ Ⓓ Ⓔ
22. Ⓐ Ⓑ Ⓒ Ⓓ Ⓔ
23. Ⓐ Ⓑ Ⓒ Ⓓ Ⓔ
24. Ⓐ Ⓑ Ⓒ Ⓓ Ⓔ
25. Ⓐ Ⓑ Ⓒ Ⓓ Ⓔ

Speech-Language Pathology

1. Ⓐ Ⓑ Ⓒ Ⓓ Ⓔ
2. Ⓐ Ⓑ Ⓒ Ⓓ Ⓔ
3. Ⓐ Ⓑ Ⓒ Ⓓ Ⓔ
4. Ⓐ Ⓑ Ⓒ Ⓓ Ⓔ
5. Ⓐ Ⓑ Ⓒ Ⓓ Ⓔ
6. Ⓐ Ⓑ Ⓒ Ⓓ Ⓔ
7. Ⓐ Ⓑ Ⓒ Ⓓ Ⓔ
8. Ⓐ Ⓑ Ⓒ Ⓓ Ⓔ
9. Ⓐ Ⓑ Ⓒ Ⓓ Ⓔ
10. Ⓐ Ⓑ Ⓒ Ⓓ Ⓔ
11. Ⓐ Ⓑ Ⓒ Ⓓ Ⓔ
12. Ⓐ Ⓑ Ⓒ Ⓓ Ⓔ
13. Ⓐ Ⓑ Ⓒ Ⓓ Ⓔ
14. Ⓐ Ⓑ Ⓒ Ⓓ Ⓔ
15. Ⓐ Ⓑ Ⓒ Ⓓ Ⓔ
16. Ⓐ Ⓑ Ⓒ Ⓓ Ⓔ
17. Ⓐ Ⓑ Ⓒ Ⓓ Ⓔ
18. Ⓐ Ⓑ Ⓒ Ⓓ Ⓔ
19. Ⓐ Ⓑ Ⓒ Ⓓ Ⓔ
20. Ⓐ Ⓑ Ⓒ Ⓓ Ⓔ
21. Ⓐ Ⓑ Ⓒ Ⓓ Ⓔ
22. Ⓐ Ⓑ Ⓒ Ⓓ Ⓔ
23. Ⓐ Ⓑ Ⓒ Ⓓ Ⓔ
24. Ⓐ Ⓑ Ⓒ Ⓓ Ⓔ
25. Ⓐ Ⓑ Ⓒ Ⓓ Ⓔ

Vocational General Knowledge

1. Ⓐ Ⓑ Ⓒ Ⓓ Ⓔ
2. Ⓐ Ⓑ Ⓒ Ⓓ Ⓔ
3. Ⓐ Ⓑ Ⓒ Ⓓ Ⓔ
4. Ⓐ Ⓑ Ⓒ Ⓓ Ⓔ
5. Ⓐ Ⓑ Ⓒ Ⓓ Ⓔ
6. Ⓐ Ⓑ Ⓒ Ⓓ Ⓔ
7. Ⓐ Ⓑ Ⓒ Ⓓ Ⓔ
8. Ⓐ Ⓑ Ⓒ Ⓓ Ⓔ
9. Ⓐ Ⓑ Ⓒ Ⓓ Ⓔ
10. Ⓐ Ⓑ Ⓒ Ⓓ Ⓔ
11. Ⓐ Ⓑ Ⓒ Ⓓ Ⓔ
12. Ⓐ Ⓑ Ⓒ Ⓓ Ⓔ
13. Ⓐ Ⓑ Ⓒ Ⓓ Ⓔ
14. Ⓐ Ⓑ Ⓒ Ⓓ Ⓔ
15. Ⓐ Ⓑ Ⓒ Ⓓ Ⓔ
16. Ⓐ Ⓑ Ⓒ Ⓓ Ⓔ
17. Ⓐ Ⓑ Ⓒ Ⓓ Ⓔ
18. Ⓐ Ⓑ Ⓒ Ⓓ Ⓔ
19. Ⓐ Ⓑ Ⓒ Ⓓ Ⓔ
20. Ⓐ Ⓑ Ⓒ Ⓓ Ⓔ
21. Ⓐ Ⓑ Ⓒ Ⓓ Ⓔ
22. Ⓐ Ⓑ Ⓒ Ⓓ Ⓔ
23. Ⓐ Ⓑ Ⓒ Ⓓ Ⓔ
24. Ⓐ Ⓑ Ⓒ Ⓓ Ⓔ
25. Ⓐ Ⓑ Ⓒ Ⓓ Ⓔ

ABOUT THE PRAXIS II: SUBJECT ASSESSMENTS

Praxis II: Subject Assessments offers tests measuring mastery of content and teaching techniques in a wide range of school subjects and specialties and subspecialties within those subjects. Many of these tests have limited use because their subject matter is specific to a particular state, such as accounting in Pennsylvania, or because the subject itself is not widely taught, such as Japanese, or simply because not many states require beginning teachers to prove their proficiency in those subjects.

For more detailed information about all the Subject Assessments in the Praxis Series, contact:

The Praxis Series
Educational Testing Service
P.O. Box 6051
Princeton, NJ 08541-6051

This final section of the book provides sample questions similar to those used on the most popular Subject Assessments given nationwide. You will find an answer key for all of these Subject Assessments test questions beginning on page 209.

BIOLOGY AND GENERAL SCIENCE (0030)

Time: 2 hours
Number of Questions: 160
Format: Multiple-choice questions

Purpose of the Test

Designed to measure the preparation of prospective secondary school biology and/or physical science teachers

Content Categories

- History, Philosophy, and Methodology of Science; Science, Technology, and Society—(10 percent)
- Molecular and Cellular Biology of Prokaryotes and Eukaryotes—(15 percent)
- Biology of Plants, Animals, Fungi, and Protists—(20 percent)
- Evolution—(12 percent)
- Ecology—(13 percent)
- Chemistry—(10 percent)
- Physics—(10 percent)
- Earth and Space Science—(10 percent)

Category Descriptions

History, Philosophy, and Methodology of Science; Science, Technology, and Society

1. Relevant history, philosophy, and methodology of science
2. Issues related to the intersection of science, technology, and society, including environmental issues

Molecular and Cellular Biology of Prokaryotes and Eukaryotes

1. Structure and function of cells and biologically important macromolecules
2. Molecular biology of genes and gene function, including viruses
3. Cellular bioenergetics, including photosynthesis and respiration

Biology of Plants, Animals, Fungi, and Protists

1. Principles of Mendelian and classical genetics
2. Characteristics, structure and function, reproduction and development, regulation and control, and behavior

Evolution

Mechanisms, population genetics, origin of life, systematics, and phylogeny

Ecology

1. Dynamics, intraspecific competition, and life-history patterns of populations
2. Energetics, interspecific relationships, and characteristics of communities
3. Aquatic and terrestrial systems, interrelationships, and biogeochemistry of ecosystems
4. Environmental issues

Chemistry

1. Structures, states, and properties of matter
2. Reactions and kinetic theory, including acids/bases, oxidation/reduction, and catalysts

Physics

1. Mechanics, energy and heat, electricity and magnetism, wave phenomena, atomic and nuclear physics
2. Environmental issues related to physics

Earth and Space Science

1. Astronomy, geology, oceanography, and meteorology
2. Environmental issues related to Earth and space science

Biology and General Science

Directions: Each question or incomplete statement is followed by five answer choices. For each question, decide which answer or completion is best, and blacken the letter of your choice on the answer sheet.

1. If the apparatus shown below is placed in a moderately warm location, within a few hours the

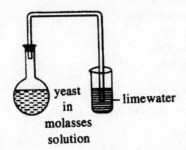

yeast in molasses solution — limewater

   (A) molasses solution will flow into the beaker.
   (B) molasses solution will turn brown.
   (C) limewater will turn milky.
   (D) limewater will flow into the flask.
   (E) None of these

Base your answers to questions 2, 3, and 4 on the pedigree chart below, where individual B is a hemophiliac male who is heterozygous for brown eyes. Individual A is his blue-eyed wife, who does not carry any genes for hemophilia.

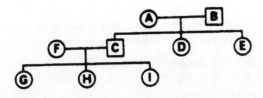

2. What is the probability that individual D is a hemophiliac?

   (A) 0

   (B) $\frac{1}{1}$

   (C) $\frac{1}{2}$

   (D) $\frac{1}{3}$

   (E) $\frac{1}{4}$

3. Which best represents the genetic makeup for eye color of individual H?

   (A) Homozygous brown
   (B) Homozygous blue
   (C) Heterozygous brown
   (D) Heterozygous blue
   (E) It cannot be determined from the information given.

4. If individual E marries a male who is a hemophiliac, which statement is true?

   (A) All of her sons must be hemophiliacs.
   (B) All of her daughters must carry at least one gene for hemophilia.
   (C) All of her daughters must be hemophiliacs.
   (D) Fifty percent of her sons can be hemophiliacs, but none of her daughters can be hemophiliacs.
   (E) Fifty percent of her daughters can be hemophiliacs, but none of her sons can be hemophiliacs.

5. The image formed by a convex mirror compared to the object is usually

   (A) inverted and imaginary.
   (B) erect and smaller.
   (C) real and inverted.
   (D) erect and imaginary.
   (E) inverted and larger.

6. Unicellular organisms ingest large molecules into their cytoplasm from the external environment without previously digesting them. This process is called

   (A) pinocytosis.
   (B) peristalsis.
   (C) plasmolysis.
   (D) osmosis.
   (E) transpiration.

7. Which of the following compounds stores energy that is immediately available for active muscle cells?

   (A) Creatine phosphate
   (B) Glycogen
   (C) Glucose
   (D) Glycine
   (E) Messenger RNA

8. The ciliary muscle is used for the process of

   (A) locomotion.
   (B) food transportation.
   (C) blinking.
   (D) accommodation.
   (E) respiration.

9. An atom of chlorine, atomic number 17 and atomic weight 35, contains in its nucleus

   (A) 35 protons.
   (B) 17 neutrons.
   (C) 35 neutrons.
   (D) 18 neutrons.
   (E) 18 electrons.

10. The structure that does NOT include nucleic acid is the

    (A) gene.
    (B) chromosome.
    (C) centriole.
    (D) ribosome.
    (E) chromatin.

Questions 11 and 12 refer to the figure below.

Diagram X represents the nucleus of a somatic cell of a mature spermatocyte. The following questions relate to the six numbered diagrams immediately below Diagram X.

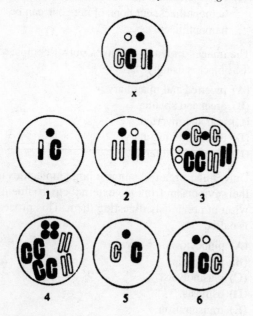

11. A functional sperm nucleus from a pollen grain produced by this plant could resemble

    (A) 1.
    (B) 2.
    (C) 5.
    (D) 4.
    (E) 6.

12. If meiotic division had NOT accompanied the formation of both gametes, a nucleus of the zygote formed would most likely have resembled

    (A) 1.
    (B) 2.
    (C) 3.
    (D) 4.
    (E) 5.

13. An organism having characteristics of both plants and animals is the

    (A) amoeba.
    (B) paramecium.
    (C) sponge.
    (D) euglena.
    (E) planaria.

14. Under the Linnaean system of classification, each kingdom is divided into related

    (A) phyla.
    (B) classes.
    (C) families.
    (D) genera.
    (E) species.

15. The major portion of ultraviolet radiation that reaches the earth is absorbed in the

    (A) troposphere.
    (B) stratosphere.
    (C) mesosphere.
    (D) thermosphere.
    (E) hydrosphere.

16. Cirrus, dew point, fronts, and isotherm are terms commonly associated with the field of

    (A) meteorology.
    (B) archaeology.
    (C) oceanography.
    (D) mineralogy.
    (E) seismology.

17. Which one of the following pairs is composed of the two LEAST related members?

    (A) Sea cucumber—sea lily
    (B) Horseshoe crab—octopus
    (C) Nautilus—garden slug
    (D) Scallop—squid
    (E) Hydra—sea anemone

18. In organic chemistry, the prefix is an important indication of the structure of the compound. For example:

Prefix	Number of carbons
meth-	1
eth-	2
pro-	3
but-	4
pent-	5

Given the compounds $CH_3CH_2CH_2CH_3$ and

$$CH_3 — CH — CH_3$$
$$|$$
$$CH_3$$

These compounds are both

(A) alkynes.
(B) alkenes.
(C) isomers of butane.
(D) isomers of propane.
(E) isomers of pentane.

19. How does the heat from the sun reach the earth?

(A) Conduction
(B) Convection
(C) Condensation
(D) Sublimation
(E) Radiation

Questions 20–23 are based on the following schematic diagram.

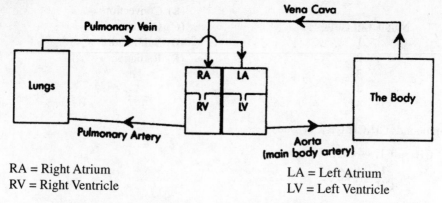

RA = Right Atrium
RV = Right Ventricle

LA = Left Atrium
LV = Left Ventricle

The above diagram indicates how blood circulates in the human body.

20. According to the diagram, in which direction do arteries carry blood?

(A) To the heart
(B) Away from the heart
(C) Both to and from the heart
(D) Only to the body
(E) Between the body and lungs

21. To which of the following does the left ventricle pump blood?

(A) The pulmonary artery
(B) The vena cava
(C) The pulmonary vein
(D) The left atrium
(E) All parts of the body

22. The blood found in the pulmonary vein has just left the lungs. Which of the following statements is true about this blood?

(A) It is rich in iron.
(B) It is poor in oxygen.
(C) It is rich in oxygen.
(D) It has no blood cells.
(E) It lacks the ability to fight germs.

23. Which of the following sequences shows the actual flow of blood?

(A) Lungs, the heart, right atrium, right ventricle
(B) The body, the lungs, vena cava, aorta
(C) Vena cava, right atrium, left ventricle, aorta
(D) Right ventricle, pulmonary artery, lungs, pulmonary vein
(E) Right ventricle, right atrium, vena cava, the lungs

24. It is LEAST likely to rain when the clouds in our sky are

(A) nimbostratus.
(B) nimbus.
(C) cirrus.
(D) altocumulus.
(E) cumulonimbus.

25. A form of binary fission in which one of the two offspring is smaller than the other is

(A) spermatogenesis.
(B) budding.
(C) mitosis.
(D) parthenogenesis.
(E) cogenesis.

BUSINESS EDUCATION (0100)

Time: 2 hours
Number of Questions: 120
Format: Multiple-choice questions. Calculators without
QWERTY keyboards are allowed.

Purpose of the Test

Designed to measure the preparation of those planning to teach in business education programs at the high school level

Content Categories

- U.S. Economic Systems—(10 percent)
- Money Management—(14 percent)
- Business and Its Environment—(11 percent)
- Professional Business Education—(20 percent)
- Processing Information—(17 percent)
- Office Procedures and Management, Communications, and Employability Skills—(14 percent)
- Accounting and Marketing—(14 percent)

Category Descriptions

U.S. Economic Systems

1. Free enterprise, entrepreneurship, and business organization/management: principles of management, business plans, and forms of business organizations

2. Government and banking: fiscal and monetary policies, GDP, taxation, and regulations

3. Economic principles: inflation, deflation, supply and demand, price systems, international trade, labor-management relations

Money Management

1. Business mathematics: calculations related to interest rates, financial management, budgets, loans, and extensions

2. Consumer education: budgeting, marketplace decisions, information resources, and consumer rights

3. Finance: banking, investing, credit, current value theory

Business and Its Environment

1. Business and consumer law: contracts, agent and principal, insurance, consignment, negotiable instruments, tort law, bankruptcy, consumer legislation, discrimination, negotiation, and global economy

2. Job standards, work standards, business ethics, and policies: peer relationships, employee evaluations, productivity measures

Professional Business Education

1. Current trends and issues: equipment, curriculum, instructional materials, interpretation and use of research

2. Student organizations: PBL, DECA, FBLA, Junior Achievement, Business Professionals of America

3. Professionalism: work ethics, human relations, professional organizations and literature, public relations

4. Methodology/teaching strategies: cooperative, simulation, competency-based, skill areas, group and individual, working with special-needs students, interactive computer software, selecting and/or determining standards for skilled and non-skilled subjects

5. Community relations: advisory committees, partnerships/alliances, visits

6. Federal vocational legislation: Carl D. Perkins Vocational Education Act of 1963 and subsequent amendments

7. Mission/objectives of business education: occupational preparation, responsibility to the business community, responsibility to society, personal-use skills, economic, literacy, training and retraining

8. Curriculum planning and program development: technological concerns, needs assessments, prescription of program outcomes, determination of content and materials, teaching strategies, activities, and evaluation

9. Department management: organization of a department, program evaluation, staffing, budgets, and equipment

10. Classroom management: record keeping, equipment safety, organizing and using classroom resources, managing classroom time and space

11. Counseling in business education: orientation, career awareness, career exploration, preparation, employment information and trends

Processing Information

1. Keyboarding, production, word processing, proofreading, editing, formatting, and entering and verifying data

2. Specialized types of information: statistical, legal, medical

3. Graphics, reprographics

4. Records management, database applications, spreadsheets, data security

5. Processing mail, shorthand and transcription systems, equipment use

6. Simulation productivity

7. Computer literacy, Internet technology

Office Procedures and Management, Communications, and Employability Skills

1. Business communications: written communications, oral communications, telecommunications, listening skills, communication barriers

2. Employability skills: self-assessment techniques, applications, references, job-search techniques, termination, advancement

3. Office procedures and management: workflow topics, assessing references, records management, record keeping, managing travel and meetings, handling mail

Accounting and Marketing

1. Accounting: accounting concepts; terminology and applications; accounting systems; basic accounting cycle of source documents, verifications, analyzing, recording, posting, trial balance, and statement

2. Marketing: sales techniques, advertising, display, buying, wholesale/retail, distribution, service occupations, market analysis, warehousing, inventory control

Business Education

> *Directions:* Each question or incomplete statement is followed by five answer choices. For each question, decide which answer or completion is best, and blacken the letter of your choice on the answer sheet.

1. The accounting equation is correctly stated as

   (A) Owner's Equity = Assets + Liabilities
   (B) Owner's Equity – Assets = Liabilities
   (C) Owner's Equity = Liabilities – Assets
   (D) Assets = Liabilities + Owner's Equity
   (E) Assets + Liabilities + Owner's Equity = 1

2. The purpose of a petty cash fund is to

   (A) take the place of the cash account.
   (B) provide a common drawing fund for the owners of the business.
   (C) provide a fund for making currency expenditures.
   (D) provide a valuation account for cash.
   (E) create a voucher file.

3. The bookkeeper should prepare a bank reconciliation mainly to determine

   (A) which checks are outstanding.
   (B) whether the checkbook balance and the bank statement balance are in agreement.
   (C) the total number of checks written during the month.
   (D) the total amount of cash deposited during the month.
   (E) the monthly net cash flow.

4. Which is the correct procedure for calculating the rate of merchandise turnover?

   (A) Gross Sales divided by Net Sales
   (B) Cost of Goods Sold divided by Average Inventory
   (C) Net Purchases divided by Average Inventory
   (D) Gross Purchases divided by Net Purchases
   (E) Closing Inventory minus Starting Inventory

5. What does the abbreviation CPA represent?

   (A) Certified Professional Accountant
   (B) Certified Public Accountant
   (C) Certified Professional Auditor
   (D) Certified Public Auditor
   (E) Certified Private Auditor

6. A set of instructions that guides the processing of data by an electronic computer is called a

   (A) file.
   (B) diagram.
   (C) program.
   (D) record.
   (E) flowchart.

7. The selling price of a share of stock as published in a daily newspaper is called the

   (A) book value.
   (B) face value.
   (C) par value.
   (D) market value.
   (E) maturity value.

8. Which type of endorsement is shown below?

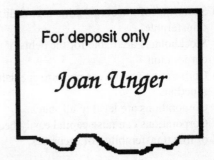

   (A) Restrictive
   (B) Blank
   (C) Full
   (D) Qualified
   (E) Contingent

9. Which phase of the data processing cycle is the same as calculating net pay in a manual system?

   (A) Input
   (B) Processing
   (C) Storing
   (D) Output
   (E) Printing

10. A business check guaranteed for payment by the bank is called a

    (A) bank draft.
    (B) certified check.
    (C) cashier's check.
    (D) personal check.
    (E) money order.

11. Which of the following CANNOT be used as input into a computer?

    (A) Punched card
    (B) Magnetic tape
    (C) Optical scanner
    (D) Printer
    (E) Keyboard

12. Which item on the bank reconciliation statement would require the business to record a journal entry?

    (A) A deposit in transit
    (B) An outstanding check
    (C) A canceled check
    (D) A bank service charge
    (E) A deposit made after the reconciliation closing date

13. Which statement is NOT true of the American corporation?

    (A) Securities of the corporation are readily transferable.
    (B) Stockholders are liable for the debts of the corporation.
    (C) Corporation employees perform specialized functions.
    (D) Corporations are legal in all states.
    (E) Corporations can raise capital easily because of free transferability of securities.

14. Of the following, which one corresponds to a fixed cost?

    (A) Payments for raw materials
    (B) Labor costs
    (C) Transportation charges
    (D) Insurance premiums
    (E) Manager's salary

15. The statement "Today, the dollar is worth about forty-five cents" describes

    (A) inflation.
    (B) prices.
    (C) supply and demand.
    (D) taxation.
    (E) deflation.

16. The consumer price index, an economic measure published by the U.S. government, may rise in response to certain domestic or foreign events. Which of the following headlines would be LEAST likely to cause an increase in the consumer price index?

    (A) "Bumper Harvest Expected in California"
    (B) "Thousands of Chickens Slaughtered in Southeastern Drought"
    (C) "Frost Hits Orange Groves in Coldest Florida Winter"
    (D) "U.S. Imposes Tariffs on Imported Autos"
    (E) "U.S. Embargo on Asian Microchips"

17. Personal income minus personal income taxes is called

    (A) real income.
    (B) gross income.
    (C) elastic income.
    (D) disposable income.
    (E) wages or salary.

18. The Taft-Hartley Act of 1947 provided for all of the following EXCEPT

    (A) permitting employers to sue unions.
    (B) requiring a sixty-day cooling-off period before strikes.
    (C) permitting union contributions to political campaigns.
    (D) requiring union leaders to take oaths that they were not Communist party members.
    (E) requiring unions to make public financial statements.

19. Which of the following is responsible for investigating fraudulent advertising and the sale of harmful products?

    (A) Federal Trade Commission
    (B) Securities and Exchange Commission
    (C) Department of Labor
    (D) Interstate Commerce Commission
    (E) Department of Human Services

20. In order to compute the income taxes you owe the federal government this year, your employer is required to give you a _____ that lists your earnings and withholdings for the past year.

    (A) 1040A form
    (B) W2 form
    (C) Social Security form
    (D) exemption statement
    (E) W4 form

21. The basic components of total demand are

    (A) human resources, natural resources, and capital resources.
    (B) consumption, investment, and government spending.
    (C) inflation, deflation, and taxes.
    (D) imports and exports.
    (E) food, clothing, and housing.

22. Americans pay many different types of taxes to federal, state, and local governments. Choose the best example of a tax that we do NOT pay in the United States.

    (A) Payroll tax
    (B) Excise tax
    (C) Value-added tax
    (D) Sales tax
    (E) Income tax

23. Susan Johnson earned $15,000 last year. Sam Milner earned $63,000 last year. Each person was required to pay a special tax of $350. Which of the following terms best describes this tax?

    (A) Proportional
    (B) Regressive
    (C) Inexpensive
    (D) Progressive
    (E) Unearned

24. Payments to a worker, his/her dependents, and/or survivors in the event of retirement, disability, or death are generally covered by the system of insurance known as

    (A) unemployment compensation.
    (B) Social Security.
    (C) workers' compensation.
    (D) pension fund.
    (E) profit sharing.

25. A short period of somewhat decreased business activity is known as a

    (A) boom.
    (B) depression.
    (C) recession.
    (D) crash.
    (E) demand.

CHEMISTRY (0240)

Time: 2 hours
Number of Questions: 120
Format: Multiple-choice questions

Purpose of the Test

Designed to measure the preparation of those planning to teach secondary school chemistry

Content Categories

- Structure of Matter—(17 percent)
- States of Matter—(17 percent)
- Reactions of Matter—(48 percent)
- Particulate Samples of Matter—(8 percent)
- Laboratory Handling of Matter; Environmental Issues Related to Chemistry—(10 percent)

Category Descriptions

Structure of Matter

1. Atomic and nuclear structure
2. Bonding
3. Intermolecular forces

States of Matter

1. Phase changes
2. Gases, liquids, and solids
3. Solutions: noncolligative and colligative properties, concentrations

Reactions of Matter

1. Acids and Bases
2. Kinetics
3. Thermodynamics
4. Equilibrium
5. Electrochemistry and oxidation-reaction
6. Stoichiometry

Particulate Samples of Matter

1. Periodic properties and trends

2. Types of organic compounds and their principal reactions and important inorganic compounds

3. Familiar metals and nonmetals

4. Names and formulas

Laboratory Handling of Matter; Environmental Issues Related to Chemistry

1. Safety precautions

2. Data handling

3. Important techniques and experiments

4. Environmental issues related to chemistry

Chemistry

Directions: Each question or incomplete statement is followed by five answer choices. For each question, decide which answer or completion is best, and blacken the letter of your choice on the answer sheet.

1. If redox reactions are forced to occur by use of an externally applied electric current, the procedure is called

   (A) neutralization.
   (B) esterification.
   (C) electrolysis.
   (D) hydrolysis.
   (E) saponification.

2. Given the equation:

   $$C_6H_{12}O_6 \xrightarrow{\text{zymase (from yeast)}} 2C_2H_5OH + 2CO_2$$

   The reaction represented by the equation is called

   (A) polymerization.
   (B) fermentation.
   (C) esterification.
   (D) saponification.
   (E) neutralization.

3. The structure ⬡ represents a molecule of

   (A) cyclopentane.
   (B) cyclopropane.
   (C) toluene.
   (D) benzene.
   (E) cyclohexane.

4. Which particle has a negative charge and a mass that is approximately $\frac{1}{1,836}$ the mass of a proton?

   (A) A neutron
   (B) An alpha particle
   (C) An electron
   (D) A positron
   (E) A photon

5. In 6.20 hours, a 100-gram sample of $^{112}_{47}Ag$ decays to 25.0 grams. What is the half-life of $^{112}_{47}Ag$?

   (A) 1.60 hours
   (B) 3.10 hours
   (C) 6.20 hours
   (D) 12.4 hours
   (E) 18.6 hours

6. Which ion is the conjugate base of H_2SO_4?

   (A) SO_3^{2-}
   (B) S^{2-}
   (C) HSO_3^-
   (D) HSO_4^-
   (E) $H_3SO_4^+$

7. What is the name of the process that begins with the joining of monomer molecules?

   (A) Fermentation
   (B) Polymerization
   (C) Esterification
   (D) Hydrogenation
   (E) Isomerization

8. A 9.90-gram sample of a hydrated salt is heated to a constant mass of 6.60 grams. What was the percent by mass of water contained in the sample?

   (A) 66.7
   (B) 50.0
   (C) 33.3
   (D) 16.5
   (E) 133.3

9. Which process occurs when dry ice, $CO_2(s)$, is changed into $CO_2(g)$?

   (A) Crystallization
   (B) Condensation
   (C) Sublimation
   (D) Solidification
   (E) Decomposition

10. How many moles of water are contained in 0.250 mole of $CuSO_4 \cdot 5H_2O$?

    (A) 62.5
    (B) 40.0
    (C) 4.62
    (D) 4.50
    (E) 1.25

11. Which is the formula for magnesium sulfide?

    (A) MgS
    (B) $MgSO_3$
    (C) MnS
    (D) $MnSO_3$
    (E) $MgSO_4$

12. Which formula represents a polar molecule?

    (A) CH_4
    (B) Cl_2
    (C) NH_3
    (D) N_2
    (E) CO_2

13. Which of the following gases is monatomic at STP?

    (A) Hydrogen
    (B) Chlorine
    (C) Oxygen
    (D) Helium
    (E) Nitrogen

14. The type of reaction represented by the equation $C_2H_4 + H_2 \rightarrow C_2H_6$ is called

    (A) substitution.
    (B) polymerization.
    (C) addition.
    (D) esterification.
    (E) dehydration.

15. The four single bonds of a carbon atom are spatially directed toward the corners of a regular

    (A) triangle.
    (B) rectangle.
    (C) square.
    (D) tetrahedron.
    (E) cube.

16. Which equilibrium expression best represents the ionization constant (K_a) for the weak-acid equilibrium below?

$$HX(aq) \rightleftharpoons H^+(aq) + X^-(aq)$$

(A) $K_a = \dfrac{\left[H^+\right] + \left[X^-\right]}{\left[HX\right]}$

(B) $K_a = \dfrac{\left[HX\right]}{\left[H^+\right] + \left[X^-\right]}$

(C) $K_a = \dfrac{\left[H^+\right]\left[X^-\right]}{\left[HX\right]}$

(D) $K_a = \dfrac{\left[HX\right]}{\left[H^+\right]\left[X^-\right]}$

(E) $K_a = \dfrac{\left[H^+\right] - \left[X^-\right]}{\left[HX\right]}$

17. Which hydrocarbon is a member of the alkane series?

(A)

(B)

(C)

(D)

(E)

18. The graph below illustrates the change in the volume of a gas sample as its temperature rises at constant pressure.

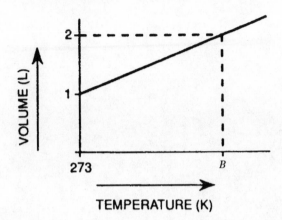

What temperature is represented by point *B*?

(A) 546 K
(B) 298 K
(C) 273 K
(D) 0 K
(E) 400 K

19. What is the heat of vaporization of water in calories per gram?

(A) 79.7
(B) 273
(C) 373
(D) 539
(E) 100

20. Which electron configuration represents an atom in the excited state?

(A) $1s^2 2s^1$
(B) $1s^2 2s^2 2p^6$
(C) $1s^2 2s^2 2p^6 4s^1$
(D) $1s^2 2s^2 2p^6 3s^2 3p^3$
(E) $1s^2 2s^2 2p^6 3s^1$

21. Which sublevel configuration correctly represents a completely filled third principal energy level?

(A) $3s^2 3p^6 3d^8$
(B) $3s^2 3p^2 3d^{10}$
(C) $3s^2 3p^6 3d^{10}$
(D) $3s^2 3p^6 3d^5$
(E) $3s^2 3p^5 3d^9$

22. One of the products of a fermentation reaction is a(n)

(A) alcohol.
(B) alkane.
(C) salt.
(D) ester.
(E) ketone.

23. Which salt forms a colored aqueous solution?

(A) $Mg(NO_3)_2$
(B) $NaNO_3$
(C) $Ca(NO_3)_2$
(D) $Ni(NO_3)_2$
(E) $BaCl_2$

24. The graph below represents a solid being heated at a uniform rate, starting at a temperature below its melting point.

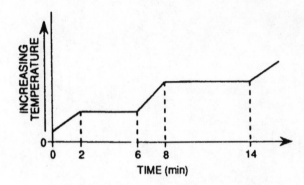

Once the solid reaches its melting point, how many minutes are required to completely melt the solid?

(A) 6
(B) 2
(C) 8
(D) 4
(E) 5

25. Given the reaction:

$$2SO_2(g) + O_2(g) \rightarrow 2SO_3(g)$$

What is the total number of liters of $O_2(g)$, measured at STP, that will react completely with 4.00 moles of SO_2?

(A) 1.00 L
(B) 0.500 L
(C) 22.4 L
(D) 44.8 L
(E) 67.2 L

EARLY CHILDHOOD EDUCATION (0020)

Time: 2 hours
Number of Questions: 120
Format: Multiple-choice questions

Purpose of the Test

Designed to measure the preparation of prospective teachers of preschool through primary-grade students

Content Categories

- Understanding the Nature of the Growth, Development, and Learning of Young Children—(31 percent)
- Recognizing Factors that Influence Individual Growth and Development—(10 percent)
- Recognizing Appropriate and Inappropriate Applications of Developmental and Curriculum Theory—(12 percent)
- Planning and Implementing Curriculum—(29 percent)
- Evaluating and Reporting Student Progress and the Effectiveness of Instruction—(12 percent)
- Understanding Professional and Legal Responsibilities—(6 percent)

Category Descriptions

Understanding the Nature of the Growth, Development, and Learning of Young Children

1. Language development: oral language development, including speaking (bilingual skills, storytelling), listening comprehension, developing vocabulary and understanding language systems; written language development, such as invented spelling, print awareness, and ideas in writing

2. Cognitive development: concepts of the physical world and of causal relationships and signing in all communication systems, such as art, mathematics, and music; skill development in areas such as manipulative skills, symbol recognition, and logical reasoning

3. Personal/social development: self-concept, locus of control, learning style, temperament, sex, gender roles, stages of social behavior, effect of discrimination, stereotypes, and aggression

4. Physical development: typical and atypical growth and development, symptoms of illness, fine and gross motor development, safety, and health

Recognizing Factors that Influence Individual Growth and Development

1. Familial factors: family relationships, parental attitudes, birth order, and siblings

2. Physiological factors: effects of genetic and congenital maturational factors

3. Nutritional/hygienic factors: diet, sleep, exercise, and environmental conditions

4. Cultural factors: effects of the interaction of cultural values; roles of the primary transmitters of the culture (schools, community, family, and the mass media); and effects of political, economic, and cultural influences, including ethnic, regional, and religious influences

Recognizing Appropriate and Inappropriate Applications of Developmental and Curriculum Theory

1. Understanding major early childhood curriculum models and approaches, such as Montessori, Froebel, Bank Street, Bereiter/Engelmann, Kamii, Weikert, Head Start, Emergent Literacy, developmentally appropriate practice, play-based and integrated curriculums

2. Understanding the contributions of major streams of developmental and learning theory to early childhood education practices, such as psychoanalytic, social-learning, behaviorist, and cognitive theories

Planning and Implementing Curriculum

1. Organizing and managing the physical learning environment: use of materials, indoor space, outdoor space, and equipment

2. Managing interpersonal interactions in the classroom: recognizing how teachers' behavior and attitudes affect children's learning and development, helping children learn to manage their behavior

3. Utilizing outside resources in curriculum planning and implementation: family and community

4. Planning, selecting, and implementing appropriate curriculum experiences and instructional strategies: whole language, language experience, and basal approaches; mathematics manipulatives; inquiry and discovery in science; physical/motor experiences; aesthetic and affective experiences; social experiences

Evaluating and Reporting Student Progress and the Effectiveness of Instruction

1. Maintaining useful records of a child's development and progress in learning

2. Using formal and informal assessment results in planning for a class and for individuals

3. Selection and use of formal and informal assessment instruments for evaluating developmental progress and effectiveness of curriculum experiences

4. Communicating effectively with parents about a child's total development progress

Understanding Professional and Legal Responsibilities

1. Being cognizant of legal responsibilities and regulations that affect teaching in the early childhood setting

2. Maintaining effective interactions with other adults who function within the learning setting

Early Childhood Education

Directions: Each question or incomplete statement is followed by five answer choices. For each question, decide which answer or completion is best, and blacken the letter of your choice on the answer sheet.

1. In establishing early childhood management, a teacher asks a child to assume responsibility for her actions, discusses the effect of the action, and has the child make a plan of how she will handle the situation the next time. These factors are all components of

   (A) life space interview.
   (B) time out.
   (C) reality therapy.
   (D) managing surface behavior.
   (E) behavior modification.

2. In organizing the curriculum of an early childhood class, one should

   I.   provide a variety of learning centers.
   II. use a thematic approach in the teaching of various concepts.
   III. use a developmental approach to provide for differences in learning style.
   IV. provide the students with a lot of factual material, such as photographs and books, to increase cognitive ability.

   (A) II, III, and IV only
   (B) I and II only
   (C) I, II, and III only
   (D) I only
   (E) III and IV only

3. All of the following statements would describe the cognitive development of a preschool youngster EXCEPT

   (A) the preschool youngster has little concept of clock time.
   (B) the preschool youngster can tell sex differences.
   (C) the preschool youngster sees many divergent objects as equivalent.
   (D) the preschool youngster cannot recognize pictures depicting various emotional responses.
   (E) the preschool youngster does not understand irony and metaphor.

4. Which educational theorist does NOT subscribe to the open educational approach to early childhood education?

   (A) Pestalozzi
   (B) Froebel
   (C) Montessori
   (D) Dewey
   (E) Hewlett

5. Which skills are often neglected in a first- and second-grade language arts curriculum?

   I.   How to use and enjoy reading
   II. Thinking skills
   III. How to interpret the symbols of reading
   IV. Answering of *wh* questions

   (A) III and IV only
   (B) I and III only
   (C) II and IV only
   (D) I and II only
   (E) All of the above

6. Which would be an appropriate social studies question to ask of a first-grade student?

   (A) Where would you go to get a prescription?
   (B) Why did the Pony Express end?
   (C) Why do more people live in the United States than in Canada?
   (D) Which animal quacks?
   (E) How does a government get money to pay for goods and services?

7. All of the following are good ways to manage a preschool classroom EXCEPT

   (A) having the day planned in advance for the students.
   (B) using specific social-behavioral procedures to minimize classroom discipline problems.
   (C) using color codes for identifying materials and classifying books.
   (D) organizing furniture to make the room as easily accessible as possible.
   (E) teaching rules as they need to learn them during the course of the year.

8. How would you describe the social-emotional behavior of a typical six-year-old child from a middle-class background?

    (A) Socially interacts with members of the opposite sex
    (B) Sparing in affection
    (C) A member of a gang
    (D) Well on the way to developing an independent identity
    (E) Scorns all things childish

9. This educator stresses the use of multiage groupings and self-correcting material in creating a prepared environment to meet a child's need to organize the world. The theory being described is that of

    (A) Piaget.
    (B) Bruner.
    (C) Rousseau.
    (D) Montessori.
    (E) Pestalozzi.

10. Part of an early childhood music curriculum is teaching children to identify, play, and explain the purpose of various types of instruments. Which of the instruments below is considered a rhythm instrument?

    (A) Wrist bells
    (B) Xylophone
    (C) Marimba
    (D) Guitar
    (E) Ukulele

11. Which does NOT describe four- to six-year-old children in the preoperational stage of development?

    (A) Rapidly acquiring language and learning new words
    (B) Constantly exploring, manipulating, and experimenting with the environment
    (C) Beginning to see the viewpoints of people other than themselves
    (D) Concrete understanding of the physical environment
    (E) Good understanding of concepts that reflect physical and tactile alternatives reflecting a common characteristic

12. All of the following are ways parents can play a part in a child's learning progress EXCEPT

    (A) observing their child reading, giving reports, and writing essays.
    (B) following through on classroom assignments.
    (C) extending their own education to better educate their child.
    (D) inquiring to make sure the curriculum fits with their moral standards.
    (E) being a classroom volunteer.

13. Using a basal reading approach, a first-grader will learn all the following decoding and/or comprehension skills EXCEPT

    (A) CVC words.
    (B) consonant blends and digraphs.
    (C) recalling facts of a story.
    (D) syllabication of multisyllable words.
    (E) sequencing.

14. Which does NOT illustrate the social behavior of a nursery school child?

    (A) Preschool children develop a vocabulary of scatology.
    (B) A preschooler's social life revolves around the world of play.
    (C) Boys and girls settle property disputes by snatching and fleeing.
    (D) Whereas boys engage in physical combat, girls use their tongues as weapons.
    (E) Boys and girls rarely resort to crying if they are hurt or angry.

15. All of the following are examples of reading readiness skills EXCEPT

    (A) auditory discrimination.
    (B) sequencing.
    (C) visual discrimination.
    (D) identification of initial blends.
    (E) recognition of uppercase and lowercase letters.

16. In teaching multiplication to a third-grade student, which method should lead to the greatest understanding of the concept?

    (A) Drilling of basic facts
    (B) Teaching that multiplication is a faster way of adding
    (C) Weaning children away from the multiplication table
    (D) First teaching the concept of partial products
    (E) Prohibiting the use of calculators

17. Which concepts are developed by using blocks in a preschool setting?

    I.   Measurement, area, spatial relations, and seriation
    II. Balance, gravity, and stability
    III. Oral language usage
    IV. Prereading skills such as visual discrimination and matching

    (A) I, II, and III only
    (B) I and II only
    (C) I, II, III, and IV
    (D) II, III, and IV only
    (E) II only

18. An effective management technique used in kindergarten to let children know how many students can play at a learning center at one time is to

    (A) assign which children can use each center at the beginning of the week.
    (B) let the students choose who can be at each learning center.
    (C) set up colored clothespins at each center and let each child using the center take one and return it after play.
    (D) set up a check chart for the students to fill in.
    (E) color code the objects at each center.

19. Which type of play is most characteristic of a four-to six-year-old child?

    I.   Solitary play
    II. Onlooker play
    III. Associative play
    IV. Cooperative play

    (A) I, II, and III only
    (B) II only
    (C) IV only
    (D) II and IV only
    (E) III and IV only

20. Pouring a set amount of water from a tall, thin glass to a thick, fat one illustrates

    (A) transduction.
    (B) conservation.
    (C) cross-classification.
    (D) volume.
    (E) cause and effect.

21. All of the following are disadvantages of a basal reading approach EXCEPT

    (A) the vocabulary is unrelated to a child's experiences.
    (B) there is minimal child input.
    (C) it contains little student-student interaction.
    (D) there is little room for individualization.
    (E) it is highly structured.

22. Which factors describe the role of play in the preschool and early childhood years?

    I.   A child makes a game of everything he does.
    II. A child can separate reality from fantasy.
    III. Play is a way of trying on different roles.
    IV. Imagination tends to increase due to expanding knowledge and emotional range.

    (A) I, III, and IV only
    (B) II, III, and IV only
    (C) III and IV only
    (D) I and II only
    (E) I, II, and III only

23. Which is a good game to improve spelling skills informally?

    (A) Hangman
    (B) Mystery sheet
    (C) Create poem booklets
    (D) Secret code for letters
    (E) Play "find the bell"

24. Which reading approach for lower-grade students encourages the instructor to write down exactly what is said so that the child can get the idea that print is talk written down and that he or she can read it?

    (A) Organic reading
    (B) Directed reading-thinking approach
    (C) Individualized reading
    (D) Language experience
    (E) Cloze

25. Many early childhood theorists believe that an effective learning environment should be one that meets the social, emotional, motor, and cognitive needs of a child. Such an environment would be based on all of the following beliefs EXCEPT

    (A) children grow and learn at different rates unrelated to chronological age.
    (B) children need to be motivated to learn, and they learn best when they follow an organized structure directed by the teacher.
    (C) learning is something a child does rather than something done to him.
    (D) play is a child's way of working and learning.
    (E) children learn from each other.

EDUCATIONAL LEADERSHIP: ADMINISTRATION AND SUPERVISION (0410)

Time: 2 hours
Number of Questions: 120
Format: Multiple-choice questions

Purpose of the Test

Designed to assess a candidate's knowledge of the functions of an administrator or supervisor

Content Categories

- Determining Educational Needs—(8 percent)
- Curriculum Design and Instructional Improvement—(13 percent)
- Development of Staff and Program Evaluation—(16 percent)
- School Management—(33 percent)
- Individual and Group Leadership Skills—(30 percent)

Category Descriptions

Determining Educational Needs

1. Expectations concerning students at various developmental and instructional levels
2. Assessments of community needs, expectations, and population projects
3. Recognition of specific needs of diverse populations and mobile populations
4. Awareness of national perspective on education
5. Interpretation of research and assessment data for decision making

Curriculum Design and Instructional Improvement

1. Curriculum goals, decision processes in design, strategies for implementation, and determination of instructional objectives
2. Instructional methods and techniques, such as team teaching, direct teaching, group instruction, contract method, individualized instruction, and interdisciplinary instruction
3. Instructional resources and research data related to curriculum needs, such as personnel, materials, technology, finance, business and industry, advisory groups, community agencies, and institutions
4. Learning theories and learning processes

Development of Staff and Program Evaluation

1. Assessment of staff abilities and determination of their needs
2. Establishment and implementation of staff development
3. Strategies for behavioral change
4. Indicators of achievement relating to goals and objectives
5. Knowledge of types, methods, and procedures of evaluation and instructional staff assessment
6. Applications of evaluation and research findings in goal setting and change

School Management

1. Organizational and operational features of school management, including structures, programs and services, and personnel selection and evaluation procedures

2. Governing and control features of school management, including educational functions of local, state, and federal agencies; formal and informal agencies; and the process of participatory government involving students and faculty and community members

3. Business and fiscal features of school management, including financial resources, support services, and budgeting

4. Legal features, including negotiations and bargaining, due process for staff members and students, and judicial and legislative provisions

Individual and Group Leadership Skills

1. Understanding individual behavior and divergent behavior of students and staff and community members

2. Understanding and affecting group dynamics

3. School–community relations, including diverse values and use of community resources

4. Communication skills

5. Creating and maintaining a positive affective environment, such as existing school cultures, communication flow, and informal leadership

Educational Leadership: Administration and Supervision

Directions: Each question or incomplete statement is followed by five answer choices. For each question, decide which answer or completion is best, and blacken the letter of your choice on the answer sheet.

1. Frederick Taylor, Henri Fayol, Luther Gulick, and Lyndall Urwick are all associated with

   (A) Leadership Theory.
   (B) Scientific Management Theory.
   (C) Humanistic Theory.
   (D) Social Systems Theory.
   (E) Bureaucratic Theory.

2. A social studies teacher tries to get her students to relate abstract concepts to a particular situation. According to Bloom, she would ask questions focusing on which developmental level?

   (A) Comprehension
   (B) Evaluation
   (C) Analysis
   (D) Application
   (E) Synthesis

3. All are associated with the application of social systems theory to organizational and administrative structures EXCEPT

   (A) Parsons.
   (B) Barnard.
   (C) Getzels.
   (D) Etzioni.
   (E) Weber.

4. Teacher education programs at the college level during the 1970s and 1980s focused on the development of

   (A) techniques to pass standardized national examinations in the area of education.
   (B) competency-based objectives that had to be met by each candidate.
   (C) the application of liberal arts to teaching in the schools.
   (D) a more *laissez-faire* attitude due to a decrease in state testing of new teachers.
   (E) criteria to increase the ability level of those students entering the education field.

5. The dichotomy between the monocratic, bureaucratic type of organization and the pluralistic, collegial type of organization has been defined by Theory X and Theory Y according to which of the following?

   (A) Maslow
   (B) McGregor
   (C) Argyris
   (D) Herzberg
   (E) Weber

6. All are major teacher personnel problems today in the field of education EXCEPT

   (A) states refusing to give money to retool teachers.
   (B) less able students entering teaching.
   (C) the women's movement making education a more attractive field to enter.
   (D) salaries of urban teachers not keeping pace with those of the suburbs.
   (E) teacher education programs not training teachers to deal with an urban environment.

7. Which of the following are some reasons why an unannounced observation is an effective supervisory technique?

   I.   The supervisor sees what is really going on in the classroom.
   II. The personality characteristics of a supervisor do not impinge when observing in this manner.
   III. A teacher's lesson will be more spontaneous.
   IV. This technique reduces teacher anxiety.

   (A) IV only
   (B) I, II, and III only
   (C) I only
   (D) I, III, and IV only
   (E) II only

8. In terms of organizational structure, "span of control" means

    (A) that every person knows to whom and for what he/she is responsible.
    (B) the development of standardized procedures for routinizing administrative operations.
    (C) assigning each administrator no greater a number of persons than the administrator can supervise directly.
    (D) the delegation of authority from superordinates to subordinates.
    (E) having a single executive head responsible for all decisions.

9. Which is NOT an aspect of clinical supervision?

    (A) The teacher selects the area he or she wishes to improve.
    (B) A supervisor directly informs the teacher of his or her strengths and weaknesses without any teacher input.
    (C) Its purpose is to develop and improve instructional competencies.
    (D) The teacher determines the faults of his or her lesson.
    (E) Follow-up observation activities are developed jointly by the instructor and supervisor.

10. Public education is not a right according to the U.S. Constitution. Nonetheless, a part of the Constitution has been interpreted by the courts as prohibiting a state from denying to a child an equal education because he or she is handicapped or emotionally disturbed. This interpretation is based on (the)

    (A) Fourteenth Amendment.
    (B) Tenth Amendment.
    (C) Sections eight and ten of Article One.
    (D) Fifth Amendment.
    (E) First Amendment.

11. Ned Flanders is associated with a model relating to

    (A) clinical supervision.
    (B) micro-teaching.
    (C) interaction analysis.
    (D) needs assessments.
    (E) teacher effectiveness.

12. A tenured teacher is having difficulty in the classroom. He cannot manage the class, and students often leave and roam the halls. His pacing is so slow that he tends to lose the students who do stay in his class. The noise level in his room is deafening. How should a building principal deal with this situation?

    I. Give the teacher the minimal number of students legally possible
    II. Remove the teacher from teaching duties because he is doing great damage to the students
    III. Allow the teacher to teach in another area if he is competent to do so
    IV. Have the teacher immediately dismissed for incompetence

    (A) III and IV only
    (B) I and III only
    (C) II and IV only
    (D) III only
    (E) I and II only

13. Edmund, Rosenshine, and Berliner are best known for their research in

    (A) clinical supervision.
    (B) developing performance objectives for teachers.
    (C) effective teaching techniques.
    (D) cooperative learning.
    (E) shared decision making.

14. A high-quality classroom teacher would exhibit all of the following behaviors EXCEPT

    (A) helping pupils to explore, discuss, check, or test questions or ideas.
    (B) responding to pupils' answers by reflecting them back to the class to provide further questioning, thought, and discussion.
    (C) smiling or appearing relaxed and cheerful.
    (D) responding to pupils' questions or ideas with scorn.
    (E) acknowledging his/her own errors.

15. It is easiest to charge and dismiss a tenured teacher for

    (A) inefficiency.
    (B) incompetency.
    (C) failure to maintain license.
    (D) conduct unbecoming a teacher.
    (E) insubordination.

16. The concept that leadership effectiveness is "dependent upon the appropriate matching of the individual's leadership style of interacting and the influence which the group situation provides" was postulated by

    (A) Lipham.
    (B) Stogdill.
    (C) Fiedler.
    (D) Getzels.
    (E) Berelson.

17. A new principal is appointed to a public school. His goal is to improve the school's academic achievement. What is the first thing he should do as an administrative leader?

    (A) Give a needs assessment to the teachers and then form a representative committee to prioritize the information
    (B) Form a committee to carry out the changes he recommends for the school
    (C) Abandon the policies of the previous principal and start from scratch
    (D) Create a new reading curriculum based upon the latest research
    (E) At the first faculty conference, outline approximately twelve important changes to be made in the school

18. Effective schools have all of the following characteristics EXCEPT

    (A) high expectations.
    (B) an emphasis on academic achievement and high-quality instruction.
    (C) a school climate or atmosphere emphasizing discipline.
    (D) an emphasis on crisis management.
    (E) constant pupil evaluation.

19. According to most research, a principal's time is mostly taken up with

    (A) discipline problems.
    (B) paperwork.
    (C) instructional leadership.
    (D) supervision.
    (E) scheduling.

20. The author most closely associated with the theory of clinical supervision is

    (A) Fiedler.
    (B) Cogan.
    (C) Flanders.
    (D) Berliner.
    (E) Getzels.

21. Direct instruction is the teaching of large groups by focusing on factual or literal questions and using controlled practice techniques. According to research, direct instruction

    (A) benefits low-functioning students.
    (B) benefits average students.
    (C) develops abstract thinking skills.
    (D) shows the need to individualize instruction with weaker students.
    (E) should be modified by using more open approaches.

22. A trend that will probably affect public education is that

    (A) parents will place a greater emphasis on literacy due to multinational competition.
    (B) a larger percentage of the school-age population will be made up of minority groups.
    (C) education is becoming a federal responsibility.
    (D) there will be greater choice between public and private schools.
    (E) economic restructuring will force more women back into education.

23. Upward mobiles, indifferents, and ambivalents are three personality types that impact upon the social structure of an organization. This social systems approach was developed by

    (A) Barnard.
    (B) Etzioni.
    (C) Presthus.
    (D) Carlson.
    (E) Griffiths.

24. Before the 1950s, studies in leadership focused on

    I.   great men.

    II. an interactional or group approach.

    III. studies of traits.

    IV. a social systems approach.

    (A) I, II, and III only

    (B) III and IV only

    (C) II, III, and IV only

    (D) I and III only

    (E) I only

25. In terms of dismissing tenured teachers for incompetence, most state laws

    (A) put the onus on the school district to help the teacher improve his or her skills.

    (B) allow an informal hearing for dismissal.

    (C) allow the district to determine who will be on any arbitration panel.

    (D) put the burden on the teacher as to why little effort was made to improve his or her skills.

    (E) allow for immediate contract termination if the instructor is employed for less than a minimal period of time.

ELEMENTARY EDUCATION: CONTENT AREA EXERCISES (0012)

Time: 2 hours
Number of Questions: 4
Format: Essays

Purpose of the Test

Designed to measure how well prospective teachers of students in the elementary grades can respond to extended exercises that require thoughtful, written responses

Content Categories

- Reading/Language Arts—(25 percent)
- Mathematics—(25 percent)
- Either Science or Social Studies—(25 percent)
- Understanding of Interdisciplinary Instruction in Subject Areas (does not include physical education and fine arts)—(25 percent)

Content Descriptions

Reading/Language Arts

1. Learner objectives
2. Balanced reading, writing, speaking, and listening
3. Sequence and scope of skills and materials
4. Understanding and knowledge of topics, procedures, and methods
5. Word recognition
6. Determining reading levels
7. Vocabulary and word usage
8. Writing techniques
9. Listening, spelling, and memorization skills
10. Informal assessments
11. Traditional and standardized assessments
12. Analysis of student work

Mathematics

1. Number concepts: counting, comparing, and classifying objects; exploring and ordering sets; number patterns
2. Curriculum components: sequence and scope of skills and materials
3. Addition, subtraction, multiplication, and division
4. Number theory
5. Problem solving
6. Geometry
7. Probability and statistics
8. Measurement
9. Rational numbers
10. Classroom management and motivation
11. Hand-held calculators and computers
12. Analysis of students' work

Science

1. Use of materials and technology
2. Model building and forecasting
3. Science as inquiry
4. Life science, earth science, and physical science

Social Studies

1. History, geography, and government
2. Social structures
3. Social organizations and human behavior in society
4. Students' development of appropriate concepts and skills

Interdisciplinary Instruction

Understanding of integrated subject areas, such as the integration of reading/language arts and social studies

Elementary Education:
Content Area Exercises

Question 1

This question refers to a student's response to an informal reading inventory based upon a basal reader in a second-grade class. The teacher is using this information to group the child in an appropriate group and determine which skills the student needs to learn.

walk   slow   at   home   look   fist   watch

Jeff walked slowly out of the house. He looked for fish in the water.

    was   rad   racks   look   fist   spook

There were some red and green rocks. One looked like a fish. Jeff spoke

    wash   was have fist   wash   was

to it. "I wish you were a live fish," he said. I wish you were in my pet

fist calling   pick   racks

fish collection." He picked up the rocks.

     look   did

Then Jeff looked for pets in the woods. He was not happy. He didn't

     saw   calling   look

have one pet to show the next day at the collection club. He looked down

   racks   side on   feet   pick

at some rocks. He let them slide under his foot. He picked them up and

walk sew   did   help

walked slowly home. Jeff didn't have much hope.

    calling   ask

"Where is your collection, Jeff?" asked the teacher the next day. Jeff

did   could   look said

didn't have one, but he couldn't say it. Katie looked sad for her friend.

   jump   racks   fall   Jeff feet

Jeff jumped up to go. Then rocks came falling down on Jeff's foot.

Student's responses to the reading comprehension questions:

Why did Jeff go to the water and wood?

Student response: There was some rad racks.

What is the best title for this story?

Student response: Racks and fists

What did Jeff want?

Student response: Then racks come fell down on Jeff's feet.

What do you think Jeff would use as a collection?

Student response: I don't know.

1. List four (4) important aspects of the student's reading problem that this informal reading inventory is showing.

2. Describe two (2) ways the teacher can develop the reading skills of this student. The first example should focus on the student's decoding skills and the second example should focus on reading comprehension.

<u>Outline</u>

inability to include suffixes

the switching of vowels

the replacement of words

/

Question 2

This question refers to math problems performed by a fifth-grade student during a math test that focused on problem-solving skills. The students who best learn to solve problems based upon real-world situations and concepts are usually taught using a constructionist approach.

Problem 1:

The Jamison family is traveling from New York to Detroit by car taking a northern route. They complete one half of the trip on the first day of their journey. They started late on the second day and completed only a third of what remained of the trip. As a fraction, how much of the total trip remains to be completed on the third day? Write down your answer as steps.

[handwritten notes in right margin: for adding must have same denominator; numerator → 2; denominator → 8]

[handwritten notes in left margin: $\frac{2}{6} ; \frac{5}{6}$; $\frac{3}{6}$; $\frac{1}{3\times2} + \frac{1 \times 3}{3 \times 4} = \frac{5}{9}$; $\frac{1}{2} + \frac{1}{3}$]

Step 1

$$\frac{1}{2}$$
$$+\frac{1}{3}$$
$$\overline{\frac{2}{5}}$$

[handwritten: $\frac{5}{6}$]

Step 2

$$1-\frac{2}{5}$$

Step 3

$$1=\frac{5}{5}$$
$$-\frac{2}{5}$$
$$\overline{\frac{3}{0}}$$

Problem 2:

Based on the information acquired in question one, if the total trip was 900 miles, how many miles more does the Jamison family have to drive to get to Detroit on the third day of the trip?

$$900-\frac{3}{0}=\frac{897}{0}$$

1. Analyze at least three (3) math weaknesses the student has based upon the answers that were given to problems 1 and 2.

2. Relate how you will go about teaching the two prerequisite skills necessary to solve problem 1, and teaching another two prerequisite skills to solve problem 2.

Outline

_____

_____

_____

_____

_____

_____

_____

_____

_____

_____

_____

_____

_____

_____

_____

_____

_____

_____

_____

_____

_____

_____

_____

_____

_____

Question 3

Social Studies

This question refers to the following essay produced by a fifth-grade student who had to write a document-based essay. The student's work was scored using a four-point rubric. For a student to reach Level Three, the student

- answers most aspects of the task by using documents
- generally uses accurate data
- develops ideas satisfactorily with adequate supporting evidence
- develops an answer, using a general plan of organization
- generally expresses ideas clearly

Essay guidelines for the student:

Using the documents and answers to the documents as well as your knowledge of social studies, write a well-organized essay about how changes in transportation contributed to the growth of the United States before the Civil War.

In your essay, remember to

- tell about what transportation was like before and during the nineteenth century in the United States
- include an introduction, body, and conclusion
- include details, examples, or reasons to develop your ideas
- use the information from the documents in your answer

I know that by 1700 the United States still had bad transportation. People had to use horses on dirt roads. It took a lot of days to get from one city to another. But transportation got better after 1800. The government started to build roads. One road went West with pioneers. A lot of canals were built for boats. Steamships were invented and carried goods in rivers. Steamships went faster than sail boats. Another invention was the railroad. The railroads carried people and goods to the West. People needed to work making railroads and they came from China and Japan.

1. Describe three (3) ways in which the student does or does not meet the above standards for a Level Three document-based social studies essay.

2. Describe three (3) specific skills the student has to learn to be able to write a document-based essay that will meet the standards at Level Three.

Outline

Question 4

This question refers to an interdisciplinary unit to be developed by a sixth-grade teacher based on Standard Two "Mathematics as Communication in the Curriculum and Evaluation Standards for School Mathematics" as outlined by the National Council of Teachers of Mathematics (NCTM, 1989).

In this unit, the teacher has to incorporate many mathematical concepts into the reading context. The teacher has to use the skills of reading, listening, and viewing to interpret and evaluate mathematical ideas.

The teacher has the class read a variety of literary and content area materials concerning ancient Egypt. The students have to use reading to place several mathematical concepts into a meaningful context. The students must do this by putting numbers into good use within the structure of literature they are reading. Within this interdisciplinary unit, the students will work in cooperative groups investigating, questioning, and planning to find answers that will support many concepts that will increase reading and mathematical literacy.

1. Describe four (4) math concepts that will be developed within this reading/math interdisciplinary unit on the Egyptians.
2. Describe two (2) reading skills that will be developed within this reading/math interdisciplinary unit on the Egyptians.

Outline

ELEMENTARY EDUCATION: CONTENT KNOWLEDGE (0014)

Time: 2 hours
Number of Questions: 120
Format: Multiple-choice questions

Purpose of the Test

Designed to measure the preparation of prospective teachers of children in the elementary grades

Content Categories

- Language Arts—(25 percent)
- Mathematics—(25 percent)
- Social Studies—(25 percent)
- Science—(25 percent)

Content Descriptions

Language Arts

1. Literature of all types, reading instruction, including recognition of words and reading comprehension and writing skills

2. Literacy acquisition

3. Reading instruction

4. Grammar and usage

5. Vocabulary in context

6. Cultural, social, and historical influences

7. Communication skills

Mathematics

1. Critical thinking

2. Meaning and use of numbers

3. Number patterns

4. Factors and multiples

5. Ratio, proportion, and percent

6. Algebraic concepts

7. Properties of zero and one

8. Patterns

9 Equalities and inequalities

10. Basic geometry and measurement

11. Combinations and permutations

12. Mean, median, and mode

Social Studies

1. World history, geography, and political science
2. Social structures
3. Social organizations
4. Economic systems

Science

1. Life, earth, and physical sciences
2. Data gathering and organizing
3. Science, technology, and society
4. History and nature of science

Elementary Education: Content Knowledge

> *Directions:* Each question or statement is followed by four answer choices. For each question, decide which answer or completion is best, and blacken the letter of your choice on the answer sheet.

Language Arts

1. It has been concluded that children whose parents read to them show improved academic achievement. Recent research has shown that

   (A) most parents stop reading to their children after age 9.
   (B) children do not need constant reinforcement to become lifelong readers.
   (C) there is little correlation between reading and parents' education attainment levels.
   (D) reading skill only slightly correlates with socioeconomic status.

2. Which of the following is the LEAST effective method for improving reading comprehension?

   (A) Activating background knowledge
   (B) Having students predict what will happen next in a story
   (C) Teaching the meaning of Greek and Latin prefixes
   (D) Visualizing events within a story

3. Which of the following are effective methods for teaching students critical reading skills?

   I. Interpreting editorials about a particular subject from different newspapers
   II. Reading and interpreting three different reviews on a movie
   III. Identifying and categorizing different propaganda techniques
   (A) I and II only
   (B) II and III only
   (C) III only
   (D) I, II and III only

4. *Neither boys nor the girls like the science lab.*

   Which of the following statements about the above sentence is true?

   (A) The sentence is written correctly.
   (B) The subject and verb do not agree.
   (C) The incorrect conjunction is used.
   (D) The construction is not parallel.

Questions 5 and 6 refer to the following:

> Edouard Manet was one of the foremost painters of the mid- and late nineteenth century. Although he was a friend of the Impressionists, he never became one of them. He chose not to exhibit with them in an effort to remain fixed in the public's mind as the finest painter of the era. While experimental in his style and techniques, he did not go as far as Impressionists, such as Degas and Pissaro or his sister-in-law, Berthe Morisot. Manet's paintings, however, served as a model for younger painters looking for different ways to capture light, movement, detail, and color. Manet himself had studied earlier painters and owed much to the Spanish, Italian, and Dutch masters.

5. The purpose of the passage is to

   (A) describe the difference between Manet's work and that of the Impressionists.
   (B) discuss Manet's relationship to Impressionism.
   (C) discuss Manet's legacy to later painters.
   (D) discuss Manet's ego.

6. The phrase "he did not go as far as Impressionists" means that

   (A) Manet's works were more traditional than those of the Impressionists.
   (B) Manet was less creative.
   (C) the Impressionists exhibited more than Manet did.
   (D) Manet was less interested in public opinion.

Mathematics

7. Which one of the following quantities has the least value?

    (A) $\frac{4}{5}$

    (B) $\frac{7}{9}$

    (C) $\frac{5}{7}$

    (D) .76

8. Round 825.6347 to the nearest hundredth.

    (A) 800
    (B) 825.63
    (C) 825.64
    (D) 825.635

9. Which of the following quantities is NOT equal to 75(32 + 88)?

    (A) $75 \times 32 + 75 \times 88$
    (B) $75 \times 32 + 88$
    (C) $75 (88 + 32)$
    (D) $(88 + 32) \times 75$

10. Of the following, the unit that would most likely be used to measure the distance from New York to Albany is the

    (A) liter.
    (B) kilometer.
    (C) centigram.
    (D) millimeter.

11. The cost of 30 sandwich rolls at $1.50 per dozen is

    (A) $3.00
    (B) $3.45
    (C) $3.75
    (D) $4.50

12. If 1 ounce is approximately equal to 28 grams, then the number of grams in a 1-pound box of candy is most nearly

    (A) 250 grams.
    (B) 350 grams.
    (C) 250 grams.
    (D) 550 grams.

13. In two hours, the minute hand of a clock rotates through an angle of

    (A) 90°
    (B) 180°
    (C) 360°
    (D) 720°

14. A shopper bought apples at 30 cents each and grapefruit at 50 cents each. If the shopper spent exactly ten dollars, which of the following could NOT be the number of grapefruit purchased?

    (A) 2
    (B) 4
    (C) 8
    (D) 1

15. If a recipe for a cake calls for $2\frac{1}{2}$ cups of flour, and Mary wishes to make three such cakes, the number of cups of flour she must use is

    (A) 5

    (B) $6\frac{1}{2}$

    (C) $7\frac{1}{2}$

    (D) 9

Social Studies

16. The citizen's constitutional right to protection from unwarranted arrest is provided by

    (A) right of eminent domain.
    (B) writ of assistance.
    (C) writ of habeas corpus.
    (D) bill of attainder.

17. The basic reason for the support of public education in the United States has been to provide which of the following?

    (A) Skilled workers for industry
    (B) Trained persons for the professions
    (C) Informed citizens for a democratic society
    (D) Educated leaders for government services

18. What is the term of a United States Senator?

    (A) two years
    (B) six years
    (C) four years
    (D) eight years

19. The Appalachian mountains are located in

    (A) the eastern part of the United States.
    (B) the western part of the United States.
    (C) Switzerland.
    (D) Asia.

Science

20. Research indicates that cigarette smoking results in which of the following conditions?

    (A) Measles
    (B) Cardiovascular stress
    (C) Hepatitis
    (D) Whooping cough

21. The process by which rocks are broken down into smaller fragments by the atmosphere and other factors in the environment is called

    (A) erosion.
    (B) weathering.
    (C) sorting.
    (D) glaciation.

22. Which of the following describes a solar eclipse?

    (A) The earth prevents the light of the sun from reaching the moon.
    (B) The shadow of the moon falls on the sun.
    (C) The moon prevents the light of the sun from reaching the earth.
    (D) The sun prevents the reflected moonlight from reaching the earth.

23. Which of the following is NOT a form of energy?

    (A) Light
    (B) Electricity
    (C) Temperature
    (D) Heat

24. Sound travels fastest when it moves through which of the following?

    (A) Wire
    (B) Water
    (C) Light
    (D) Air

25. The San Andreas fault is associated most frequently with

    (A) tidal waves in Japan.
    (B) geyser actions in Oregon.
    (C) volcanoes in Washington.
    (D) earthquakes in California.

ELEMENTARY EDUCATION: CURRICULUM, INSTRUCTION, AND ASSESSMENT (0011)

Time: 2 hours
Number of Questions: 110
Format: Multiple-choice questions

Purpose of the Test

Designed to measure the preparation of prospective elementary education teachers in their knowledge of principles and processes

Content Categories

- Reading/Language Arts
- Mathematics
- Science
- Social Studies
- Arts and Physical Education
- General Information about Curriculum, Instruction, and Assessment

Category Descriptions

Reading/Language Arts

1. Learner objectives
2. Balanced reading, writing, speaking, and listening
3. Sequence and scope of skills and materials
4. Understanding and knowledge of topics, procedures, and methods
5. Word recognition
6. Determining reading levels
7. Vocabulary and word usage
8. Writing techniques
9. Listening, spelling, and memorization skills
10. Informal assessments
11. Traditional and standardized assessments
12. Analysis of student work

Mathematics

1. Number concepts: counting, comparing, and classifying objects; exploring and ordering sets; number patterns

2. Curriculum components: sequence and scope of skills and materials

3. Addition, subtraction, multiplication, and division

4. Number theory

5. Problem solving

6. Geometry

7. Probability and statistics

8. Measurement

9. Rational numbers

10. Classroom management and motivation

11. Hand-held calculators and computers

12. Analysis of students' work

Science

1. Use of materials and technology

2. Model building and forecasting

3. Science as inquiry

4. Life science, earth science, and physical science

Social Studies

1. History, geography, and government

2. Social structures

3. Social organizations and human behavior in society

4. Students' development of appropriate concepts and skills

Arts and Physical Education

1. Basic music and arts concepts

2. Basic physical education concepts

3. Teaching strategies for music, arts, and physical education

4. Curriculum planning and evaluation of student achievement

General Information about Curriculum, Instruction, and Assessment

1. Understanding and knowledge of topics dealing with emotional, personal, and social development of children

2. Classroom management

3. Curriculum components

4. General principles of instruction

5. Learning theories

6. Evaluation of student progress

Elementary Education: Curriculum, Instruction, and Assessment

> *Directions:* Each question or incomplete statement is followed by five answer choices. For each question, decide which answer or completion is best, and blacken the letter of your choice on the answer sheet.

1. Mr. Unger is teaching a lesson in social studies called "Building New Lives." Which of the following incorporates English and Language Arts into this lesson?

   (A) Students will pretend to be late nineteenth-century European immigrants and write a letter back to relatives in their respective countries about life in New York.

   (B) Students will create a graph about changes in immigration patterns from 1900 to 2003.

   (C) Students will study the different types of engines found in steam ships that crossed the ocean during the first half of the twentieth century.

   (D) Students will create a blueprint of a tenement in New York City and label different parts of the building.

2. One school district decides that it wants informal rather than state- and citywide reading tests as the primary measures of reading ability. All of the following are informal measures of reading ability EXCEPT

   (A) portfolios.

   (B) IRIs.

   (C) diagnostic/prescriptive measures.

   (D) interest inventories.

3. Mrs. Reiss is developing a communication arts curriculum for the early childhood classes in her elementary school. According to research, communication skills develop in which sequence?

   (A) Listening, speaking, reading, and writing

   (B) Speaking, listening, reading, and writing

   (C) Listening, speaking, writing, and reading

   (D) Writing, reading, listening, and speaking

4. Geography today focuses on social history as well as geography. All of the following are basic themes in teaching geography today EXCEPT

   (A) understanding the reasons for and the importance of human migration.

   (B) understanding the interaction between humans and the natural environment through time.

   (C) understanding the world regions and the interrelated impact of cultural and global interdependence.

   (D) understanding the difference among various symbols within maps of countries in conflict.

5. Dr. Levy is teaching sixth-grade social studies, including a unit on ancient Greece. She assigned the reading of Antigone, Socrates, an anthology of myths, and excerpts from the history of the ancient world by Herodotus. The reason these books were assigned was to

   (A) make history more interesting.

   (B) use literature to teach social studies.

   (C) cover issues in depth.

   (D) teach the difference between fiction, plays, philosophy, and nonfiction.

6. Ms. Hernandez is teaching a unit on the role of religion in history. She knows that this may be a sensitive topic and that religion must be taught in a comparative manner. All are appropriate topics for her unit EXCEPT

   (A) contrasting the differences among the Moslem, Jewish, and Christian religions.

   (B) exploring the role of religion in the development of educational institutions.

   (C) exploring the origins of the three major Western religions.

   (D) exploring the role the prophets played in predicting events that happened in the future.

7. Mr. Small is taking a course entitled *Theoretical Thoughts in Education*. Which of the following authors would most help Mr. Small to understand the underlying effects of poverty on academic achievement?

   (A) Dewey
   (B) Maslow — *needs*
   (C) Piaget
   (D) Ravitch

8. Luis is a seventh-grade student preparing for a science fair. He would like to incorporate his interest in music with his project. Which of the following would be most appropriate?

   I. Comparing the sound from different CDs to determine which one is the loudest
   II. Determining the effect music has on emotions
   III. Determining whether the price of different CDs is dependent upon the complexity of the music
   IV. Determining the effect of different types of music upon common houseplants

   (A) I and II only
   (B) I, II, and III only
   (C) I, II, and IV only
   (D) I, II , III, and IV

9. A fourth-grade teacher developed a card game in which students matched different fractions. The shapes contained within each card were the same, while the number of parts shaded were different. In this rummy-type game, the student with the most pairs won the game. This activity is being used to teach the concept of

   (A) proper and improper fractions.
   (B) equivalent fractions.
   (C) sequencing fractions.
   (D) converting fractions.

10. In a fourth-grade math program, symbols such as $\frac{1}{4}$ and $\frac{1}{2}$ should be

    (A) introduced immediately so that students can write the answers to fractional examples.
    (B) memorized in their correct order so students gain an understanding of number sequence.
    (C) converted into fractions containing their like denominators so students will understand that all fractions are equivalent.
    (D) introduced only after children have developed the concepts and oral language necessary for these forms to have meaning and be connected to language.

11. Ms. Smith teaches a lesson in which students must recognize that $\frac{1}{4}$ is the same as 0.25. They use this relationship to determine that .15 and .20 are slightly less than $\frac{1}{4}$ and that 0.30 and 0.38 are a little more than $\frac{1}{4}$. Which of the following concepts is (are) being taught in this lesson?

    I. Numeration skills for decimals —
    II. Relationships between fractions and decimals
    III. Fractional conversions
    IV. Place value of decimals

    (A) III only
    (B) I only
    (C) II and IV only
    (D) I and II only

12. In a social studies class, Mr. Kapinski presents a morally ambiguous situation and asks his students what they would do. Using this technique, Mr. Kapinski is applying the theory developed by

    (A) Kohlberg. — *moral reasoning*
    (B) Bruner.
    (C) Piaget.
    (D) Bandura.

13. In science lab, students are given wires, bulbs, switches, and dry cells and are told to create a circuit that will increase the brightness of each bulb. Before the experiment, the teacher discussed how electricity flows through wires and what generates the electric charge. This approach to instruction

    (A) uses a taxonomy of basic thinking skills.
    (B) uses a cooperative learning approach.
    (C) uses a constructivist approach.
    (D) helps students understand scientific methodology.

14. Students in a first-grade class receive three books on a particular literary theme each week. The student then reads or has the parent read one of the books. The student or the parent then writes one or two sentences about the book. Finally, the child chooses from about five different activities that illustrate or depict a part of the book. This reading strategy is derived from which of the following reading approaches?

    (A) A linguistic approach to reading
    (B) The Gattegno approach to reading remediation
    (C) A whole language approach to reading
    (D) The application of whole-word methodology

15. Two first-grade students are having difficulty with words in which initial consonants must be blended. They pronounce blends as single consonants even when the words are used over and over. Using the whole language approach, how would a teacher develop decoding skills in these students?

    (A) She would teach a lesson blending *bl, sl, cl,* and *fl* words to the whole class, so the two students would not be embarrassed.

    (B) She would have the students recognize blends by having them pick out similar blended words in children's magazines.

    (C) She would teach a mini lesson on blending to these students, using the words in the picture book that they are reading.

    (D) She would totally avoid teaching phonics because the development of sound/symbol relations is not taught within this philosophical approach.

16. Mr. Smith, Assistant Principal, wants to introduce cooperative learning to his teachers. Cooperative learning was central to the teaching ideas of all of the following theorists EXCEPT

    (A) Rousseau.
    (B) Pestalozzi.
    (C) Dewey.
    (D) Flavell.

17. Mrs. Chang is teaching a second-grade class. The poor readers have difficulty identifying the organization of a passage, so their comprehension is suffering. How can Mrs. Chang increase her students' abilities to structure the passage to increase reading comprehension?

    (A) Have them look up new vocabulary concepts in a simplified children's dictionary
    (B) Create a semantic concept map of the story
    (C) Have the students read the passage with their parents at home for reinforcement
    (D) Create an extensive list of comprehension questions that the students will answer after the passage is read silently in class

18. Mr. Posner wants an essay question for a test on heredity to tap into divergent thinking. He wants creative, critical-thinking answers. Which of these four questions tap into divergent thinking skills?

    (A) "How can PKU be detected?"
    (B) "What improvements can you suggest for the environment in which you live?" *many dif. answers*
    (C) "Why do no two people have the same fingerprints?"
    (D) "Why do most states require newborn infants to have urine tests to detect PKU?"

19. Mrs. Garcia was chosen by her principal to speak to the parents of kindergarten students about preparing preschool children for reading success. In her workshop, she described all of the following predictors of success EXCEPT

    (A) a preschooler's ability to recognize and name letters of the alphabet.
    (B) a preschooler's awareness of phonemes.
    (C) literacy preparation, such as playing with refrigerator letters, being read to, or watching *Sesame Street*.
    (D) a wide range of concept development and information.

20. According to the latest research, which statement is true about learning how to read?

    (A) Children with no experiences with print have just as good a chance to learn how to read as children whose parents read with them daily.
    (B) Differences in reading potential are not strongly related to poverty, handedness, dialect, gender, IQ, and mental age.
    (C) Musical ability is positively correlated to reading ability.
    (D) All children who value reading as a means of entertainment, information, and communication learn how to read at the same rate.

21. Mr. Schwartz's fourth-grade class was given the fundamental rules and scoring of baseball, including such information as at-bats, runs batted in, hits, errors, innings pitched, outs, and walks. From these box scores, the students create word problems. What goal does Mr. Schwartz have in this lesson?

    (A) Increasing confidence in making sense of the world using mathematical ideas
    (B) Using complex problems that have no right or wrong answer
    (C) Developing the ability to communicate mathematically using complex symbols and terms
    (D) Developing good reasoning skills

22. Mrs. Korenge is teaching estimation to a fifth-grade class. One activity is estimating the number of pennies in a jar. All of the following are grade-level activities EXCEPT

    (A) finding the mean, mode, and median of the guesses.
    (B) showing the fractional part of the whole group.
    (C) estimating your bill in a fast-food restaurant.
    (D) telling if the guesses are odd or even.

23. As part of her reading program, Mrs. Marango reads to her second-grade students for 20 minutes just after lunch. Which of the following are valid reasons for reading aloud to children?

    I. Exposing children to more classic types of literature
    II. Modeling good reading practices
    III. Quieting and calming students after a high level of activity
    IV. Filling in a transitional period of time between two low-interest activities

    (A) I, II, and III only
    (B) I and IV only
    (C) II, III, and IV only
    (D) I and II only

24. During a teacher-directed reading lesson, Mrs. Devlin asks the following questions:

    "What is this whole story about?"

    "What is the author's purpose in writing this story?"

    "What can we learn from this story?"

    The teacher is using these questions to

    (A) confuse the students.
    (B) engage in structured comprehension.
    (C) engage the students in answering different drawing-conclusions questions.
    (D) increase question-comprehension skills.

25. Which of the following statements is true of the discovery approach to learning science?

    I. Students do less well on standardized science tests using this approach.
    II. Students do not have to discover every fact, principle, and concept they need to know.
    III. Students do not understand how ideas are connected using this method.
    IV. Most schools cannot use this approach because the materials needed are very expensive.

    (A) II and IV only
    (B) II only   *Brunner - discovery learning*
    (C) IV only
    (D) I and III only

FAMILY AND CONSUMER SCIENCES (0120)

Time: 2 hours
Number of Questions: 120
Format: Multiple-choice questions

Purpose of the Test

Designed to measure the preparation of prospective family and consumer sciences teachers in middle through senior high schools

Content Categories

- The Family—(14 percent)
- Human Development—(11 percent)
- Management—(12 percent)
- Consumer Economics—(12 percent)
- Nutrition and Food—(15 percent)
- Clothing and Textiles—(9 percent)
- Housing—(8 percent)
- Family and Consumer Sciences Education—(19 percent)

Category Descriptions

The Family

1. Family structures and stages
2. Family functions, including education and development of family members, and the physical and psychological support of family members
3. Factors affecting family relationships

Human Development

1. Theories of development: Gesell and Ilg, Havinghurst, Erikson, Piaget, and Maslow
2. Development tasks and processes: physical, social, psychological/emotional, and intellectual and moral development
3. Development requiring special resources, including special needs, gifted conditions, drug and alcohol abuse, teenage pregnancies, and teen suicide

Management

1. Management theory: work simplification, time management, and organization of activities
2. Management processes and techniques: goal setting; decision making; assessing and using resources; strategies for change; and identification and clarification of family values, goals, and standards in decisions

Consumer Economics

1. Consumer rights and responsibilities: legal and ethical considerations
2. Social influences on consumer decisions
3. Consumer resources: private and government
4. Selection of services and products
5. Financial planning and management
6. Consumer protection

Nutrition and Food

1. Factors influencing nutritional needs
2. Functions and sources of nutrition
3. Nutritional guidelines
4. Related health problems as well as prevention and treatment strategies
5. Sociocultural aspects of food
6. Meal/food management
7. Food selection and purchase topics
8. Food preparation, storage, and preservation

Clothing and Textiles

1. Wardrobe management
2. Types and characteristics of fibers, production of properties of fabrics

Housing

1. Functions and types of housing
2. Factors that affect consumer decisions

Family and Consumer Sciences Education

1. Philosophical and professional concerns: quality of life; sex-role stereotypes; dual home/work role preparation; integration of the cognitive, affective, and psychomotor skills; and role of professional organizations
2. Characteristics of family/consumer education and of occupational family and consumer sciences education
3. Planning, implementation, and evaluation of community advisory committees, laboratory settings, demonstrations, youth organizations, special needs, and assessments

Family and Consumer Sciences

> *Directions:* Each question or incomplete statement is followed by five answer choices. For each question, decide which answer or completion is best, and blacken the letter of your choice on the answer sheet.

1. Which of the following is NOT a myth?

    (A) Vitamins give you "pep" and "energy."
    (B) Timing of vitamin intake is crucial.
    (C) Vitamin C "protects" against the common cold.
    (D) Synthetic vitamins, manufactured in the laboratory, are identical to natural vitamins in their effect on the body.
    (E) The more vitamins, the better.

2. The unit of electrical energy most commonly associated with the use of electrical appliances is the

    (A) horsepower.
    (B) watt.
    (C) kilowatt-hour.
    (D) amp.
    (E) volt.

3. Which of the following is a high-fiber food?

    (A) Grapefruit
    (B) White rice
    (C) Lettuce
    (D) Peeled potatoes
    (E) Brown rice

4. The introduction of solid food to a baby's diet is normally recommended at the age of

    (A) 1 to 3 months.
    (B) 2 to 4 months.
    (C) 4 to 6 months.
    (D) 6 to 8 months.
    (E) 8 to 10 months.

5. Which of the following has the greatest number of calories?

    (A) Four celery sticks
    (B) A small apple
    (C) A large green pepper
    (D) Ten mushrooms
    (E) A small tomato

6. If 3 teaspoons   = 1 tablespoon
   16 tablespoons = 1 cup
   2 cups   = 1 pint

   then $\frac{1}{2}$ pint is equivalent to how many teaspoons?

    (A) 10
    (B) 12
    (C) 21
    (D) 24
    (E) 48

7. All of the following are faucet components EXCEPT

    (A) stem.
    (B) O ring.
    (C) escutcheon.
    (D) washer.
    (E) float ball.

Questions 8 and 9 are based on the following bill.

SW **Valley Water Company** INCORPORATED
360 West End Road • Redwood, New York 10994

BILLING DATE		SERVICE ADDRESS		
JUN 05		15 Jones AVE		45-110-13

METER NUMBER	FOR THE PERIOD		NO OF DAYS IN PERIOD	RATE CODE	METER READINGS		CONSUMPTION IN 100 CU. FT.	BILLING CODE	AMOUNT
	FROM	TO			PREVIOUS	PRESENT			
05445024	0221	0331	38		1355	1364	9		31.19
30664421	0331	0522	52		0000	0022	22		62.71
					SUMMER RATE				
					WINTER RATE				

BUDGET PAYMENT PLAN	
COST FOR WATER	BALANCE IN PLAN
CONSUMED THIS PERIOD	AFTER PAYMENT OF AMOUNT DUE

ONE HUNDRED CUBIC FEET EQUALS 748 GALLONS. YOUR CONSUMPTION FOR THE CURRENT BILLING PERIOD WAS **23,188** GALLONS.

AMOUNT DUE **$93.90**

PAYABLE ON OR BEFORE **JUN 20 05**

8. Based on this bill, how many gallons of water were used from February 21 to March 31?

  (A) 1,364
  (B) 6,732
  (C) 16,456
  (D) 28,424
  (E) Cannot be determined from the information given

9. How much does 100 cubic feet of water cost in the winter, given the fact that the winter rate ends on March 31?

  (A) $1.42
  (B) $1.46
  (C) $3.02
  (D) $3.47
  (E) $6.97

10. Do not use lightweight plastic containers such as margarine tubs in a microwave because they

  (A) reflect the microwaves causing sparks.
  (B) inhibit the cooking process.
  (C) melt.
  (D) burn the corners of the heated item.
  (E) cause pitting on the oven walls.

11. Local authorities are most likely to receive the greatest part of their revenues from

  (A) sales taxes.
  (B) property taxes.
  (C) payroll taxes.
  (D) personal income taxes.
  (E) corporate income taxes.

12. How many square yards of carpet are required to completely cover the floor of a room 9 ft × 12 ft?

  (A) 6
  (B) 12
  (C) 27
  (D) 54
  (E) 108

13. It is recommended that each of the following not be frozen EXCEPT

  (A) cream cheese.
  (B) hard-cooked eggs.
  (C) mayonnaise.
  (D) mashed potatoes.
  (E) carbonated drinks.

14. Which of the following sentences is NOT true with respect to preventing or retarding mildew growth?

(A) Avoid putting away any clothing or material items when wet.
(B) Poorly lighted areas help prevent growth of and can even kill the mildew.
(C) Disinfectant can slow or stop growth.
(D) Silica gel is effective against mildew growth.
(E) Proper air flow helps prevent growth.

15. The tool used to locate a point directly below a ceiling hook is a

(A) plumb bob.
(B) line level.
(C) transit.
(D) drop gauge.
(E) vertical shaft.

16. A recession may be best described as

(A) a limited period when unemployment rises and business activity slows down.
(B) a limited period of rising prices, increased industrial output, and falling wages.
(C) the extended aftermath of a long depression.
(D) a sudden and acute rise in unemployment, business activity, and industrial output.
(E) an extended period in which wages, prices, employment, and industrial output rise and fall rapidly and inexplicably.

17. In a sample survey, questions are asked of a group of people who

(A) volunteer to participate in the sample.
(B) are able to understand the goals of the researcher.
(C) are carefully selected to be representative of a larger group.
(D) are familiar with statistical techniques.
(E) are chosen at random from the population at large.

18. The short form of the 1980 census asked questions on all of the following EXCEPT

(A) whether a person was of Spanish/Hispanic origin or descent.
(B) whether a person was married.
(C) whether a home had complete indoor plumbing.
(D) whether a person was African-American.
(E) whether a person was heterosexual.

19. In a well-known experiment, psychologists frustrated young children by placing a wire fence between the children and a pile of toys. When finally allowed to play with the toys, the children smashed and destroyed them. This reaction is an example of

(A) displaced aggression.
(B) absence of aggression.
(C) dormant aggression.
(D) rational aggression.
(E) sustained aggression.

20. A convertible mortgage is which of the following?

(A) An adjustable-rate mortgage that, at the buyer's option, can be converted to a fixed-rate loan
(B) A fixed-rate mortgage that, at the buyer's option, can be converted to an adjustable-rate loan
(C) A fixed-rate mortgage that, at the lender's option, can be converted to an adjustable-rate loan
(D) An adjustable-rate mortgage that, at the lender's option, can be converted to a fixed-rate loan
(E) A balloon mortgage that, at the buyer's option, can be converted to a fixed-rate loan

21. The federal agency that insures deposits in savings and loan associations and savings banks is the

(A) FNMA.
(B) FHA.
(C) FSB.
(D) FSLIC.
(E) FHLMC.

22. Which instrument is specially designed for fixed-income and retiree homeowners who have little or no mortgage debt, offering them the ability to receive monthly payments to supplement income while still retaining home ownership?

(A) Reverse-annuity mortgage
(B) Conventional mortgage
(C) Balloon mortgage
(D) Variable-rate mortgage
(E) Second mortgage

23. All of the following draw funds from a deposit account EXCEPT

    (A) an ATM card.
    (B) an asset card.
    (C) a credit card.
    (D) a debit card.
    (E) check writing.

24. Insurance that extends the liability coverage beyond the underlying limits for auto and home, usually up to $1 million dollars, is called

    (A) whole-life coverage.
    (B) umbrella coverage.
    (C) overinsured coverage.
    (D) accidental coverage.
    (E) extended-benefit coverage.

25. This type of insurance has no savings or investment component, is relatively inexpensive pure insurance for young people, and is coverage for a defined number of years and must then be renewed; its premiums increase with age. It is called

    (A) whole life.
    (B) straight life.
    (C) limited payment life.
    (D) term life.
    (E) endowment.

INTRODUCTION TO THE TEACHING OF READING (0200)

Time: 2 hours
Number of Questions: 100
Format: Multiple-choice questions

Purpose of the Test

Designed to measure the preparation of prospective elementary or secondary school teachers in the area of reading

Content Categories

- Reading as a Language-Thought Process—(13–17 percent)
- Text Structure—(8–12 percent)
- Instructional Process in the Teaching of Reading—(38–42 percent)
- Affective Aspects—(13–17 percent)
- Environmental/Sociocultural Factors—(18–22 percent)

Category Descriptions

Reading as a Language-Thought Process

1. Theoretical approaches to the reading process, acquisition and understanding of language, metacognition
2. Relationships between listening, speaking, and writing, especially reading/writing connection

Text Structure

1. Structure for narrative and expository text, syntactic complexity, organization, vocabulary, and story grammar
2. Clues in semantics, syntax, graphemes, and experience

Instructional Processes in the Teaching of Reading

1. Use of strategies, such as reciprocal teaching, critical questioning, monitoring, scaffolding, schema, language expansion, story grammars, scripts, organizational patterns, and guided oral and silent reading
2. Age-appropriate strategies
3. Classroom management, including cooperative groups, use of paraprofessionals, centers, peer grouping, and computers
4. Content area reading
5. Study skills
6. Use of criterion-based tests, achievement tests, and individual and group assessment strategies

Affective Aspects

Use of art expression, drama, and media to motivate reading and writing

Environmental/Sociocultural Factors

1. Understand factors that influence literacy and biliteracy development, including parental support, home/school congruence, approaches, and teacher expectations

2. Recognize influence of family and peers and of the differences between socio-economics, regional, and cultural linguistics

3. Select appropriate instructional strategies to address above factors

Introduction to the Teaching of Reading

Directions: Each question or incomplete statement is followed by five answer choices. For each question, decide which answer or completion is best, and blacken the letter of your choice on the answer sheet.

1. Using an Informal Reading Inventory, the instructional level measuring inferential comprehension would be approximately

   (A) 70 percent.
   (B) 90 percent.
   (C) below 60 percent.
   (D) 99–100 percent.
   (E) 90–95 percent.

2. Which is NOT a major contribution to poor reading scores in school?

   (A) Emotional factors causing academic blockage
   (B) Limited and fragmented instructional programs
   (C) Inadequately prepared teachers
   (D) Dependency on workbooks and ditto sheets
   (E) Improper use of reading materials

3. A sixth-grade student of average potential has comprehension skills on grade level. She is asked to find several factual details about the Lewis and Clark Expedition from her textbook. The most probable reason the student may be unable to do this activity is because she

   (A) may have difficulty reading the material.
   (B) does not know how to use the table of contents or index.
   (C) has poor inference skills.
   (D) cannot organize the information.
   (E) is reading material above her grade level.

4. According to research, which is NOT an effective way of teaching vocabulary and improving concept development in children?

   (A) Teach cloze to develop context clues.
   (B) Teach words for which children have an immediate need.
   (C) Develop work-study skills in the context of need.
   (D) Teach prefixes and roots.
   (E) Teach multiple meanings and figurative language.

5. Which is an example of teaching phonics synthetically?

   (A) Introducing letters and then related sounds
   (B) Teaching sounds using a multisensory approach
   (C) Using computer-assisted instruction to develop sound relationships
   (D) Using phonograms rather than individual sounds to develop word analysis skills
   (E) Teaching letter-sound relationships from sight words already known

6. Which is a good definition of reading according to psycholinguistic theory?

   (A) Reading is the ability to discriminate letters and sounds.
   (B) Reading is the act of identifying the symbol and obtaining meaning from the identified symbol.
   (C) Reading is the translation of symbols into sounds.
   (D) Reading reconstructs a message encoded by a writer in graphic language.
   (E) Reading is thinking and the reconstructing of the ideas of others.

7. There are a variety of reading programs and strategies available in the teaching of reading to students of average intellectual ability. According to research, which of the programs below is the MOST effective?

   (A) A basal approach
   (B) Initial teaching alphabet
   (C) A rebus approach
   (D) A basal approach using strong word-attack applications
   (E) A language experience approach

8. Some effective approaches in developing reading readiness in preschool are

   I. labeling objects in a classroom.
   II. teaching sound-symbol relationships using specialized workbooks.
   III. reading picture books about a variety of subjects.
   IV. formal teaching of auditory discrimination skills.

   (A) I, II, and III only
   (B) I and III only
   (C) II and IV only
   (D) I only
   (E) II only

9. Who attributed reading difficulty to neurological immaturity and failure to establish cerebral dominance?

   (A) Chall
   (B) Chomsky
   (C) Fernald
   (D) Orton
   (E) Delacato

10. The use of the cloze technique comes from which reading theory?

    (A) Linguistics
    (B) Psycholinguistics
    (C) Process theory
    (D) Organic model
    (E) Compensatory comprehension model

11. Results of standardized tests

    I. show how well children are reading compared to other children.
    II. help determine in which reading group a child should be placed.
    III. determine in which skills students are deficient.
    IV. are expressed in grade and age scores.

    (A) I and II only
    (B) II and III only
    (C) I, II, and III only
    (D) I, II, and IV only
    (E) II and IV only

12. The primary focus of reading in the middle grades is

    (A) reading to gather information from various materials.
    (B) analyzing different points of views.
    (C) synthesizing information from various sources.
    (D) drawing conclusions from open-ended stories.
    (E) teaching affixes and nonphonetic words to improve decoding ability.

13. Recent research has shown that the use of colored lenses with some learning disabled students

    (A) does not reduce extraneous stimuli when reading.
    (B) decreases reversals and transpositions while reading.
    (C) helps them improve their ability to comprehend material.
    (D) does not significantly improve reading problems in such students.
    (E) tends to increase word blindness.

14. Teaching reading readiness in kindergarten should emphasize

    I. the teaching of initial letter sounds.
    II. the teaching of sight vocabulary.
    III. the use of a variety of informal language activities.
    IV. playing recordings and showing filmstrips containing a variety of stories.

    (A) III only
    (B) I and II only
    (C) III and IV only
    (D) IV only
    (E) II and III only

15. Research has shown that when students learn to read at three years of age,

    (A) these students are more intelligent than those pupils who do not learn how to read until seven years of age.
    (B) there is no significant difference in reading ability between them and the late readers by the time these students are in third and fourth grade.
    (C) such students are more likely to go on to higher education than those who first read at seven or eight years.
    (D) comprehension skills develop before perceptual skills.
    (E) academically oriented preschool programs will improve their achievement along with that of all children.

16. Sylvia Ashton Warner is most associated with the

    (A) basal approach.
    (B) multisensory approach.
    (C) organic approach.
    (D) phonics approach.
    (E) linguistic approach.

17. Examples of reading diagnostic tests are the

    I.   Metropolitan Achievement Test.
    II. Durrell Analysis of Reading Difficulty.
    III. California Reading Test.
    IV. Roswell-Chall Auditory Blending Test.

    (A) I, III, and IV only
    (B) I and III only
    (C) III and IV only
    (D) II, III, and IV only
    (E) II and IV only

18. Recognition of figurative language is an example of a

    (A) word-recognition skill.
    (B) word-meaning skill.
    (C) comprehension skill.
    (D) study skill.
    (E) appreciation skill.

19. A reading system using a 44-character core alphabet to avoid inconsistencies in sound-letter relationships describes

    (A) i/t/a.
    (B) linguistic readers.
    (C) simplified spelling.
    (D) DMS.
    (E) Unifon.

20. If a student constantly repeats words and phrases while reading passages, it can be concluded that he or she may have

    (A) visual perceptual problems.
    (B) tracking problems.
    (C) visual discrimination problems.
    (D) memory problems.
    (E) language-processing problems.

21. A child is given a passage slightly above his ability so as to analyze his miscues. He constantly omits the final *s* in almost all verbs and plural nouns. It can be concluded that the errors made may possibly be due to

    (A) problems in grammar development.
    (B) inability to see obvious mistakes.
    (C) variations in dialect.
    (D) graphic similarity between the miscue and the actual word.
    (E) auditory similarity between the miscue and the actual word.

22. A teacher writes on the board:

    Rearrange these items so that each subgroup is placed under its proper heading.

    The instructor is

    (A) developing study and organization skills.
    (B) planning to teach the concept of developing main ideas.
    (C) developing a skill in word meaning.
    (D) developing word-recognition skills.
    (E) teaching students to separate important from unimportant details.

23. Having first-grade students supply missing letters sequentially in groups teaches

    (A) letter-recognition skills.
    (B) dictionary skills.
    (C) organizational skills.
    (D) sound-symbol skills.
    (E) discrimination skills.

24. This program develops reading skills by stimulating discussion, creating a story, and developing word skills. Which approach is being described?

    (A) The whole-language approach
    (B) Individualized reading
    (C) The language-experience approach
    (D) The organic approach
    (E) The basal approach

25. Words such as *few*, *oil*, *out*, *should*, *toy*, and *buy* contain

    (A) vowel digraphs.
    (B) silent vowels.
    (C) vowel diphthongs.
    (D) phonically irregular words.
    (E) short vowels.

MATHEMATICS: CONTENT KNOWLEDGE (0061)

Time: 2 hours
Number of Questions: 50
Format: Multiple-choice questions, graphing calculator required

Purpose of the Test

Designed to assess the mathematical knowledge necessary for a teacher of secondary school mathematics

Content Categories

- Arithmetic and Basic Algebra—(35 percent)
- Functions and Their Graphs—(35 percent)
- Probability and Statistics—(30 percent)

Category Descriptions

Arithmetic and Basic Algebra

1. Geometry
2. Trigonometry
3. Analytic Geometry

Functions and Their Graphs

1. Calculus

Probability and Statistics

1. Discrete Mathematics
2. Linear Algebra
3. Computer Science
4. Mathematical Reasoning and Modeling

Mathematics: Content Knowledge

Directions: Each of the questions below is followed by four possible answers or completions. Choose the best answer for each question.

---

1. The graph of $\dfrac{x^2 + x - 6}{x - 2}$ has which of the following properties at $x = 2$?

   (A) A vertical asymptote
   (B) A horizontal asymptote
   (C) A hole
   (D) A root (a zero)

2. What is the third term in the expansion of $(x - 2y)^6$?

   (A) $15x^4 y^2$
   (B) $60x^4 y^2$
   (C) $60x^2 y^4$
   (D) $-60x^4 y^2$

3. If $f(x) = \dfrac{x+1}{x-1}$, which of the following is $f^{-1}(x)$?

   (A) $\dfrac{x+1}{x-1}$

   (B) $\dfrac{x-1}{x+1}$

   (C) $\dfrac{2}{x-1}$

   (D) $-\left(\dfrac{x-1}{x+1}\right)$

4. $\displaystyle\int \dfrac{\ln 2x}{x^2}\,dx =$

   (A) $-\dfrac{1}{x}\left(\ln 2x - \dfrac{1}{x}\right) + C$

   (B) $-\dfrac{1}{x}\left(\ln 2x + 1\right) + C$

   (C) $-\dfrac{1}{x}\left(\ln 2x - 1\right) + C$

   (D) $\dfrac{1}{2x}\left(\ln 2x - 2\right) + C$

5. What is the equation of the normal line to the ellipse $2x^2 + y^2 = 18$ at the point $(1, 4)$?

   (A) $y + 4 = -2(x - 1)$
   (B) $y + 4 = 2(x - 1)$
   (C) $y - 4 = -2(x - 1)$
   (D) $y - 4 = 2(x - 1)$

6. What is the area of the circle $x^2 - 6x + y^2 + 4y - 23 = 0$?

   (A) 36π
   (B) 23π
   (C) 18π
   (D) 6π

7. Which of the following applies to $\displaystyle\sum_{k=0}^{\infty} \dfrac{1}{k!}$?

   (A) Converges to π
   (B) Converges by the Ratio Test
   (C) Diverges by the Ratio Test
   (D) Inconclusive by the Ratio Test

8. Solve for x and y:

   $$\begin{bmatrix} 3 & 4 \\ 1 & -2 \end{bmatrix}\begin{bmatrix} x \\ y \end{bmatrix} = \begin{bmatrix} 5 \\ 5 \end{bmatrix}$$

   (A) $x = 1$ and $y = -3$
   (B) $x = -1$ and $y = 3$
   (C) $x = 3$ and $y = 1$
   (D) $x = 3$ and $y = -1$

9. What is the phase shift of the function:

   $$f(x) = 3\sin\left(\dfrac{2x}{3} - \dfrac{2\pi}{9}\right) - 8?$$

   (A) $\dfrac{2\pi}{9}$ units to the left

   (B) $\dfrac{2\pi}{9}$ units to the right

   (C) $\dfrac{\pi}{3}$ units to the right

   (D) $\dfrac{\pi}{3}$ units to the left

10. What is the remainder when $x^3 - 4x^2 + 1$ is divided by $x + 1$?

(A) −4
(B) −1
(C) 1
(D) 4

11. A spinner is divided into 4 equal spaces as shown. A player bets $2 on a given letter. If the spinner lands on that letter, he is paid $8 and gets his $2 back. If the spinner lands on any letter not chosen, the player loses the $2. What is the expected value of the game? (Any spin landing on a division line between the lettered sections is voided and the spinner is re-spun.)

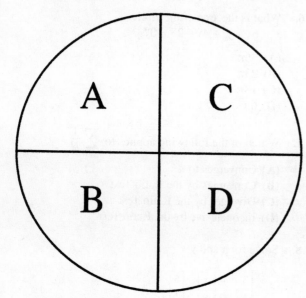

(A) Lose $0.50
(B) Lose $0.30
(C) Gain $0.30
(D) Gain $0.50

12. If $\log_b N = 2$ what is the value of $\log_{\frac{1}{b}} N$?

(A) −2

(B) $-\dfrac{1}{2}$

(C) $\dfrac{1}{2}$

(D) 2

13. A 75-sided regular polygon has how many diagonals?

(A) 2,775
(B) 2,770
(C) 2,700
(D) 2,706

14. Which of the following expresses $y^{\frac{1}{3}} \times x^{\frac{3}{4}}$ as a single radical?

(A) $\sqrt[7]{x^3 y}$

(B) $\sqrt[7]{x^3 y^4}$

(C) $\sqrt[12]{x^7 y^8}$

(D) $\sqrt[12]{x^9 y^4}$

15. If the height of the cylinder is four times the radius, express the lateral area in terms of the volume. ($V = \pi r^2 h$ and Lateral Area $= 2\pi r h$)

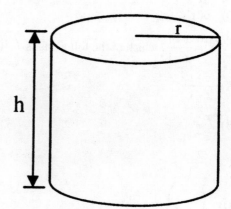

(A) $\sqrt[3]{6\pi V^2}$

(B) $2\sqrt[3]{2\pi V^2}$

(C) $2\sqrt[3]{4\pi V^2}$

(D) $4\sqrt[3]{2\pi V^2}$

16. Solve: $\dfrac{x+3}{x-4} \geq 0$

(A) $(-\infty,-3) \cup (4,\infty)$

(B) $(-\infty,3] \cup [4,\infty)$

(C) $(-\infty,-3] \cup (4,\infty)$

(D) $(-\infty,3) \cup [4,\infty)$

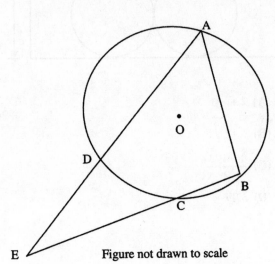

Figure not drawn to scale

17. If $\overline{AB} = 8$ and arcs $AB{:}BC{:}CD{:}DA$ are in the ratio of $10{:}7{:}7{:}12$, what is the length of $\overline{EB}$ to the nearest integer?

(A) 50

(B) 37

(C) 31

(D) 29

18. $\dfrac{\sin 2\theta}{1 + \cos 2\theta}$ is equivalent to which of the following?

(A) $\sin 2q + \tan 2q$

(B) $\sin q \, \cos q$

(C) $\sec q$

(D) $\tan q$

19. What is the equation of the circle with center $(1, -2)$ and tangent to the line $x - 2y = 2$?

(A) $5(x-1)^2 + 5(y+2)^2 = 9$

(B) $9(x-1)^2 + 9(y+2)^2 = 5$

(C) $7(x-1)^2 + 7(y+2)^2 = 3$

(D) $3(x-1)^2 + 3(y+2)^2 = 7$

20. Find the product of $2\left(\cos\dfrac{\pi}{3} + i\sin\dfrac{\pi}{3}\right)$ and $3\left(\cos\dfrac{5\pi}{6} + i\sin\dfrac{\pi}{6}\right)$.

(A) $6\left(\sqrt{3} - 2i\right)$

(B) $-\sqrt{3} - 3i$

(C) $-3\sqrt{3} - 3i$

(D) $-6\sqrt{3}\left(1 + 2i\right)$

21. A 3-person committee is to be formed by selecting from a group of 5 men and 6 women, one of whom is Dawn. What is the probability of selecting a committee with 1 man and 2 women, one of whom *must* be Dawn?

(A) $\dfrac{2}{11}$

(B) $\dfrac{5}{11}$

(C) $\dfrac{5}{24}$

(D) $\dfrac{5}{33}$

22. Which of the following sentences is the application of DeMorgan's Law to the sentence: *It is not the case that it is blue or not red*?

(A) It is not blue or it is red.

(B) It is red and blue.

(C) It is not red and not blue.

(D) It is not blue and it is red.

23. What is the maximum value of the objective function $6x + 4y$ subject to the following constraints:

$$2x + y \le 8$$
$$x + 2y \le 10$$
$$x > 0$$
$$y > 0$$

(A) 36
(B) 32
(C) 28
(D) 24

24. Find: $\lim\limits_{x \to 0} \dfrac{3^x - 1}{x}$

(A) e^3
(B) $3 \ln 3$
(C) $\ln 3$
(D) $-1 + \ln 3$

25. Five identical circles of radius 1 are packed in a rectangle as shown in the diagram. What is the minimum value of x for such a rectangle?

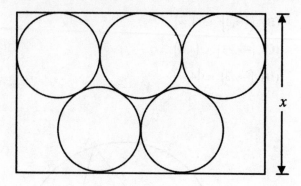

(A) $2 + \sqrt{3}$

(B) $1 + 2\sqrt{2}$

(C) $\dfrac{1 + 4\sqrt{3}}{2}$

(D) 3.99

MUSIC EDUCATION (0110)

**Time: 2 hours, comprised of a 40-minute listening section
and an 80-minute written section**
Number of Questions: 150 (45 of which are based on taped musical excerpts)
Format: Multiple-choice questions

Purpose of the Test

Designed to measure the preparation of prospective K–12 music educators

Content Categories

- Music History and Literature—(20 percent)
- Music Theory—(21 percent)
- Performance Skills—(19 percent)
- Curriculum, Instruction, and Professional Concerns—(40 percent)

Category Descriptions

Music History and Literature

1. Music of all periods, with emphasis on eighteenth, nineteenth, and twentieth centuries

2. Style periods and their characteristics

3. Composers

4. Genres

5. Music literature

6. Performance media

7. Approximately half of the music history questions are based on taped musical excerpts

Music Theory

1. Compositional organization and acoustics

2. Approximately half of the music theory questions are based on taped musical excerpts

Performance Skills

1. Conducting

2. Interpretation of style and symbols

3. Improvisational techniques and performance literature

4. Critical listening and performance error recognition

5. Acoustical considerations involving rehearsal rooms and performance areas

6. Approximately half of the performance skills questions are based on taped musical excerpts

Curriculum, Instruction, and Professional Concerns

1. Course offerings from K-12

2. Course content includes psychomotor, cognitive and affective behaviors, conceptual elements of music, learning sequence, grade-level performance skills, interdisciplinary aspects, student evaluation, pedagogical approaches, appropriate vocal and instrumental materials, and classroom management skills

3. Sociology, philosophy, psychology, and history of music education

4. Professional literature, practices, organizations, and ethics

5. Several curriculum, instruction, and professional concerns questions may be based on taped excerpts.

Music Education

> *Directions:* Each question or incomplete statement is followed by five answer choices. For each question, decide which answer or completion is best, and blacken the letter of your choice on the answer sheet.

Sample Questions for the Taped Section (On the actual test, you will hear an excerpt from a well-known chorus.)

1. Name the composer.

   (A) J. S. Bach
   (B) W. A. Mozart
   (C) R. Schumann
   (D) G. F. Handel
   (E) L. van Beethoven

2. Name the type of cadence used in this music.

   (A) Authentic
   (B) Half
   (C) Plagal
   (D) Deceptive
   (E) Imperfect

3. This example is part of a large work called a(n)

   (A) oratorio.
   (B) symphony.
   (C) tone poem.
   (D) opera.
   (E) sonata.

(On the actual test, you will hear a short excerpt from the following march.)

4. Name the composer of this famous march.

   (A) J. P. Sousa
   (B) K. L. King
   (C) P. Tchaikovsky
   (D) F. Mendelssohn
   (E) J. Brahms

Sample Questions for the Nontaped Section

5. Identify the most important form of early polyphonic music during the Middle Ages.

    (A) Trio sonata
    (B) Homophonic
    (C) Motet
    (D) Tone row
    (E) Quartet

6. The figured bass for a deceptive cadence is

    (A) V–I
    (B) II–V
    (C) I–VI
    (D) IV–I
    (E) V–VI

7. Pivot chords are used in

    (A) adagio.
    (B) augmentation.
    (C) atonal.
    (D) odd meter.
    (E) modulation.

8. Which of the following was NOT performed during the Baroque period?

    (A) Atonal
    (B) Cantata
    (C) Opera
    (D) Motet
    (E) Fugue

9. In order to produce a good characteristic tone, wind instrumental students must have the correct

    (A) rosin.
    (B) embouchure.
    (C) sticks.
    (D) music.
    (E) rhythm.

10. Classroom eurythmic activities would include

    (A) singing.
    (B) testing.
    (C) marching.
    (D) talking.
    (E) listening.

11. Which one of the following was a twentieth-century composer?

    (A) C. Ives
    (B) J. Brahms
    (C) C. P. E. Bach
    (D) F. Liszt
    (E) G. Verdi

12. The music of the Classical period includes the works of which composer?

    (A) S. Prokofiev
    (B) F. Haydn
    (C) A. Toscanini
    (D) S. Earnhart
    (E) A. Berg

13. In teaching beginning music reading, which of the following should be avoided?

    (A) Staff
    (B) Clef
    (C) Note values
    (D) Note names
    (E) Syncopation

14. The largest music educator's association is the

    (A) A.P.B.S.A.
    (B) N.A.R.D.
    (C) N.E.M.C.
    (D) N.A.S.A.
    (E) D.O.T.

15. While conducting a fund-raising project, the music teacher should

    (A) deposit all money into a personal account.
    (B) delegate all responsibilities to the students.
    (C) expect compensation for the time spent fund-raising.
    (D) keep all money in the teacher's desk.
    (E) avoid using classroom time to conduct the project.

16. The main purpose for music education in the public schools is to

    (A) win contests.
    (B) prepare students for careers in music.
    (C) provide music for school functions.
    (D) provide experience for future music consumers.
    (E) teach discipline.

17. The first note a beginning violinist should play is

    (A) concert B flat.
    (B) middle C.
    (C) second space A.
    (D) first space F.
    (E) third line D.

18. One technique that can be used in teaching vocal sight reading is

    (A) a periodic chart.
    (B) solfeggio.
    (C) cantata.
    (D) madrigal.
    (E) arpeggio.

19. Which of the following scales does NOT share characteristics with the other four?

    (A) Major
    (B) Minor
    (C) Dorian
    (D) Mixolydian
    (E) Pentatonic

20. A curved line connecting two of the same note is called a

    (A) phrase marking.
    (B) tie.
    (C) slur.
    (D) staccato.
    (E) mistake.

21. The notations above are used to designate

    (A) chords.
    (B) glissandos.
    (C) arpeggios.
    (D) slurs.
    (E) staccatos.

22. The excerpt above is an example of

    (A) four-part harmony.
    (B) sotto voce.
    (C) elementary music.
    (D) polyrhythm.
    (E) lyre.

Credo in unum Deum, Patrem omni-potentem

23. The music above would have been performed during the

    (A) Gregorian period.
    (B) Baroque period.
    (C) Classical period.
    (D) Romantic period.
    (E) Modern period.

24. A capella vocal music should be performed

    (A) with a rhythm section only.
    (B) with a full orchestra.
    (C) with piano accompaniment.
    (D) with a cap.
    (E) unaccompanied.

25. Which of the following does NOT belong in an elementary classroom music curriculum?

    (A) Singing folk songs
    (B) Music reading
    (C) Music listening
    (D) Four-part dictation
    (E) Music writing

PHYSICS (0260)

Time: 2 hours
Number of Questions: 100
Format: Multiple-choice questions

Purpose of the Test

Designed to measure the preparation of prospective junior and senior high school physics teachers

Content Categories

- Major Concepts, Heat and Thermodynamics, Environmental Issues—(28 percent)
- Mechanics—(25 percent)
- Electricity and Magnetism—(20 percent)
- Wave Motion, Atomic and Nuclear Physics—(27 percent)

Category Descriptions

Major Concepts, Heat and Thermodynamics, Environmental Issues

1. Nature and properties of matter

2. Interaction of energy and matter, including conservation, thermal effects, electrical effects, quantum effects, kinetic molecular theory, and nuclear reactions

3. Heat and thermodynamics: basic laws, friction, heat pumps, transfer, thermal properties, and expansion and contraction effects

4. Environmental issues

Mechanics

1. Motion: linear, curvilinear, and periodic

2. Dynamics, conservation, gravity

3. Fluid mechanics of noncompressible fluids

4. Relativistic mechanics related to special theory only

Electricity and Magnetism

Static electricity, electric current, and magnetic fields

Wave Motion, Atomic and Nuclear Physics

1. Wave motion: properties, models, phenomena, sound and vibrations in matter, electromagnetic radiation, and geometrical and physical optics

2. Atomic and nuclear physics: fundamental particles, quantum theory, models, and wave/particle duality

Physics

Directions: Each question or incomplete statement is followed by five answer choices. For each question, decide which answer or completion is best, and blacken the letter of your choice on the answer sheet.

1. The diagram below represents a block sliding along a frictionless surface between points *A* and *G*.

As the block moves from point *A* to point *B*, the speed of the block will be

(A) decreasing.
(B) increasing.
(C) constant but not zero.
(D) zero.
(E) decreasing and then increasing.

2. A person travels 6 meters north, 4 meters east, and 6 meters south. What is the total displacement?

(A) 16 m east
(B) 6 m north
(C) 6 m south
(D) 4 m east
(E) 4 m west

3. The diagram below shows a graph of distance as a function of time for an object in straight-line motion.

According to the graph, the object most likely has a(n)

(A) constant momentum.
(B) decreasing acceleration.
(C) decreasing mass.
(D) increasing speed.
(E) increasing mass.

4. If an object's velocity changes from 25 meters per second to 15 meters per second in 2.0 seconds, the magnitude of the object's acceleration is

(A) 5.0 m/s^2
(B) 7.5 m/s^2
(C) 13 m/s^2
(D) 20 m/s^2
(E) 25 m/s^2

5. Which vector below represents the resultant of the concurrent vectors *A* and *B* in the diagram at the right?

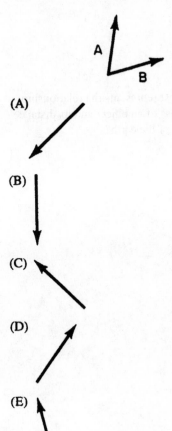

6. Four forces are acting on an object as shown in the diagram.

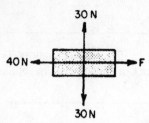

If the object is moving with a constant velocity, the magnitude of force *F* must be

(A) 0 N
(B) 20 N
(C) 30 N
(D) 40 N
(E) 100 N

7. A force of 50 newtons causes an object to accelerate at 10 meters per second squared. What is the mass of the object?

(A) 500 kg
(B) 60 kg
(C) 5.0 kg
(D) 0.20 kg
(E) 0.10 kg

8. Which graph best represents the relationship between the mass of an object and its distance from the center of the earth?

(A)

(B)

(C)

(D)

(E)

9. Gravitational force of attraction *F* exists between two point masses *A* and *B* when they are separated by a fixed distance. After mass *A* is tripled and mass *B* is halved, the gravitational attraction between the two masses is

(A) $\frac{1}{6}F$

(B) $\frac{2}{3}F$

(C) $\frac{3}{2}F$

(D) $\frac{9}{4}F$

(E) $6F$

10. Which terms represent scalar quantities?

(A) Power and force
(B) Work and displacement
(C) Time and energy
(D) Distance and velocity
(E) Mass and acceleration

11. What is the approximate thickness of this piece of paper?

(A) 10^2 m
(B) 10^1 m
(C) 10^0 m
(D) 10^{-2} m
(E) 10^{-5} m

12. A negatively charged object is brought near the knob of a negatively charged electroscope. The leaves of the electroscope will

(A) move closer together.
(B) move farther apart.
(C) become positively charged.
(D) become neutral.
(E) be unaffected.

13. Which diagram below shows correct current direction in a circuit segment?

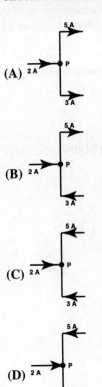

14. Which circuit segment has an equivalent resistance of 6 ohms?

(A) —3Ω—2Ω—

(B) [3Ω, 2Ω parallel]

(C) —2Ω—2Ω—2Ω—

(D) [2Ω, 2Ω, 2Ω parallel]

(E) —2Ω— [2Ω, 2Ω parallel]

15. Which diagram best represents the magnetic field near the poles of a horseshoe magnet?

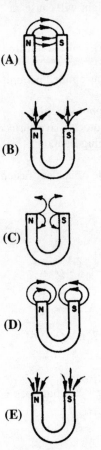

16. In the diagram below, ray *XO* is incident upon the concave (diverging) lens. Along which path will the ray continue?

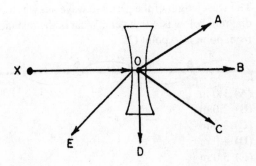

(A) *OA*
(B) *OB*
(C) *OC*
(D) *OD*
(E) *OE*

17. A beam of blue light causes photoelectrons to be emitted from a photoemissive surface. An increase in the intensity of the blue light will cause an increase in the

    (A) maximum kinetic energy of the emitted photoelectrons.
    (B) number of photoelectrons emitted per unit of time.
    (C) charge carried by each photoelectron.
    (D) work function of the photoemissive surface.
    (E) frequency of the impinging light.

18. Which reaction is an example of nuclear fusion?

    (A) $^{226}_{88}Ra \rightarrow ^{222}_{86}Rn + ^{4}_{2}He + Q$

    (B) $^{214}_{83}Bi \rightarrow ^{214}_{84}Po + ^{0}_{-1}e + Q$

    (C) $^{235}_{92}U + ^{1}_{0}n \rightarrow ^{92}_{36}Kr + ^{141}_{56}Ba + 3^{1}_{0}n + Q$

    (D) $^{3}_{1}H + ^{1}_{1}H \rightarrow ^{4}_{2}He + Q$

    (E) $^{235}_{92}U + ^{1}_{0}n \rightarrow ^{141}_{56}Ba + ^{92}_{36}Kr + 3^{1}_{0}n + Q$

19. In the reaction $^{24}_{11}Na \rightarrow ^{24}_{12}Mg + x$, what does x represent?

    (A) An alpha particle
    (B) A beta particle
    (C) A neutron
    (D) A positron
    (E) A proton

20. The wavelength of the periodic wave shown in the diagram below is 4.0 meters. What is the distance from point B to point C?

    (A) 1.0 m
    (B) 2.0 m
    (C) 3.0 m
    (D) 4.0 m
    (E) 5.0 m

21. The half-life of an isotope is 14 days. How many days will it take 8 grams of this isotope to decay to 1 gram?

    (A) 14
    (B) 21
    (C) 28
    (D) 42
    (E) 49

22. The diagram below shows an object traveling clockwise in a horizontal, circular path at constant speed. Which arrow best shows the direction of the centripetal acceleration of the object at the instant shown?

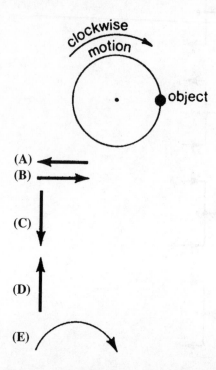

23. The graph below represents the relationship between the temperature of a gas and the average kinetic energy (KE) of the molecules of the gas.

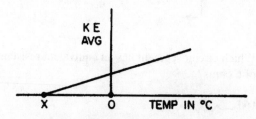

The temperature represented at point X is approximately

    (A) 273°C
    (B) 0°C
    (C) –273°C
    (D) –373°C
    (E) –1,000°C

24. What is the mass number of an atom with 9 protons, 11 neutrons, and 9 electrons?

    (A) 9
    (B) 18
    (C) 20
    (D) 23
    (E) 29

25. Which of the following electromagnetic waves has the LOWEST frequency?

    (A) Violet light
    (B) Green light
    (C) Yellow light
    (D) Red light
    (E) Blue light

READING SPECIALIST (0300)

Time: 2 hours
Number of Questions: 145
Format: Multiple-choice questions

Purpose of the Test

Designed to measure the preparation of prospective supervisory or instructor positions in reading instruction K–12

Content Categories

- Linguistic and Cognitive Bases of the Reading Process—(15 percent)
- Comprehension—(20 percent)
- Word Identification—(15 percent)
- Vocabulary Development—(10 percent)
- Methodologies—(20 percent)
- Diagnosis and Program Improvement—(20 percent)

Category Descriptions

Linguistic and Cognitive Bases of the Reading Process

1. Language as a communication system, including relationships of listening, thinking, reading, writing, and speaking and linguistic differences

2. Language and cognitive development, including abilities, major theories, learning styles, and sociolinguistics

Comprehension

1. Literal and interpretive: teaching strategies, content area integration, and signals

2. Critical and evaluative: criteria for evaluation, propaganda, stereotyping, teaching styles, content area integration, and development of creative thinking

3. Reference and study skills, including SQ3R, reading rate, graphic interpretation, test-taking, and graphic organizers

Word Identification

1. Interrelatedness of identification skills and comprehension

2. Knowledge of word-identification strategies

3. Knowledge of individual and group activities for mastery

Vocabulary Development

1. Interrelatedness of vocabulary development and comprehension

2. Strategies for teaching

3. Word origins

Methodologies

1. Research and theories on teaching and learning

2. Environment organization for diagnostic instruction

3. Special needs concerns

4. Fostering enjoyment and appreciation of reading

Diagnosis and Program Improvement

1. Prescription, organization, and implementation of instruction on the basis of individual or group diagnosis

2. Community interaction in the planning and development of a program

3. Curriculum development and instructional planning

4. Identification of needs and initiation and implementation of improvement in programs

Reading Specialist

> *Directions:* Each question or incomplete statement is followed by five answer choices. For each question, decide which answer or completion is best, and blacken the letter of your choice on the answer sheet.

1. A reading-impaired student who cannot learn individual phonic sounds can best be taught using all of the following techniques EXCEPT

   (A) identifying word endings.
   (B) putting together and separating compound words.
   (C) teaching syllabication skills by emphasizing that each word part contains a vowel.
   (D) identifying separate diphthongs and r-controlled patterns.
   (E) identifying root prefixes and suffixes.

2. A reading disability can best be defined as a

   (A) significant discrepancy between reading level and intellectual potential as measured by standardized tests.
   (B) gap of at least two years below grade level as measured by an Informal Reading Inventory.
   (C) significant discrepancy between literal comprehension and decoding ability.
   (D) problem caused by severe perceptual and neurologic deficits.
   (E) blockage primarily caused by a combination of emotional and cognitive factors.

3. Techniques for dealing with high school students who have low reading ability include all of the following EXCEPT

   (A) introducing text by building concepts and developing new vocabulary.
   (B) asking many factual questions using a structured approach.
   (C) emphasizing discussion and oral reading.
   (D) giving students a great deal of independent seatwork.
   (E) giving students high-interest/low-vocabulary supplementary material.

4. Which of the following are examples of mature reading material to use with a fifteen-year-old non-reader?

   I. Operation Alphabet
   II. Picture-word cards
   III. Merrill Linguistic Readers
   IV. *Readers' Digest* Skill Texts

   (A) I and II only
   (B) I, II, and IV only
   (C) I and IV only
   (D) III and IV only
   (E) II, III, and IV only

5. A student who reads up to grade level on standardized tests but is still not functioning to his potential is usually considered an underachiever. Often, this student lacks outside reading interests. Such a student usually has problems with higher-level reading skills in high school. Which is the LEAST effective remedial technique for such an underachiever?

   (A) Choose material that will motivate the student to read further on his own.
   (B) Give comprehension exercises dealing with separate content area fields.
   (C) Increase vocabulary by developing a notebook of new words and sentences.
   (D) Teach Latin and Greek prefixes and roots.
   (E) Emphasize oral reading so the student hears what a story is about.

6. A teacher says groups of four words, three with the same sound. She says each group a second time and the children clap at the word that does not begin with the sound being taught. The instructor is trying to enhance auditory

   (A) memory.
   (B) closure.
   (C) discrimination.
   (D) sequencing.
   (E) blending.

7. Which of these skills should be taught last?

    (A) Syllabication
    (B) Phrasing and expression
    (C) Context clues
    (D) Blending
    (E) Nonphonetic words

8. A student glances over chapter headings and turns them into questions. Then the student answers these questions while looking away from the book while he writes down the information to review the lesson to understand its major points. The technique being described is

    (A) advanced organizing.
    (B) outlining.
    (C) SQ3R.
    (D) summarizing.
    (E) semantic mapping.

9. In teaching initial consonants and blends to disabled readers, which of the following procedures should be followed?

    I.   Present them in uppercase and lowercase with pictures whose content is mature in format.
    II. Teach four to five sounds in a single lesson.
    III. Have children name each object pictured to avoid confusion.
    IV. Choose letters that are similar in appearance and sound to enhance discrimination skills.

    (A) I, II, and IV only
    (B) IV only
    (C) I, III, and IV only
    (D) I, II, and III only
    (E) II, III, and IV only

10. How would you lower the anxiety of a pupil taking a standardized reading test?

    (A) Tell the student that the test will not count.
    (B) Cut out hard questions.
    (C) Read the test to him.
    (D) Tell him that the questions will get easier during the session.
    (E) Tell him to take the test slowly to avoid mistakes.

11. A high school student with a bright-average IQ is reading at the second-grade level. He has extreme difficulty decoding words. All of the following are good techniques to use EXCEPT

    (A) using other media to reinforce learning.
    (B) assigning books at his independent reading level.
    (C) using recorded audio books.
    (D) introducing spelling and writing gradually and only when necessary.
    (E) engaging the student in various shop activities to develop a technical vocabulary.

12. It is important to have poor readers read aloud, alternating paragraphs with an instructor, to help the student with

    I.   phrasing.
    II. expression.
    III. comprehension.
    IV. learning new words.

    (A) I, II, and IV only
    (B) I, II, and III only
    (C) II, III, and IV only
    (D) II and III only
    (E) I and II only

13. Poor high school readers need to develop test-taking skills. All of the following are ways to develop such skills EXCEPT

    (A) explaining the purpose of various tests.
    (B) starting with short quizzes.
    (C) relating questions directly to material covered.
    (D) having pupils correct the test and deemphasizing marks.
    (E) stressing the rightness or wrongness of answers.

14. In remediating reading-disabled students, word recognition skills must be taught in a systematic and simplified fashion. Which skill should probably be taught first?

    (A) Long vowel sounds
    (B) Initial consonants
    (C) Sight words
    (D) Syllabication
    (E) Consonant digraphs

15. What is the importance of developing a large sight vocabulary?

   (A) It teaches students to figure out words phonetically.
   (B) Failure to develop this prevents fluency.
   (C) It increases a student's comprehension of vocabulary concepts.
   (D) A large sight vocabulary prevents students from using configuration clues.
   (E) It is essential in developing alphabetization skills.

16. Which is an example of a visual-motor method in teaching irregular sight words?

   (A) Child looks at a word, tries to remember it with eyes closed, then writes it down
   (B) Teacher makes repetitive use of picture-word cards created from magazine photographs
   (C) Small groups engage in oral reading of stories at children's own level with teacher supplying missing words repeatedly until they are recognized by sight
   (D) Child looks at word, traces it with finger while pronouncing each sound, then writes word without a model
   (E) Teacher uses tachistoscope to mechanically flash sight words at shorter and shorter intervals

17. An approach to help a high school student who cannot read beyond the second-grade level would include

   (A) teaching blending skills using a newspaper.
   (B) teaching words from signs, labels, medicines, and menus.
   (C) teaching words using only capitals.
   (D) emphasizing syllabication skills in dealing with context-area vocabulary.
   (E) using cloze techniques at a student's potential reading level.

18. According to the latest research, the best prognosis for remediating nonreaders is when

   (A) emphasis is placed on pull-out programs.
   (B) focus is placed on structural analysis.
   (C) functional words are emphasized.
   (D) a multimodal approach is used.
   (E) remediation begins at a young age.

19. Library techniques must be taught to facilitate research skills. All of the following library skills should be taught EXCEPT

   (A) the use of reference material.
   (B) the use of a computer database to search for specific authors, titles, or subjects.
   (C) the use of microfiche material.
   (D) the structure of the Dewey Decimal or Library of Congress systems.
   (E) how to find fiction books using a card catalog.

20. A student completes a whole story for the first time, although he or she has struggled through decoding the words. The student feels proud of his or her accomplishment. The teacher's next step would be to

   (A) ask multiple questions about the content.
   (B) have the student look back in the story to substantiate specific facts.
   (C) find explanatory phrases to elaborate specific points.
   (D) encourage spontaneous discussion.
   (E) focus on answering main idea questions.

21. All are effective ways to help students improve their vocabularies EXCEPT

   (A) using a dictionary to look up many unknown words.
   (B) teaching words that have multiple meanings.
   (C) reminding students to use context to figure out unknown words.
   (D) teaching the origin of words by using dramatic examples.
   (E) teaching technical vocabulary groups.

22. Which of the following skills would probably be taught LAST?

   (A) Pronunciation of words derived from foreign languages
   (B) Adjusting reading rate
   (C) Following directions
   (D) Drawing conclusions
   (E) Finding the main idea

23. Why is it advisable to postpone the teaching of the short *e* until the other vowels are learned?

    (A) The *e* sound can sometimes be silent.
    (B) There are many vowel sounds for *e*.
    (C) Many children have considerable difficulty distinguishing between the short sounds of *a* and *e*.
    (D) The short *e* should be taught in combination with blends and digraphs.
    (E) It is best to teach the short *e* as a CVC combination.

24. Having students read cookbooks, magic books, math problems, and science experiments teaches them how to

    (A) find the main idea.
    (B) draw conclusions.
    (C) recall facts.
    (D) follow directions.
    (E) determine effective research skills.

25. Which is the LEAST important factor interfering with comprehension of content area material?

    (A) Limited intelligence
    (B) Unfamiliarity with basic concepts of the subject matter
    (C) Lack of interest in the material
    (D) Meager vocabulary
    (E) Reading rate

SCHOOL GUIDANCE AND COUNSELING (0420)

Time: 2 hours
Number of Questions: 140 (45 based on listening section)
Format: Multiple-choice questions
(approximately one third based on taped interactions)

Purpose of the Test

Designed to measure the preparation of prospective public school counselors

Content Categories

- Counseling and Guidance—(55 percent)
- Consulting—(20 percent)
- Coordinating—(15 percent)
- Professional Issues—(10 percent)

Category Descriptions

Counseling and Guidance

Communication, special populations, appraisal, transition

Consulting

Indirect services to other students, including consultation with staff members, families, and community agencies

Coordinating

1. Management and organization
2. Information acquisition and dissemination
3. Program evaluation

Professional Issues

1. Legal and ethical concerns
2. Resources for professional development

School Guidance and Counseling

> *Directions:* Each question or incomplete statement is followed by five answer choices. For each question, decide which answer or completion is best, and blacken the letter of your choice on the answer sheet.

1. After twelve weeks, a junior high counselor has to terminate counseling services to a student who initially was having difficulty adjusting to being in a departmentalized program. All are effective ways for the counselor to end counseling EXCEPT

   (A) avoiding discussing any new counseling material during the last two or three weeks.
   (B) leaving on a positive note—celebrating the student's progress and gains.
   (C) telling the student he can come when he needs to even though they will not be meeting regularly.
   (D) forewarning the student how many sessions they have left.
   (E) asking the student's homeroom teacher to tell him that he no longer needs to come to counseling because he has adjusted well to junior high school.

2. The type of therapy that builds a positive relationship between client and therapist and then emphasizes that each person assumes responsibility for his own behavior by setting goals and making responsible decisions illustrates

   (A) reality therapy.
   (B) play therapy.
   (C) behavioral counseling.
   (D) rational-emotive therapy.
   (E) client-centered counseling.

3. Lawrence Kohlberg's research on moral development emphasizes a three-level, six-stage approach. Using his theory, if a student says that he will do something because his conscience tells him it is right, this student is at the

   (A) punishment and obedience stage.
   (B) law and order stage.
   (C) social contract stage.
   (D) universal ethics stage.
   (E) instrumental relativism stage.

4. Which of the following LEAST describes the role of a guidance counselor?

   (A) He or she tries to develop school adjustment strategies.
   (B) He or she emphasizes personal and career development.
   (C) He or she should experiment in the use of different disciplinary techniques to control management problems in the classroom.
   (D) He or she develops structured learning activities or lessons that guide students to understand themselves and others.
   (E) He or she helps students understand and meet academic goals.

5. In the 1920s,

   (A) a guidance counselor's primary function was measurement of personality traits using standardized tests.
   (B) school counselors emphasized mental health due to rapid changes in society.
   (C) school guidance encouraged talented youths to attend college if aptitude in math and science were shown.
   (D) school guidance focused primarily on developing vocational skills and choices.
   (E) school guidance coordinated the transition between school and the world of work for students with developmental delays.

6. The developmental approach to school guidance

   I.   identifies certain skills and experiences students need to be successful in school.
   II. clarifies behaviors and tasks a student will need to facilitate adjustment.
   III. emphasizes the learning of tasks through a guidance curriculum.
   IV. develops interpersonal skills in students after crisis situations.

   (A) I and III only
   (B) II, III, and IV only
   (C) III only
   (D) I, II, and III only
   (E) I and II only

7. Which is a limitation of using teachers as guidance advisers in lieu of trained counselors?

   (A) Differential staffing makes better use of school personnel.
   (B) Such an approach depends on administrative as well as teacher knowledge and support.
   (C) It fosters a positive learning environment.
   (D) More students receive guidance services in the school.
   (E) It lowers counselor–student ratios dramatically.

8. In an elementary school, a guidance counselor does all of the following EXCEPT

   (A) help develop guidance units that evolve from student needs.
   (B) consult with teachers and administrators about counseling interventions being done with various students.
   (C) serve as a resource to teachers about behavior changes a student may be having.
   (D) help identify students with special needs or problems and help find alternative educational or guidance services for them.
   (E) serve as a liaison between the school and public health and rehabilitation agencies.

9. This type of student needs less verbal counseling. He or she needs more concrete and operational forms of assistance. This student needs to gain insight by doing instead of talking. The student being described

   (A) is learning disabled.
   (B) has mental retardation.
   (C) has a conduct disorder.
   (D) has an attention deficit disorder.
   (E) is socially maladjusted.

10. A student describes to a guidance counselor several ways he has tried to harm his parents because they are abusive to him. It is the counselor's responsibility at this point to

   (A) keep the matter confidential.
   (B) refer the student to someone more qualified.
   (C) secretly inform the authorities.
   (D) tell the student he must inform the authorities for his own protection.
   (E) talk the student out of any further harmful actions.

11. Rational-emotive therapy is most associated with

   (A) Carl Rogers.
   (B) Albert Ellis.
   (C) Virginia Axline.
   (D) B. F. Skinner.
   (E) William Glasser.

12. The best way for a guidance counselor to begin to develop study skills and habits in underachieving students would be to

   (A) give out a list of effective study approaches.
   (B) have these underachieving students observe the study habits of excelling students.
   (C) drill such students in various study approaches.
   (D) encourage students to talk about study habits from their own experiences.
   (E) have them view filmstrips about various study approaches.

13. A student broke up with his girlfriend several days ago. He tells the school counselor that last night he thought about putting a pillow over his head. What should the counselor do at this point?

   (A) Engage in therapeutic-intervention techniques
   (B) Refer the student to a mental health center
   (C) Call the police to have the student hospitalized
   (D) Immediately have the student suspended from school
   (E) Refer the student for family therapy

14. How are school counseling and psychotherapy different?

   (A) School guidance and psychotherapy utilize totally different theories of counseling.
   (B) Psychotherapy must be done by someone with a medical degree, while counseling can be done by lay personnel trained in various techniques.
   (C) School counseling deals with students who are within the normal range of functioning, while psychotherapy deals with people in a clinical setting who are very dysfunctional and need to gain insight into their problems through exploration of the past.
   (D) Psychotherapy uses a behavioral approach to change dysfunctional behaviors, while school counseling focuses more on a psychosexual model of therapy to help clients gain insight into the reasons for their behaviors.
   (E) There is no significant difference in approach between school counseling and psychotherapy.

15. All of the following contributed to the development of school guidance and counseling EXCEPT

    (A) more humane care of the mentally disturbed, which began in the nineteenth century.
    (B) scientific methods in the study of affective behavior.
    (C) the concept that one's environment contributes to development.
    (D) John Dewey's emphasis on the importance of the student in the educational process.
    (E) Piaget's theory of child development.

16. School guidance at the primary level focuses on

    (A) the testing and evaluation of middle-grade students.
    (B) the setting up of school schedules and programming.
    (C) individual counseling of those students who are having academic difficulty.
    (D) intervening in order to avoid crisis situations.
    (E) developing a consultative role with teachers and administrators.

17. A student confides in her guidance counselor that she is having sex with her boyfriend. She is afraid that if her parents find out, they will severely punish her and try to end her relationship. How should the counselor deal with this situation?

    (A) Tell the student's parents about the problem in a nonjudgmental way.
    (B) Tell the student to abstain from sex to avoid catching a venereal disease or AIDS.
    (C) Show the student a filmstrip about the consequences of such immoral behavior.
    (D) Discuss with the student various methods of birth control.
    (E) Advise the student to seek the counsel of a priest, minister, or rabbi.

18. A leader in the vocational guidance movement in the early twentieth century was

    (A) Carl Rogers.
    (B) A. S. Neil.
    (C) Jesse B. Davis.
    (D) Fritz Redl.
    (E) Bruno Bettelheim.

19. There are four approaches to guidance and counseling in the schools: crisis, remedial, preventive, and developmental. Which of the following are examples of the developmental approach?

    I.   Assisting in the development of life skills
    II. Acting as a mediator
    III. Teaching students how to interact in a positive manner
    IV. Helping in the development of interpersonal skills

    (A) I, III, and IV only
    (B) II, III, and IV only
    (C) I, II, and III only
    (D) II only
    (E) IV only

20. Individual counseling is considered the best approach for all of the following students EXCEPT

    (A) a student who lacks self-confidence.
    (B) a student who feels others neither understand nor care about his/her situation.
    (C) a student who lacks social skills and who is rejected by others.
    (D) a student whose siblings may be involved in illegal activities.
    (E) a class clown engaging in attention-seeking behavior.

21. A counselor has initiated counseling with a student who is being described by his teacher as uncooperative. The student pays no attention to classwork, constantly talks, and is sullen. How should this counselor initiate discussing the boy's problem?

    (A) State to the student that he is being seen because he is in trouble with his teacher.
    (B) State that the principal feels the student should be taken out of his present class.
    (C) Ask a series of open-ended questions pertaining to school.
    (D) Immediately describe to the student various strategies on how to improve class adjustment.
    (E) Threaten suspension if the student does not change his behavior.

22. In a developmental guidance curriculum, the goal of recognizing how one's self-esteem and attitude are related to the way in which a goal is approached describes

(A) motivation.
(B) study skills and habits.
(C) self-assessment.
(D) decision making and problem solving.
(E) educational planning.

23. The theory focuses on goal orientation within a social context, emphasizing that people should see themselves as individuals who have the capacity to make decisions and choices and to gain insight into their behavior for the purpose of finding alternatives to solving problems. This describes

(A) psychoanalytic theory.
(B) Adlerian psychology.
(C) transactional analysis.
(D) Gestalt theory.
(E) multimodal theory.

24. An adolescent coming from an inner-city environment has trouble relating to students and teachers. He has been suspended several times. Which is the best approach to deal with this student?

(A) The counselor needs to discuss childhood conflicts with the student using the psychoanalytic approach.
(B) The student should be involved in counselor-led group activities where interpersonal skills could be discussed and practiced.
(C) The counselor should mediate any conflicts between the student and other school personnel.
(D) The counselor should use play therapy so the student can act out his negative impulses in private.
(E) The counselor should call in the student's parents to discuss a possible referral to an outside agency for the purpose of beginning family therapy.

25. Which of the following are either classroom guidance methods or programs?

I. DUSO
II. Magic Circle
III. Classroom meetings
IV. DISTAR

(A) I only
(B) I and II only
(C) II, III, and IV only
(D) I, II, and III only
(E) IV only

SCHOOL PSYCHOLOGIST (0400)

Time: 2 hours
Number of Questions: 120
Format: Multiple-choice questions

Purpose of the Test

Designed to measure the preparation of prospective school psychologists

Content Categories

- Diagnosis and Fact Finding—(25 percent)
- Prevention and Intervention—(25 percent)
- Applied Psychological Foundations—(20 percent)
- Applied Educational Foundations—(12 percent)
- Ethical and Legal Considerations—(18 percent)

Category Descriptions

Diagnosis and Fact Finding

1. Initial fact gathering
2. Assessment of functioning levels, diagnostics, achievement, development, behavior, personality, and self-concept
3. Assessment of special needs

Prevention and Intervention

1. Cognitive and behavioral: techniques and major research studies
2. Interventions with special populations
3. Academic: accommodations and modifications, research, discipline, classroom management, and remediation
4. Crisis intervention and prevention
5. Other skills: developmentally appropriate intervention for ages 0–21 years, adjustment techniques, social skills, data management, computer applications, therapy recommendation, stress management, conflict/resolution, decision making, problem solving, communication skills, group facilitation, and leadership skills

Applied Psychological Foundations

1. General psychological principles: biological bases, effects of commonly prescribed medications, substance abuse signs and symptoms, research findings, life-span development, motivation, theories of intelligence, and language development
2. Knowledge of testing theory and principles

Applied Educational Foundations

Principles of learning and teaching, academic needs of exceptional students

Ethical and Legal Considerations

1. Ethical principles and professional standards

2. Laws, codes, and regulations governing the practice of school psychology, including rights, disabilities, legal liability, malpractice, negligence, and student records

School Psychologist

> *Directions:* Each question or incomplete statement is followed by five answer choices. For each question, decide which answer or completion is best, and blacken the letter of your choice on the answer sheet.

1. Drug therapy has been effectively used in treating children with behavior problems. Of the following, the best type of medications for children who have personality disorders and psychoses are

   I. psychostimulant drugs.
   II. psychotropic drugs.
   III. antidepressant drugs.
   IV. anticonvulsant drugs.

   (A) I and III only
   (B) II only
   (C) I only
   (D) III and IV only
   (E) I, II, and III only

2. Psychological testing is used for all of the following EXCEPT

   (A) detection of intellectual deficiencies for admission to special programs.
   (B) research on individual differences.
   (C) the determination of academic achievement.
   (D) the determination of potential intellectual ability.
   (E) selection and classification of personnel for various types of jobs.

3. A technique in which a psychologist compares two interpretations of a single set of behaviors—e.g., idealistic and real points of view—is called

   (A) peer nomination.
   (B) behavioral inventories or checklists.
   (C) task analysis of standardized tests of personality.
   (D) Q-Sort.
   (E) life-space interview.

4. A troublesome student is sent by a teacher to the school psychologist, along with a note. Which one of the notes below describes an inappropriate use of the psychologist's counseling services?

   (A) "The student is having a personal problem he wants to talk over."
   (B) "The child is afraid to walk into the class."
   (C) "I don't want him in my room. Keep him until the bell rings. He's out of control again."
   (D) "I've noticed excessive bruises on her arm. Please look further into this matter."
   (E) "This boy keeps falling asleep in class. Can you please see if he is having any problems? He won't open up to me at all."

5. A psychologist recommends a commercial program designed to teach affective skills. She recommends a program in which teacher-led discussions take place using a structured approach in order to help students develop skills in self-control, responsibility, and role expectations and in creating satisfactory peer relations. The clinician is describing

   (A) DUSO-R.
   (B) TAD.
   (C) Magic Circle.
   (D) TLC.
   (E) ACCESS.

6. A type of therapy that combines value clarification and social-skills learning using a modified behavioral approach has been developed by

   (A) Ellis.
   (B) Meichenbaum.
   (C) Glasser.
   (D) Coleman.
   (E) Wolfe and Moseley.

7. What is a major problem with intelligence tests, such as the WISC III and the Stanford-Binet, as a measure of mental deficiency?

   (A) The tests are heavily loaded with verbal content.
   (B) Both tests are known to have poor reliability coefficients.
   (C) They have insufficient validity.
   (D) The content is not related to the needs of society.
   (E) These tests are culturally biased in favor of a middle-class population.

8. Planned ignoring, signal interference, and proximity control are techniques used in

   (A) operant conditioning.
   (B) managing surface behavior.
   (C) contracting.
   (D) managing temper tantrums.
   (E) life-space interviewing.

9. A seven-year-old student who has normal hearing and vision but cannot pronounce even initial sounds when attempting to talk needs to be evaluated for her intellectual potential. The best test to use is the

   (A) Vineland.
   (B) K-ABC.
   (C) McCarthy Scale.
   (D) WISC III.
   (E) Leiter Scale.

10. In which situation is a middle-grade student considered a danger to himself and to others?

    (A) Throwing temper tantrums
    (B) Arguing with another student
    (C) Using profanity
    (D) Talking at inappropriate times
    (E) Refusing to follow teacher directions

11. All of the following are steps in the consultation process EXCEPT

    (A) identifying the problem.
    (B) clarifying the situation.
    (C) identifying goals and outcomes.
    (D) observing and recording behavior.
    (E) initiating the plan.

12. The classroom is out of control. The teacher constantly yells at her students in a hostile fashion, but the class is impossible to manage. The teacher has negative things to say about many students in the class. She wants you to help her find a way to improve her class. All of the following must be considered in such a situation EXCEPT that

    (A) the teacher may be resistant to change.
    (B) it can be correctly assumed that the problem rests wholly with the students.
    (C) more than one intervention may be needed.
    (D) the presenting problem may not be the real problem.
    (E) the responsibility for changing the students has to be shared.

13. Which author believed that tests of sensory discrimination could serve as a means of gauging a person's intellect?

    (A) Pearson
    (B) Galton
    (C) Binet
    (D) Sequin
    (E) Terman

14. All of the following are projective counseling techniques used by psychologists to help students express feelings they may not reveal in conversation EXCEPT

    (A) puppetry.
    (B) role playing.
    (C) play therapy.
    (D) art and music therapy.
    (E) reality therapy.

15. An event that is imposed or occurs regularly after a behavior and increases the frequency or duration of that behavior is an example of

    (A) reinforcement.
    (B) punishment.
    (C) generalization.
    (D) shaping.
    (E) discrimination training.

16. Two students are given the WISC III. One has a full-scale IQ of 91, while the other has an IQ of 109. It can be concluded that

    (A) the second student has significantly higher intellectual ability.
    (B) intelligence cannot be measured by this test because the instrument has poor internal consistency.
    (C) both students are functioning in the average range of intellectual ability.
    (D) the first student is probably below average, while the second student has above-average potential.
    (E) another IQ test should be given to truly assess their intellectual potential.

17. Some weaknesses of self-reporting personality checklists are that

    I.   individuals can hide or disguise feelings.
    II. results are highly subjective and dependent on the competence and experience of the examiner.
    III. all have poor internal consistency and stability.
    IV. many personality measures have built in lie scales.

    (A) III and IV only
    (B) II, III, and IV only
    (C) I and II only
    (D) I, II, and III only
    (E) I only

18. Which of these authors would favor an analytic approach to managing behavior?

    (A) Trieshman
    (B) Long and Newman
    (C) Algozzine
    (D) Thorndike
    (E) Redl

19. Which type of test determines whether students accept responsibility for their own behavior or assign responsibility for their behavior to other people?

    (A) Sentence-completion checklists
    (B) Locus-of-control tests
    (C) Stylistic tests
    (D) Thematic tests
    (E) Draw-a-person tests

20. An example of a peer-nominating technique is

    (A) class pictures in which a child chooses among photographs of students engaged in maladjusted or neutral behaviors.
    (B) TAT in which students describe pictures of various social events.
    (C) a technique describing how students act in different physical environments.
    (D) the use of interaction analysis to examine and analyze pupil–pupil relationships within a classroom.
    (E) the use of sociometric diagrams to determine a student's position within a class.

21. All are good ways to improve your own interview skills as a psychologist during counseling EXCEPT to

    (A) videotape yourself in interview and have others evaluate your performance.
    (B) role play an interview.
    (C) monitor yourself for defensive behaviors or responses.
    (D) write an outline of the questions to be asked.
    (E) keep extensive notes during the interview of how you responded.

22. Which of the following are examples of good interview techniques to be employed by a clinician?

    I.   Open the interview by asking nonthreatening questions.
    II. Avoid answering any direct questions posed by the respondent.
    III. Clarify unclear responses through further questioning.
    IV. Probe sensitive subject matter intensively.

    (A) I, II, and III only
    (B) I and III only
    (C) II and IV only
    (D) II, III, and IV only
    (E) I only

23. The purpose of a Rapid Deployment Team is to

    (A) evaluate students in crisis.
    (B) counsel individual students who are suicidal.
    (C) determine if a call to child welfare is necessary when abuse or neglect is suspected.
    (D) counsel students, parents, and staff in case of a death or fatal injury of a student or teacher.
    (E) counsel staff when problems in management arise.

24. This behavioral checklist is unique because it has five subscales that deal with behaviors that are indicative of the five components of the federal definition of emotional disturbance. This checklist is called the

(A) Test of Early Socioemotional Development.
(B) Behavior Evaluation Scale.
(C) Behavior Rating Scale.
(D) Thematic Apperception Test.
(E) Bailey Scale.

25. The term describing the consistency of a test is

(A) the objective measure of difficulty.
(B) standardization.
(C) validity.
(D) norm sample.
(E) reliability.

SPECIAL EDUCATION: KNOWLEDGE-BASED CORE PRINCIPLES (0351)

Time: 1 hour
Number of Questions: 60
Format: Multiple-choice questions

Purpose of the Test

Designed to measure the preparation of prospective special education teachers for preschool through high school grade levels

Content Categories

- Understanding Exceptionalities—(25 percent)
- Legal and Social Issues—(13 percent)
- Delivery of Services to Students with Disabilities—(62 percent)

Category Descriptions

Understanding Exceptionalities

1. Major historical/social movements and trends that influence the delivery of services for exceptional children

2. Basic concepts relating to exceptionality: characteristics of various exceptionalities, degrees of severity, prevalence of exceptionalities in the national population, causation and prevention, early identification and early intervention, and service provisions throughout the life span

3. Major research findings and classroom implications of research

Legal and Social Issues

1. Procedural rights of exceptional students and parents

2. Special education legislation

3. Service delivery requirements of Individuals with Disabilities Education Act (IDEA)

Delivery of Services to Students with Disabilities

1. Application of basic measurement concepts, such as validity, reliability, and standard deviation

2. Ethical use of tests: nondiscriminatory assessment, testing in the native language, use of multiple measures

3. Procedures for identifying and establishing students' eligibility for special education programs, such as multidisciplinary teams, the role of team members, complete and multifaceted assessment, observation procedures, and interpretation of formal assessment

4. Use of assessment and evaluation data to plan, implement, and monitor effectiveness

5. Individualized education programs

6. Curriculum and instruction

7. Career education, vocational planning, and post-school transitions

8. Skills related to teacher consultation

9. Classroom organization for exceptional students, including both physical and social environments

10. Techniques for managing student behavior: applied behavior analysis/behavior modification, self-management, behavioral and psychoeducational approaches to discipline

11. Teaching of social skills

12. Locating and using resources by working with a variety of individuals and groups: parents, auxiliary and related-services personnel and consultants, volunteers, paraprofessionals, tutors, and out-of-school resources

Special Education:
Knowledge-Based Core Principles

Directions: Each question or incomplete statement is followed by five answer choices. For each question, decide which answer or completion is best, and blacken the letter of your choice on the answer sheet.

1. Which of the following best describes a noncategorical resource room program?

    (A) In this program, even gifted students can be accommodated.
    (B) This disability-based program allows the teacher to service various schools within a district.
    (C) This program services only learning-disabled students.
    (D) The teacher engages in team teaching within the regular classroom.
    (E) All classwork in this program is individualized and based on the particular academic needs of each student.

2. In determining the educational needs of a special education student, a variety of assessment techniques are used. Which of the following is NOT an effective assessment technique used in evaluating a student who may be in need of special services?

    (A) Direct observation
    (B) Testing
    (C) Teacher recommendation
    (D) Review of records
    (E) Product evaluation

3. An instructor uses prescriptive teaching to determine a pupil's knowledge of shapes. The pupil is able to match two or more shapes of different sizes. The student is also able to point to particular shapes named by the teacher. However, when asked, "What shape is this?" the pupil confuses three out of five common shapes. Which of the following describes the pupil's ability to recognize shapes?

    I.   He is able to discriminate pictorial representations.
    II. The pupil has good expressive language concepts.
    III. The student's receptive understanding is adequate.
    IV. He does not understand the concept of congruence.

    (A) I, II, and IV only
    (B) II, III, and IV only
    (C) I and III only
    (D) I, III, and IV only
    (E) IV only

4. All of the following are examples of norm-referenced interpretations EXCEPT that

    (A) the student's Performance IQ is 92.
    (B) the pupil's intellectual development is two standard deviations below the mean.
    (C) the student received an 11.9 Age Equivalent Score on this measure of receptive language.
    (D) given the first-grade Dolch list, the student will correctly spell 80 percent of the words.
    (E) the student received a score above the 80th percentile on this achievement measure.

5. In this program, a teacher provides direct and indirect services to handicapped students. Although this teacher provides services to special education students, they are not the exclusive recipients of the program's benefits. Other students within a regular classroom benefit when this teacher and the general education instructor modify instruction for labeled students. The above statement is best describing

   (A) a categorical resource room.
   (B) consultant teaching.
   (C) an itinerant resource room.
   (D) a noncategorical resource room.
   (E) mainstreaming.

6. A student during informal conversation states the following: "Umm, I like the, umm, *Cosby Show*. You know, it was, umm, interesting. Bill Cosby walked down the stairs and then, umm, he fell on the rug, then he did something to whatchamacallit…" How would you describe this student's difficulty with semantic language?

   (A) Poor understanding of indefinite pronouns
   (B) Repeated use of meaningless sounds or phrases
   (C) Roundabout descriptions or circumlocutions
   (D) Overuse of verbs and nouns
   (E) Redundancies and repetitions

7. All of the following describe strategies used by fluent readers EXCEPT that the reader

   (A) shifts speed and approach to the type and purpose of reading.
   (B) predicts the endings of words and phrases.
   (C) reads to identify meaning rather than to identify letters and words.
   (D) notes the distinctive features in letters and words.
   (E) utilizes tactile reinforcement to distinguish between similar letters and words.

8. A major advantage of curriculum-based assessment is that

   (A) it connects testing with teaching.
   (B) it is based on a criterion-referenced measurement model.
   (C) national norms are being developed for this technique.
   (D) it tends to focus on anecdotal information on how a student is progressing.
   (E) these tests are informal in nature.

9. This norm-referenced reading test uses a modified cloze technique in which the student has to supply the missing word of a short sentence or passage. Which of the tests below is being described?

   (A) Woodcock Reading Mastery Test—Revised
   (B) Diagnostic Reading Scale
   (C) Gray Oral Reading Test
   (D) Informal Reading Inventory
   (E) Durrell Analysis of Reading Difficulty

10. Many special educators have to work with paraprofessionals or teacher aides. This extra person in the classroom can be either an asset or a detriment. Which of the following are good ways to improve the effectiveness of such personnel in the classroom?

    I.   Train teaching assistants in record keeping.
    II. Make sure teacher aides carry out specified remedial strategies developed and utilized by the teacher.
    III. Minimize direct teacher supervision of paraprofessionals.
    IV. Handle contradictory student–paraprofessional relationships strictly within the classroom

    (A) I and III only
    (B) II only
    (C) I only
    (D) I and II only
    (E) All of the above

11. All of the following are effective techniques in facilitating parent involvement in a student's special education program EXCEPT

    (A) scheduling parent conferences to accommodate a parent's work responsibilities.
    (B) developing a parents' brochure illustrating how to help students with their homework.
    (C) keeping parents informed by a newsletter about different school programs.
    (D) providing a resource room where parents may browse or borrow material.
    (E) informing parents of a student's progress by means of a monthly report card.

12. Computer technology is being used today to enhance the communication skills of various handicapped individuals. A device useful in helping someone who is visually impaired is a(n)

    (A) teletypewriter.
    (B) electronic page turner.
    (C) keyboard emulator.
    (D) lightpen.
    (E) viewscan.

13. Time management, listening, self-management of behavior, and the use of graphic aids are all examples of

    (A) adaptive living skills.
    (B) career education skills.
    (C) study skills.
    (D) socioemotional skills.
    (E) content-area skills.

14. Most special education students do not possess adequate test-taking ability. All of the following are effective test-taking strategies EXCEPT

    (A) teaching test-taking procedures to enhance a student's ability to understand different types of questions.
    (B) allowing unlimited time when taking standardized tests.
    (C) discussing different methods of studying for objective and essay tests.
    (D) reviewing completed tests with students in order to highlight test-taking errors.
    (E) ensuring that students know how much time is allotted for completion of a test.

15. A student continually called out answers in class. Her teacher decided to ignore this student's outbursts but rewarded her with a star every time she silently raised her hand and was called upon to give an answer. This behavior-modification technique is called

    (A) discrimination training.
    (B) differential reinforcement.
    (C) punishment.
    (D) extinction.
    (E) modeling.

16. Long and Newman are best known for their

    (A) use of contracts for facilitating behavioral changes.
    (B) strategy in the management of temper tantrums.
    (C) development of life-space interviewing.
    (D) theories on counseling using projective techniques.
    (E) techniques for managing surface behavior.

17. A seventh-grade student has been placed in a resource room program. The student has problems in developing skills in mathematics. His assessment reveals that he is having problems in visual perception and visual memory. All of the following are effective strategies for this student EXCEPT

    (A) reinforcing memorization of automatic multiplication and division facts to improve computational speed.
    (B) having frequent demonstrations, modeling, and rehearsal.
    (C) reading textbook instructions to the student.
    (D) minimizing the type or amount of information presented to the student.
    (E) allowing the student to make oral rather than written responses.

18. The LEAST effective method to remediate a student who writes too small is to

    (A) rule a midline on standard writing paper and have lowercase letters touch the midline.
    (B) practice large writing on the chalkboard.
    (C) have the student copy a correct model of several words and have him or her evaluate the size.
    (D) have the student evaluate his own writing problem so he is aware of what must be corrected.
    (E) encourage the student to write more slowly, as speed tends to affect size.

19. Which is NOT a practical remedial technique in the teaching of spelling skills to a learning-disabled student?

    (A) Have the student use a structured basal program such as *Riverside Spelling*, *Basic Goals in Spelling*, or *Silver Burdett Spelling*.
    (B) Provide a variety of writing activities that necessitate using the words learned.
    (C) Teach minimum-sized lists and use words that are of functional importance to the student.
    (D) Teach no more words than the pupil can successfully learn to spell.
    (E) Ask questions about the structural aspects of the words.

20. An eighth-grade student attending middle school has recently been evaluated. The student exhibits all the signs of learning disabilities and will be recommended for a self-contained classroom. The student is reading on the third-grade level and doing math also on the same level. Written expression is poor, and he has a low fund of general information. The student immigrated to the United States four years ago and is now somewhat proficient in both his native language and English. His mother is totally against the recommendation for this service. She does not want her child to be called a cripple, and she states that he is able to read better than she. What is the probable reason for the attitude of this parent?

(A) The evaluation team is using too restrictive a label for this parent to tolerate.

(B) The student was probably tested only in English, and, thus, the evaluation is invalid.

(C) The child's mother probably feels her due process rights have been violated.

(D) The child study team may not have taken divergent cultural factors into consideration.

(E) The child's scores better warrant a resource room program because he can probably function in a regular class for part of the day.

21. Which is NOT an example of an occupational-interest test for special education students taking career education courses in secondary school?

(A) Career Assessment Inventory
(B) Geist Inventory
(C) Strong-Campbell Inventory
(D) Kuder Survey
(E) Career Ability Placement Survey

22. The Detroit Test of Learning Ability–3 measures all of the following skills EXCEPT

(A) visual memory.
(B) visual problem-solving and reasoning.
(C) auditory memory.
(D) visual closure.
(E) auditory discrimination.

23. A teacher presents a student with a list of words and a list of endings. She asks the student to make up as many *real* words as she can using the endings. This remedial technique is mainly used to address problems with

(A) word discrimination.
(B) compound words.
(C) root words.
(D) vocabulary development.
(E) phonics.

24. In recent years, P.L. 94-142 has been amended by Congress and renamed. This federal law is now called

(A) ADA.
(B) P.L. 99-457.
(C) IDEA.
(D) Chapter 53.
(E) Chapter I.

25. A special education teacher gave a student several multiplication examples. One example was done in this way:

$$\begin{array}{r} 367 \\ \times\ 25 \\ \hline 1535 \\ 614\ \ \\ \hline 7675 \end{array}$$

In analyzing the error, how would you describe the problem this student is having?

(A) Omitting steps
(B) Format problems
(C) Regrouping incorrectly
(D) Wrong order of steps in computation process
(E) Random response

SPECIAL EDUCATION: TEACHING STUDENTS WITH MENTAL RETARDATION (0321)

Time: 1 hour
Number of Questions: 50
Format: Multiple-choice questions

Purpose of the Test

Designed to measure the preparation of those who have completed teacher training programs in the education of students with mental retardation

Content Categories

- Educational Principles and Professional Considerations—(14 percent)
- Understanding Students with Mental Retardation—(25 percent)
- Knowledge of Assessment Principles and Practices—(10 percent)
- Delivery of Services—(21 percent)
- Design and Implementation of Instruction—(30 percent)

Category Descriptions

Factors Other than Direct Instruction that Influence

1. Characteristics of children with mental retardation, such as adaptive and affective behaviors; learning and motivation; and physical, personality, and motor development
2. Definition and degrees of severity of mental retardation
3. Causation and prevention, including genetic and environmental factors
4. Public attitudes, post-school adjustment, family adjustment, early intervention, community-based training
5. History, trends, and contemporary issues, including special education philosophies
6. Characteristics of students with mental retardation with secondary disabilities such as speech impediments, physical disabilities, and behavior disorders

Delivery of Services

1. Basic measurement concepts such as validity, reliability, standard deviation, nondiscriminatory evaluation, and norm-referenced and criterion-referenced techniques
2. Ability to select, administer, and interpret teacher-administered assessments
3. Knowledge, interpretation, and application of specialized evaluations

Curriculum and Instruction

1. Teacher's role as a multidisciplinary team member

2. Knowledge of Individuals with Disabilities Education Act (IDEA)

3. Knowledge of placement options within the school and district, including appropriate least restrictive environment

4. Collaboration with other school personnel

5. Basic curriculum models and related materials, including social learning, life-centered, daily living, community-based, and functional academics

6. Appropriate use and adaptation of instructional methods, materials, and approaches, such as task analysis, diagnostic-prescriptive, direct and adapted instruction, computers, adaptive devices, and augmentative communication

7. Classroom management, including social environment, student behavior, behavior modification, and nonaversive methods

Special Education:
Teaching Students with Mental Retardation

Directions: Each question or incomplete statement is followed by five answer choices. For each question, decide which answer or completion is best, and blacken the letter of your choice on the answer sheet.

---

1. Using task analysis, a teacher has to write short-term goals to improve the fine-motor development of a student with moderate retardation. Which of the following objectives will facilitate the development of this skill?

   I. The student will push a button that is halfway through a loop using his forefinger and thumb four out of five times.
   II. The student will button his coat two out of three times.
   III. The student will use snaps on his jacket, with 80-percent accuracy.
   IV. The student will pick up small buttons from a table and push them through $\frac{1}{8}$-inch slots eight out of ten times.

   (A) I and IV only
   (B) II and III only
   (C) I and III only
   (D) II and IV only
   (E) IV only

2. Why has it been difficult to define mental retardation?

   (A) Researchers cannot define the nature of intelligence.
   (B) Different disciplines view mental retardation from their own perspectives.
   (C) It cannot be determined which abilities to include in the definition.
   (D) Intellectual and emotional factors are not independent of each other.
   (E) All of the above

3. All these statements describe trainable students with mental retardation EXCEPT

   (A) IQ between 25 and 50 on most standardized intelligence tests.
   (B) can hold an independent job if it is structured.
   (C) need to learn self-care skills and common safety rules.
   (D) need supervision, protection, and care.
   (E) can learn to walk, feed themselves, and speak single phrases but at a very slow pace.

4. Cognitive growth is seen as a continuous interaction between the individual and the environment. The more a child is stimulated, the greater his intellectual development. Accordingly, a child with mental retardation proceeds through the same intellectual stages as a normal-functioning child but at a slower pace. These ideas are best associated with

   (A) Bruner.
   (B) Bijou.
   (C) Terman.
   (D) Piaget.
   (E) Gagne.

5. Which skill would be LEAST emphasized in the education of students with severe retardation?

   (A) Self-care
   (B) Total communication
   (C) Occupational skills
   (D) Socialization
   (E) Prevocational skills

6. Why are methods and procedures used to instruct students with mental retardation also used for autistic children?

   (A) Methods to teach autistic children are not yet well developed.
   (B) Autistic children need a less structured approach to learning.
   (C) Many autistic children are functionally retarded although their intellectual development may really be higher.
   (D) Such instruction rapidly increases the intellectual and social ability of autistic children.
   (E) Both autistic and children with mental retardation benefit from small class environments.

7. Which of these people worked with the "Wild Boy of Aveyron," thus proving that intelligence was fluid and not fixed?

    (A) Binet
    (B) Itard
    (C) Sequin
    (D) Montessori
    (E) Rousseau

8. Which can best describe the development of rehabilitative practices for people with mental retardation in the 1960s and 1970s?

    (A) Judicial and legislative responsibility for them became widely recognized.
    (B) There was an increase in the institutionalization of people with mental retardation in this era.
    (C) There was a widespread formation of parent organizations for children with mental retardation during this time.
    (D) Theories disproving fixed intelligence came into existence during this period.
    (E) The teaching of children with retardation included individualized instruction—working with the whole child as well as motor and sensory education.

9. A student with moderate retardation who is 14 years old is still not independent enough to use public transportation. He is in a program that should primarily focus on

    (A) the development of any vocational aptitudes.
    (B) the use of repetitive tasks to develop physical, social, emotional, and intellectual skills.
    (C) being in a part school/part work type of program.
    (D) enhancing his sensory and motor skills.
    (E) developing self-care skills for independent living.

10. The teaching students with mild retardation today involves all of the following concepts EXCEPT

    (A) maximization of potential skills.
    (B) normalization.
    (C) use of behavioral objectives.
    (D) development of recreational and family-living skills.
    (E) attainment of statewide minimum standards for the acquisition of a high school diploma.

11. Which of these items describe(s) the mildly retarded child?

    I.   Should not focus on academic development
    II. First four years of life are important in stimulating such a child
    III. Some forms of mild retardation are reversible
    IV. Can be taught social skills

    (A) I, II, and III only
    (B) I only
    (C) III and IV only
    (D) II, III, and IV only
    (E) I, III, and IV only

12. America is about fifteenth among modern industrialized nations in the prevention of mental retardation. All of the following should be found in the establishment of effective preventive programs EXCEPT

    (A) the development of an extensive network of prenatal programs.
    (B) redesigning institutional programs to prevent problems caused by maternal deprivation or lack of stimulation.
    (C) complete maternal care for high-risk mothers.
    (D) genetic counseling and comprehensive diagnostic centers for each community.
    (E) an extensive child welfare network to prevent the abuse and neglect of children.

13. All of the following are valid techniques in the education of students with mental retardation EXCEPT

    (A) programmed instruction.
    (B) computer-assisted instruction.
    (C) task analysis.
    (D) behavior modification.
    (E) multisensory approaches.

14. Which of the following are arguments in favor of special classes for students with mental retardation?

    I.   Significant improvement in the academic achievement of such youngsters
    II. Greater opportunity for individualized instruction
    III. Protects against academic failure and social rejection
    IV. Results in the development of higher self-concepts

    (A) I and III only
    (B) I, III, and IV only
    (C) I and III only
    (D) I and IV only
    (E) III and IV only

15. An example of an independent living skill would include

    (A) banking and keeping a budget.
    (B) functional literacy.
    (C) maintaining a home.
    (D) working.
    (E) all of the above.

16. Which of the following LEAST describes the learning characteristics of a student with moderate retardation?

    (A) The student needs to be given one-step directions.
    (B) The child needs concrete, repetitive experiences in a structured environment.
    (C) The student must actively manipulate different materials.
    (D) The student has a short attention span, resulting in restlessness and physical activity.
    (E) The student needs to develop reading comprehension skills and problem solving at a slower academic pace.

17. All are contributing to a general decline in the ranks of those labeled mentally retarded EXCEPT

    (A) mental retardation is relative to a student's cultural situation.
    (B) more borderline cases are being labeled learning disabled.
    (C) learning disability is perceived as a safer label than mental retardation.
    (D) the criteria for the label have changed during the last few years.
    (E) most diseases and environmental factors causing mental retardation have been cured or drastically reduced.

18. Which of the following are valid reasons why mental retardation is NOT evenly distributed among the different segments of the population?

    I.   Incidences increase as students "age out" of educational programs
    II. Racial differences exist
    III. There is higher incidence in lower socioeconomic groups
    IV. More males than females are retarded

    (A) II, III, and IV only
    (B) I only
    (C) I and II only
    (D) III and IV only
    (E) I, II, and III only

19. Which would NOT be an appropriate economic skill to teach a student with mild retardation?

    (A) Keeping a household budget
    (B) Keeping accurate records so as to fill out income tax forms
    (C) Shopping wisely
    (D) Handling money and making change
    (E) Reading a sales receipt

20. Which of the following are achievable goals in the education of students with moderate retardation?

    I.   Development of positive self-concept
    II. Economic independence
    III. Ability to interact favorably with others
    IV. Participate in community and recreational activities

    (A) II, III, and IV only
    (B) I, III, and IV only
    (C) I, II, and III only
    (D) II only
    (E) II and III only

21. According to federal and state law, a child with an IQ below 25 on a standardized intelligence test would be labeled

    (A) profoundly retarded.
    (B) mentally retarded.
    (C) severely retarded.
    (D) moderately retarded.
    (E) mildly retarded.

22. Which of the following stated that mental retardation is the result of genetic inheritance?

    (A) Jensen
    (B) Piaget
    (C) Guiford
    (D) Terman
    (E) Bruner

23. According to such intelligence tests as the WISC III or the Stanford-Binet, a child who is considered moderately retarded would have a flat IQ score of about

    (A) 75.
    (B) 42.
    (C) 20.
    (D) 84.
    (E) 79.

24. Which is key in labeling a child as having mental retardation?

   (A) Having intellectual ability in the deficient range according to a standardized IQ test
   (B) Being labeled adaptively retarded as determined by observation and an adaptive rating scale given to a caregiver
   (C) Determining that a deficient IQ will not increase at some future time
   (D) Making sure the retardation is cognitively based and not caused by any other childhood disorder
   (E) Determining that the student is at least three years below his/her present grade level according to academic testing

25. The illusion of retardation may be created by the fact that a person considered competent in one environment may be considered incompetent in another. Which of the following are valid examples of this concept?

   I.   Computer literacy movement in education
   II. Moving from a rural to an urban area
   III. Using phonics as opposed to a whole-language approach
   IV. Moving from a halfway house to a group home

   (A) I and III only
   (B) II and IV only
   (C) III and IV only
   (D) I and II only
   (E) II only

SPEECH COMMUNICATION (0220)

Time: 2 hours
Number of Questions: 150
Format: Multiple-choice questions

Purpose of the Test

Designed to measure the preparation of prospective speech communication teachers in junior or senior high school

Content Categories

- Interpersonal Communication—(17 percent)
- Small Group Communication—(13 percent)
- Public Speaking—(17 percent)
- Media and Their Influences—(10 percent)
- Play Production—(13 percent)
- Oral Interpretation—(13 percent)
- Forensics: Classroom and Curriculum Instruction—(10 percent)
- Assessment and Evaluation Issues—(7 percent)

Category Descriptions

Interpersonal Communication

1. Communication process and competence
2. Verbal and nonverbal
3. Listening
4. Goals, skills, and outcomes of interpersonal communication
5. Intercultural communication

Small Group Communication

1. Discussion principles
2. Problem solving/Decision making
3. Group roles and functions, including leadership
4. Conflict management

Public Speaking

1. Purposes, types, and forms
2. Audience analysis
3. Organizing strategies
4. Language and style
5. Delivery, including voice and diction, projection, and movement
6. Listening, feedback, and adaptation to audience
7. Criticism and evaluation of speeches

Media and Their Influences

1. Media: television, film, radio, computer technology
2. Critical analysis and evaluation
3. Social and technological influences and effects
4. Production techniques and audiovisual

Play Production

1. Dramatic theory and criticism
2. Acting, directing, design and construction, and theater management

Oral Interpretation

1. Readers' theater, storytelling, folklore, oral history, and creative dramatics
2. Aesthetic principles, universality, individuality, imagination, principles of text
3. Analysis: thinking involved in interpretation process
4. Performance techniques

Forensics: Classroom and Curriculum Instruction

1. Argumentation and debate
2. Individual events
3. Program management

Assessment and Evaluation Issues

1. Teacher responsibilities
2. Curriculum: planning, development, appropriate assignments, textbook selection
3. Oral performance
4. Test construction

Speech Communication

Directions: Each question or incomplete statement is followed by five answer choices. For each question, decide which answer or completion is best, and blacken the letter of your choice on the answer sheet.

1. Little attention is paid in most classrooms to which areas of communication?

   I. Written language
   II. Listening
   III. Speaking
   IV. Reading

   (A) II and III only
   (B) III and IV only
   (C) I and IV only
   (D) II only
   (E) III only

2. A student can express positive and negative feelings. He can take the role of another person and take part in complex inferential communication. This student is most likely in

   (A) high school.
   (B) kindergarten.
   (C) an advanced private elementary school.
   (D) the upper-elementary grades.
   (E) middle school.

3. "Self-talk" is how we talk to ourselves so as to self-regulate our behavior and deploy strategies in routine tasks. All are examples of "self-talk" EXCEPT

   (A) finding the main idea in paragraphs.
   (B) going through the process of long division.
   (C) checking answers on tests.
   (D) memorizing a poem.
   (E) listening to foreign-language audiotapes.

4. Difficulties in listening and speaking often result in which of the following?

   I. Saying inappropriate things
   II. Being described as "weird" by peers
   III. Misinterpreting what other students and teachers say
   IV. Causing social isolation or rejection

   (A) I, II, and III only
   (B) II, III, and IV only
   (C) III only
   (D) IV only
   (E) I, II, III, and IV

5. The research of Otto and Smith identifies five levels of speaking competence seen in students. If a student appropriately uses regular and irregular verbs and eliminates double negatives, he or she is speaking

   (A) at the homely level.
   (B) at the illiterate level.
   (C) using standard informal English.
   (D) at the literacy level.
   (E) formal English.

6. A student who works to discern relationships among materials resulting in the ability to state the main idea and summarize is usually engaged in

   (A) active listening.
   (B) passive listening.
   (C) factual listening.
   (D) interpretive listening.
   (E) metacognitive listening.

7. A student says "tin" for "thin," "den" for "then," and "sin" for "sing." The most likely cause of this pupil's articulation errors is due to the fact that he

   (A) comes from a multicultural background.
   (B) speaks black English.
   (C) speaks a nonstandard regional dialect.
   (D) has little education.
   (E) comes from a lower-class group.

8. According to some theories, if a person articulates and pronounces very precisely, varying intonation patterns and using appeal tags, such as "isn't it?" or "don't you think?" this individual is probably

   (A) from the upper class.
   (B) well educated.
   (C) a woman.
   (D) an elderly man.
   (E) a teenager.

9. Using the linguistic model, the basic unit of language development is the

   (A) morpheme.
   (B) syllable.
   (C) kernel.
   (D) surface structure.
   (E) phoneme.

10. The set of rules for changing sentences into questions, imperatives, passives, or more complex sentences containing conjunctive clauses is the

   (A) transformational grammar system.
   (B) pragmatic language system.
   (C) psycholinguistic system.
   (D) structural language system.
   (E) auditory-symbolic system.

11. Study of egocentric language, in which a child's speech is manifested in such a way as not to make allowances for the perspective of the listener, characterizes the research of

   (A) Piaget.
   (B) Wiig.
   (C) Bloom.
   (D) Chomsky.
   (E) Hammill.

12. Effective speech and listening require linguistic, cognitive, and social prerequisites so as to establish coherent communication. Which are examples of a social prerequisite?

   I.   Comprehension of technical information
   II. Teacher shifting vocabulary levels
   III. Knowing grammatical verbs for interpreting sentences
   IV. Articulation of speech sounds clearly and correctly

   (A) II and IV only
   (B) II, III, and IV only
   (C) III and IV only
   (D) I and II only
   (E) III only

13. Research describes three dimensions of language—linguistic content, use, and form. Which are examples of linguistic form?

   I.   Semantics
   II. Syntax
   III. Morphology
   IV. Phonology

   (A) I, III, and IV only
   (B) II, III, and IV only
   (C) I, II, and III only
   (D) I only
   (E) IV only

14. Children from the age of 3 use various sentence types. The sentence "allgone nana" can be described as

   (A) the joining of elements to make sentences.
   (B) the development of subject–predicate sentences.
   (C) the expansion of the verb phrase.
   (D) an embedded element within a sentence.
   (E) the use of negative, declarative, and interrogative transformations.

15. Which is an example of the use of passive voice in a sentence?

   (A) "We will go to the movies."
   (B) "When can we leave?"
   (C) "We left for town on the railroad."
   (D) "If you're happy, then please smile."
   (E) "The building was destroyed by the explosion."

16. Which is an example of a bounded morpheme?

   (A) Con
   (B) Leave
   (C) Run
   (D) Book
   (E) Parties

17. Groups in which to place words relating to objects, actions, relationships, or events that share an essential feature are called

   (A) semantic categories.
   (B) syntactical categories.
   (C) object classes.
   (D) interjections.
   (E) coordinate categories.

18. Language during Piaget's concrete operational stage can best be described as

    (A) having meanings tied to concrete actions.
    (B) having more complex relationships along with broader meaning.
    (C) having meanings tied to the function performed by the word.
    (D) the discussion of complex processes from an abstract point of view.
    (E) having words used to declare, question, or exclaim.

19. It is expected that a young child would say "comed" instead of "came" and "bringed" instead of "brought." These are examples of a child's development of

    (A) phonological concepts.
    (B) morphological concepts.
    (C) syntactical concepts.
    (D) semantic concepts.
    (E) pragmatic concepts.

20. Pragmatics is the function or purpose of communication. An eight-year-old child would have which pragmatic skills?

    I.   Protesting
    II. Increasing ability to express feelings appropriately
    III. Differential adaption to listeners' perspective and personality
    IV. Ability to judge and use speech of appropriate directness

    (A) I and III only
    (B) I, II, III, IV
    (C) I, III, and IV only
    (D) I and II only
    (E) II and IV only

21. An indirect way of speaking when someone cannot retrieve a specific word for an object, action, or event is called a(n)

    (A) counterfactive.
    (B) indefinite reference.
    (C) circumlocution.
    (D) fricative.
    (E) permutation.

22. All are examples of morphological functions EXCEPT

    (A) the use of comparatives and superlatives.
    (B) the use of affixes in sentences.
    (C) the use of regular and irregular plural forms.
    (D) usage of hard and soft *g*.
    (E) the conjugation of verbal forms.

23. The sentences "You nice" and "They bad" are found in

    I.   African-American English.
    II. Southern white nonstandard.
    III. Appalachian.
    IV. nonstandard English.

    (A) I and II only
    (B) III and IV only
    (C) I only
    (D) II only
    (E) I, II, and IV only

24. The sentence "Driving cars can be dangerous" contains

    (A) a structural ambiguity.
    (B) ritualized reduplications.
    (C) a stereotypical starter.
    (D) passive reduplications.
    (E) omission of auxiliaries and modals.

25. The ability of a student to repeat sentences and words can be used as a measure of a student's short-term auditory memory.

    Many questions have been raised about the efficacy of such sentence-repetition tests. Such tests may not be a valid measure of auditory memory because

    (A) students may find too many associations among the words used.
    (B) dialectical differences may impact on a student's ability to recall cues accurately.
    (C) the syntax may be too simple for the student.
    (D) the number of perceptual units may be too small.
    (E) the vocabulary level of the sentence may be congruent with the student's ability.

SPEECH-LANGUAGE PATHOLOGY (0330)

Time: 2 hours
Number of Questions: 150
Format: Multiple-choice questions

Purpose of the Test

Designed to measure the academic preparation in and knowledge of the field of speech-language pathology

Content Categories

- Basic Human Communication Processes—(17 percent)
- Phonological and Language Disorders: Assessment and Treatment—(19 percent)
- Speech Disorders: Identification, Assessment, Treatment, and Prevention—(13 percent)
- Neurogenic Disorders—(19 percent)
- Audiology/Hearing—(5 percent)
- Clinical Management—(19 percent)
- Professional Issues/Psychometrics/Research—(8 percent)

Category Descriptions

Basic Human Communication Processes

1. Language acquisition and learning theory: normal development; theoretical models; behavior management and modification; cognitive development; and developmental, motor, and linguistic processes

2. Language science: structure, phonetics, phonology, grammatical categories, morphology, syntax, semantics, and pragmatics

3. Learning theory: theoretical models related to disorders, models of behavior management and modification, and theories of cognitive development

4. Multicultural awareness: applications of theoretical models of language in society to a variety of linguistic and cultural groups, cultural and socioeconomic factors, communicative differences between speakers of the same language, and cultural differences in use of nonverbal communication

5. Speech science: speech perception, physiological phonetics, acoustic phonetics, related anatomy and physiology, and neural bases

Phonological and Language Disorders: Assessment and Treatment

1. Articulation disorders as influenced by anomalous, oral-motor, dental, learning, or behavioral factors

2. Language disorders: developmental, motor, and linguistic processes; differentiation of normal, delayed, and disordered language development; nature of expressive and receptive language disorders; treatment of language delays and language disorders

Speech Disorders: Identification, Assessment, Treatment, and Prevention

1. Fluency disorders, including theories; neurological and psychological factors; assessment; treatment; and prevention

2. Resonance disorders as influenced by congenital anomalies, neuralgic disorders, disease, trauma, and behavioral factors

3. Assessment, treatment, and prevention of resonance disorders

4. Phonation of voice disorders as influenced by respiratory, laryngeal, and airway problems

5. Alaryngeal speech

6. Assessment, treatment, and prevention of voice disorders

Neurogenic Disorders

1. Neurological disorders: aphasia, progressive disorders, motor speech disorders, traumatic brain injury, and cognitive communication disorders

2. Dysphagia: process, cause, effect, assessment, and treatment of swallowing disorders

Audiology/Hearing

1. Principles, anatomy, and physiology of hearing

2. Congenital and acquired hearing loss in children and adults

3. Audiological assessment: screening, interpretation of audiograms and tympanograms, and referrals

4. Auditory habilitation and rehabilitation

Clinical Management

1. Assessment, use, and determining candidacy for alternative/augmentative communication devices

2. Communication of assessment and treatment plans, progress, and results to clients and appropriate professionals

3. Interpersonal communication and counseling techniques

4. Documentation and monitoring client progress, including using other agencies, communication to other professionals, data gathering and interpretation, determining termination, procedures for referral and follow-up, and writing reports

5. Efficacy in demonstration of results and determining and communicating information

6. Instrumentation used

7. Purpose, use, and applications of technological developments

8. Speech-language assessment: establishing clients' past and present status, recommendations, identifying at-risk individuals, screening, selection, and administration of standard and nonstandard evaluation procedures

9. Speech-language intervention: diagnostic, activities appropriate to age, sociocultural membership and disorder, remediation methods and strategies

10. Basic principles of relevant genetics

11. Syndromic and nonsyndromic inherited and developmental conditions and their influences

Professional Issues/Psychometrics/Research

1. Ethical practices: standards for professional conduct, referrals, obtaining permissions, client records, client privacy, and handling staff issues

2. Research methodology/psychometrics: criteria for selection of test materials, determining reliability of assessment procedures, models of research design, and test construction principles

3. Standards and laws: designing appropriate assessment and treatment, federal laws and regulations, and reporting requirements to government agencies

Speech-Language Pathology

Directions: Each question or incomplete statement is followed by five answer choices. For each question, decide which answer or completion is best, and blacken the letter of your choice on the answer sheet.

---

1. All are examples of organic causes of disorders in rhythm and speech flow EXCEPT

   (A) a predisposition to break down easily under emotional stress, thereby losing fluency.
   (B) a parent's causing the child to stutter more by labeling a normal dysfluency as defective.
   (C) a child's lack of cerebral dominance resulting in stuttering.
   (D) dysphemia, which is a neuromuscular condition characterized by nerve impulses that are poorly timed in coordinating speech musculatures.
   (E) an epileptic type of condition resulting in a series of small seizures that interrupt speech.

2. A receptive language disorder in which a child repeats words and sentences in a parrot-like fashion is usually found in

   (A) learning-disabled children.
   (B) emotionally disturbed children.
   (C) mentally retarded children.
   (D) autistic children.
   (E) hearing-impaired children.

3. Twenty years ago, specialists dealing with communication disorders focused primarily on which of the following problems?

   I.   Inability to articulate sounds
   II.   Lisps
   III. Dysfluencies
   IV.   Delayed speech

   (A) II and III only
   (B) I and IV only
   (C) I, II, and III only
   (D) II, III, and IV only
   (E) I, III, and IV only

4. According to most research, deaf children

   (A) develop language and speech in the same sequential manner as hearing students.
   (B) develop as many concepts as hearing students but take a longer time to do so.
   (C) in terms of nonverbal functioning can have as high an IQ as hearing children.
   (D) have intelligence test scores three to four years below those of hearing children.
   (E) are taught using methods similar to those used with learning-disabled students.

5. A child speaks using excessive speed, resulting in disorganized sentences. The speech is garbled with syllables and sounds that are slurred or omitted. The student tends to make excessive repetitions when vocalizing. The problem described is called

   (A) cluttering.
   (B) hypernasality.
   (C) stuttering.
   (D) dysphasia.
   (E) aphasia.

6. The remediation of language deficits will take into account all of the following factors EXCEPT

   (A) vocabulary.
   (B) voice intensity.
   (C) word meaning.
   (D) concept formation.
   (E) development of grammatical rules.

7. Which language systems are usually set before the age of 6?

   I.   Semantics
   II.   Morphology
   III. Syntax
   IV.   Phonology

   (A) II and III only
   (B) III and IV only
   (C) I, II, and III only
   (D) I, III, and IV only
   (E) II, III, and IV only

8. The LEAST effective technique to use with a child who has speech apraxia is to

    (A) have the child feel vibrations of sound by touching the teacher's face and throat.
    (B) use a computer to mimic speech sounds.
    (C) have the child observe mouth movements and shaping during the production of sound.
    (D) exercise the child's speech muscles by smiling, chewing, blowing, and laughing.
    (E) have the child practice tongue movements in front of a mirror.

9. Pronouncing /s/ in "said" as /z/ is an example of a(n)

    (A) distortion.
    (B) addition.
    (C) substitution.
    (D) omission.
    (E) lalling.

10. All of the following either are or contain oral language tests EXCEPT

    (A) Carrow.
    (B) EOWPVT-R.
    (C) PPVT.
    (D) Vocabulary subtest of the WISC III.
    (E) Word Opposites subtest of the DTLA-3.

11. A child has an expressive language delay in which he cannot remember words to be expressed. He may use words like "thing" for objects he cannot recall, or he may attempt to use circumlocutions. The child is suffering from

    (A) dyslexia.
    (B) dysnomia.
    (C) apraxia.
    (D) aphasia.
    (E) echolalia.

12. The concept that language is learned through imitation and reinforcement comes from the

    (A) linguistic view.
    (B) language arts view.
    (C) pathological view.
    (D) psycholinguistic view.
    (E) behavioral view.

13. Which author is most associated with the psycholinguistic view of language?

    (A) Myklebust
    (B) Chomsky
    (C) Piaget
    (D) Vygotsky
    (E) Roswell

14. Which of the following children would be diagnosed with a language disorder rather than a language deficit?

    (A) A student who often omits subjects when speaking
    (B) A student who often uses inappropriate words when speaking
    (C) A child who is speaking in one-word utterances in kindergarten
    (D) A seventh-grader who uses many circumlocutions while conversing
    (E) A student who has poor pragmatic language skills

15. Acquired aphasia is

    (A) the loss of ability to speak due to brain damage as a result of an accident.
    (B) a language disorder primarily affecting children.
    (C) the inability to develop receptive language skills.
    (D) a neurological dysfunction causing delays in speech.
    (E) primarily a problem in communication beginning after the age of two.

16. Children who have difficulty with pitch, stress, and juncture usually

    (A) cannot discriminate syllables.
    (B) speak in monotone and without expression.
    (C) mix up sentence order.
    (D) demonstrate considerable skill in vocabulary acquisition.
    (E) have good understanding of morphological units.

17. Which of the following describe language of inner-city children?

    I. Nonstandard language has divergencies in vocabulary, dialect, and grammatical structure.
    II. Nonstandard language can be considered as a different but equal language system.
    III. Research shows that inner-city language is functionally inadequate and structurally unsystematic.
    IV. There is frequently a mismatch between the child's language and that used by teachers.

    (A) I only
    (B) II and III only
    (C) I, II, and IV only
    (D) I and III only
    (E) I and IV only

18. All are possible organic causes of speech disorders EXCEPT

    (A) a significant hearing loss.
    (B) oral-facial abnormalities.
    (C) poor coordination of speech musculature.
    (D) dyslalia caused by parents' not stimulating speech.
    (E) high and narrow palate that leaves little room for the tongue to move.

19. According to research, the sound that is LEAST misarticulated in children is

    (A) /s/
    (B) /r/
    (C) /d/
    (D) /th/
    (E) /sh/

20. Which is the basic morphemic generalization of inner-city dialect to denote plurality?

    (A) The use of the /z/ sound added to nouns
    (B) Omission of irregular plurals
    (C) The use of appropriate quantitative adjectives without pluralizing the noun
    (D) Adding /s/ to all nouns and adjectives in a sentence
    (E) The use of qualitative adjectives without pluralizing the noun

21. All of the following are techniques you might use in teaching auditory perception and discrimination of language sounds EXCEPT

    (A) making bingo cards with consonant blends in the squares and then reading words while asking the child to cover the blend that begins each word.
    (B) saying three words, two of which have the same initial sound, and then asking the child to identify the word that begins with a different sound.
    (C) using sound boxes by putting toys, pictures, and objects in a box representing a consonant sound.
    (D) asking a child to substitute an initial sound to make a new word.
    (E) using gestures and exaggeration to help children understand the meaning of a word that symbolizes an object.

22. Which is probably the LEAST common speech problem among school-aged children?

    (A) Articulation difficulty
    (B) Stuttering
    (C) Speech problems due to hearing impairment
    (D) Cerebral palsy speech
    (E) Retarded speech development

23. John often speaks omitting verb inflections when conjugating. His problem is best described as a

    (A) communication disorder.
    (B) language disorder.
    (C) developmental aphasic response.
    (D) language disability.
    (E) language difference.

24. A student is asked to verbally list different vegetables. His list includes peas, beans, salads, orange, and fruit. The student's problem is mainly

    (A) caused by delayed speech.
    (B) in vocabulary.
    (C) in concept formation.
    (D) in the misapplication of grammatical rules.
    (E) due to problems in language comprehension.

25. Which of the following statements describe the language of a 4-year-old child?

    I.   She uses compound and complex sentences.
    II. Reversals of sounds are typically the most frequent error, with repetitions rarely present.
    III. Hesitations and repetitions are still present, although the voice is usually well controlled.
    IV. Medial consonants are often slighted.

    (A) I and II only
    (B) III and IV only
    (C) I, II, III, and IV
    (D) I and III only
    (E) II, III, and IV only

VOCATIONAL GENERAL KNOWLEDGE (0890)

Time: 2 hours
Number of Questions: 100
Format: Multiple-choice questions

Purpose of the Test

Designed to assess knowledge and understanding of a variety of disciplines and their interrelationships, including knowledge of basic facts, and ability to analyze problems and to apply principles

Content Categories

- Social Studies—(40 percent)
- Mathematics—(40 percent)
- Science—(20 percent)

Category Descriptions

Social Studies

1. U.S. history
2. Economics
3. Geography
4. Political institutions

Mathematics

1. Problem solving
2. Logical reasoning
3. Probability
4. Measurement
5. Ration, proportion, and percent
6. Interpreting charts, diagrams, and graphs
7. Estimating

Science

1. Scientific methods
2. Nutrition
3. Classification of living things
4. Gravity and nuclear force
5. Sources and transfer of energy

Vocational General Knowledge

Directions: Each of the questions below is followed by four possible answers or completions. Choose the best answer for each question.

---

1. Concrete is usually made by mixing

   (A) only sand and water.
   (B) only cement and water.
   (C) lye, cement, and water.
   (D) rock, sand, cement, and water.

2. The tool used to locate a point directly below a ceiling hook is a

   (A) plumb bob.
   (B) line level.
   (C) transit.
   (D) drop gauge.

3. When marking wood, an allowance of 1/16″ to 1/8″ should be made to allow for

   (A) drying of the wood.
   (B) absorption of water by wood.
   (C) the width of the saw.
   (D) knots in the wood.

4. High oil content or so-called "spar" varnish is used primarily for

   (A) finishing furniture.
   (B) obtaining a high-gloss finish.
   (C) finishing weather-exposed surfaces.
   (D) finishing interior trim.

5. The best electrical connection between two wires is obtained when

   (A) the insulations are melted together.
   (B) all insulation is removed and the wires are bound together with friction tape.
   (C) both are wound on a common binding post.
   (D) they are soldered together.

6. Which of the following non-metallic elements listed is the best conductor of electricity?

   (A) Mica
   (B) Carbon
   (C) Formica
   (D) Hard rubber

7. When an electric motor designed to be used on AC is plugged into a DC source, what occurs?

   (A) Excessive heat will be produced.
   (B) It will operate the same as usual.
   (C) It will continue to operate but will not get so warm.
   (D) It cannot be predicted

8. Most problems in electricity involving resistance, voltage, and current can be solved using

   (A) Ohm's Law.
   (B) Watt's Law.
   (C) Coulomb's Law.
   (D) Kirchoff's Voltage and Current Laws.

9. The ampere measures

   (A) inductance.
   (B) resistance.
   (C) voltage.
   (D) current.

10. A "hot-rodder" wants to make his/her car run faster, so he/she changes the ignition mechanism. All components are in working order, so he/she

    (A) uses a larger capacitor on the points.
    (B) retards the ignition several degrees.
    (C) puts hotter spark plugs in the engine.
    (D) checks the ignition timing.

11. Which one of the following has the LEAST resistance?

    (A) Silver
    (B) Aluminum
    (C) Copper
    (D) Iron

12. Which of the following terms can best be compared to electrical voltage?

    (A) Tension
    (B) Resistance
    (C) Flow
    (D) Pressure

13. The best way to put out a gasoline fire is to

    (A) use a bucket of water.
    (B) smother it with rags.
    (C) use a carbon dioxide extinguisher.
    (D) use a carbon tetrachloride extinguisher.

14. The best reason to overhaul a machine on a regular basis is

    (A) that overhauling is easier to do when done often.
    (B) to minimize breakdowns of the machine.
    (C) to make sure the machine is properly lubricated.
    (D) to make sure the employees are familiar with the machine.

15. Caulking a joint is

    (A) applying sealing material to the joint.
    (B) tightening the joint with wrenches.
    (C) opening the joint with wrenches.
    (D) testing the joint for leaks.

16. When drilling into a steel plate, the drill bit is most likely to break because

    (A) the drill speed is too low.
    (B) the oil lubricant is excessively cut.
    (C) there is too much drill pressure.
    (D) the bit has a dull point.

17. The volt-ohmmeter can be used in an electric circuit to measure

    (A) inductance.
    (B) power.
    (C) resistance.
    (D) capacitance.

18. The water trap in a plumbing drainage is used to

    (A) prevent water leakage.
    (B) prevent pipes from freezing.
    (C) block off sewer gases.
    (D) reduce the water pressure in the system.

19. In order to prevent damage to an air compressor, the air coming into the compressor is usually

    (A) cooled.
    (B) heated.
    (C) expanded.
    (D) filtered.

20. An electrical transformer may be utilized to

    (A) raise battery output voltage.
    (B) maintain constant battery output voltage.
    (C) lower the voltage from a 110-volt AC power line.
    (D) change the current from AC to DC.

21. Using measuring cans without any intermediate marks, 2 gallons of oil can be accurately measured from a barrel and put in a bearing using

    (A) an 8-gallon and a 4-gallon can.
    (B) two 4-gallon cans.
    (C) a 6-gallon and a 4-gallon can.
    (D) a 1-gallon and a 6-gallon can.

22. If a plant making bricks turns out 1,250 bricks in 5 days, how many bricks can be made in 20 days?

    (A) 5,000
    (B) 6,250
    (C) 12,500
    (D) 25,000

23. When one compares the cost of a 25-watt lamp burning for 100 hours to the cost of a 100-watt lamp burning for 25 hours, the cost will be

    (A) four times as much for the 100-watt lamp.
    (B) the same.
    (C) four times as much for the 25-watt lamp.
    (D) eight times as much for the 10-watt lamp.

24. What is the maximum number of 120-pound weights that can be lifted safely with a chain hoist of 1,000-pound capacity?

    (A) 7
    (B) 8
    (C) 9
    (D) 10

25. If one ounce of naphthalene is recommended for use for each 6 cubic feet, how much is needed for a space 6 feet by 8 feet by 4 feet?

    (A) 1 pound
    (B) 2 pounds
    (C) 3 pounds
    (D) 4 pounds

ANSWER KEY

Biology and General Science	Business Education	Chemistry	Early Childhood Education
1. C	1. D	1. C	1. C
2. A	2. C	2. B	2. C
3. E	3. B	3. D	3. D
4. B	4. B	4. C	4. E
5. B	5. B	5. B	5. D
6. A	6. C	6. D	6. A
7. A	7. D	7. B	7. E
8. D	8. A	8. C	8. A
9. D	9. B	9. C	9. D
10. C	10. B	10. E	10. A
11. A	11. D	11. A	11. E
12. C	12. D	12. C	12. D
13. D	13. B	13. D	13. D
14. A	14. D	14. C	14. E
15. B	15. A	15. D	15. D
16. A	16. A	16. C	16. B
17. B	17. D	17. C	17. C
18. C	18. C	18. A	18. C
19. E	19. A	19. D	19. E
20. B	20. B	20. C	20. B
21. E	21. B	21. C	21. E
22. C	22. C	22. A	22. A
23. D	23. B	23. D	23. A
24. C	24. B	24. D	24. D
25. B	25. C	25. D	25. B

Elementary Education: Content Knowledge	Elementary Education: Curriculum, Instruction, and Assessment	Family and Consumer Sciences
1. A	*(see page 221 for Explanatory Answers)*	1. D
2. C		2. C
3. D	1. A	3. E
4. D	2. C	4. C
5. B	3. A	5. B
6. A	4. D	6. E
7. C	5. B	7. E
8. B	6. D	8. B
9. B	7. B	9. E
10. B	8. C	10. C
11. C	9. B	11. B
12. C	10. D	12. B
13. D	11. D	13. D
14. D	12. A	14. B
15. C	13. C	15. A
16. C	14. C	16. A
17. C	15. C	17. C
18. B	16. D	18. E
19. A	17. B	19. A
20. B	18. B	20. A
21. B	19. D	21. D
22. C	20. B	22. A
23. C	21. A	23. C
24. A	22. D	24. B
25. D	23. D	25. D
	24. B	
	25. B	

Explanations for Elementary Education: Content Area Exercises.

Introduction to the Teaching of Reading	Mathematics: Content Knowledge	Music Education	Physics
1. A	1. C	**Taped Section**	1. B
2. B	2. B	1. D	2. D
3. B	3. A	2. C	3. D
4. D	4. B	3. A	4. A
5. E	5. D	4. D	5. D
6. E	6. A	**Nontaped Section**	6. D
7. D	7. B	5. C	7. C
8. B	8. D	6. E	8. E
9. E	9. C	7. E	9. C
10. B	10. A	8. A	10. C
11. D	11. D	9. B	11. E
12. A	12. A	10. C	12. B
13. B	13. C	11. A	13. B
14. C	14. D	12. B	14. C
15. B	15. C	13. E	15. A
16. C	16. C	14. C	16. B
17. E	17. D	15. E	17. B
18. B	18. D	16. D	18. D
19. A	19. A	17. C	19. B
20. B	20. C	18. B	20. B
21. C	21. D	19. E	21. D
22. A	22. D	20. B	22. A
23. B	23. C	21. C	23. C
24. C	24. C	22. D	24. C
25. C	25. A	23. A	25. D
		24. E	
		25. D	

Reading Specialist	School Guidance and Counseling	School Psychologist	Special Education: Knowledge-Based Core Principles
1. D	1. E	1. B	1. A
2. A	2. A	2. C	2. C
3. D	3. D	3. E	3. C
4. B	4. C	4. C	4. D
5. E	5. D	5. C	5. B
6. C	6. D	6. B	6. B
7. B	7. B	7. A	7. E
8. C	8. E	8. B	8. A
9. D	9. B	9. E	9. A
10. A	10. D	10. A	10. D
11. B	11. B	11. E	11. E
12. A	12. D	12. B	12. E
13. E	13. B	13. B	13. C
14. C	14. C	14. E	14. B
15. B	15. B	15. A	15. D
16. A	16. E	16. C	16. E
17. B	17. D	17. C	17. A
18. E	18. C	18. E	18. E
19. E	19. A	19. B	19. A
20. D	20. E	20. A	20. D
21. A	21. C	21. E	21. E
22. B	22. A	22. B	22. E
23. C	23. B	23. D	23. C
24. D	24. B	24. B	24. C
25. E	25. D	25. E	25. A

Special Education: Teaching Students with Mental Retardation	Speech Communication	Speech-Language Pathology	Vocational General Knowledge
1. A	1. A	1. B	1. D
2. E	2. A	2. D	2. A
3. B	3. E	3. C	3. C
4. D	4. E	4. D	4. C
5. C	5. C	5. A	5. D
6. C	6. D	6. B	6. B
7. B	7. A	7. E	7. A
8. A	8. C	8. B	8. A
9. A	9. A	9. A	9. D
10. E	10. A	10. A	10. D
11. D	11. A	11. B	11. A
12. E	12. D	12. E	12. D
13. B	13. B	13. B	13. C
14. C	14. A	14. C	14. B
15. E	15. E	15. A	15. A
16. E	16. A	16. B	16. C
17. E	17. A	17. C	17. C
18. A	18. C	18. D	18. C
19. B	19. C	19. C	19. D
20. B	20. D	20. C	20. C
21. B	21. C	21. E	21. C
22. A	22. D	22. D	22. A
23. B	23. A	23. E	23. B
24. B	24. A	24. C	24. B
25. D	25. B	25. A	25. B

ANSWERS AND EXPLANATIONS FOR ELEMENTARY EDUCATION: CONTENT AREA EXERCISES

Question 1

The student's response to the oral reading portion of this informal reading inventory shows that he has deficits in phonic skills. He is having difficulty consistently pronouncing CVC words and consonant clusters and following the silent *e* rule. Some examples of these errors were *rad* for red, *fist* for fish, and *spook* for spoke. The student cannot pronounce two-syllable words. He also cannot pronounce nonphonetic patterns. In addition to inconsistent phonic development, he disregards all punctuation marks. There are no pauses between sentences because he does not stop at periods. He also does not pause at commas. His substitutions were impulsive and configuration-based. Attentional aspects appear to be a factor because he does not look carefully at the words, causing him to rely more on their shape than trying to sound them out using their separate phonemes. Finally, he did not try to use context clues to figure out the words. Most substitutions had nothing to do with the story at hand. He appeared totally unaware that the word *rack* had nothing to do with any aspect of the information he was reading. That final aspect of his reading problem seems to be affecting reading comprehension. His ability to read a second-grade passage is at the frustration level of development; thus, he cannot answer any questions. Because he looks back and tries to answer in a word-for-word manner from the story, most answers are completely wrong. Responses also show that he is unable to determine where in the story he will find a probable answer.

In terms of developing decoding skills, the student first needs to develop two cueing systems to enhance pronunciations and meaning. He needs to be taught phonics explicitly to effectively develop some of the cueing strategies. Errors have to be categorized into the correct sequence of teaching phonics to determine which skills are missing or have gaps. The student may need a multisensory approach to teach the correct sequence of phonic development. He has to learn how to pronounce CVC words, clusters, and vowel digraphs/diphthongs as well as apply the silent *e* rule. This should be done not only by having the student hear the sound, but also by having the student feel the sound kinesthetically and tactily. He can focus on the shape of the mouth during sound production and feel whether vowels are voiced or unvoiced. Cueing cards can also be used. The student can learn symbols that show how to correct various errors in words. If the student cannot pronounce the silent *e*, then such words on cards should have that particular letter circled with an arrow pointing back to the vowel. The student also has to utilize his sight vocabulary along with developing phonic skills to self-correct various miscues based upon context. Finally, the student should read aloud to peers or younger children, tape record his reading errors, and participate in Reader's Theater activities to enhance flow, rhythm, and meter, so that oral reading sounds like everyday speech.

In developing reading comprehension skills, the teacher has to orally present the written material to the student to ascertain whether his comprehension is being impacted by language or still mainly by decoding. Before a student reads a story, the teacher should model the reading of that story, not only to improve decoding, but also to see if the student understands the information given if presented in another modality. Once the student orally hears the story and rehearses its reading, main idea can be taught by having the student focus on words or concepts that are mentioned more than one time in the story. Main idea can also be enhanced by having the student summarize the story that was just read to him. This will also help him focus and sequence on details of a story, thus making it easy for him to answer detail questions. Since the student also has difficulty with cause-and-effect questions, the teacher could make a graphic organizer containing probable effects and then have the student dictate facts that were causes. At all points, vocabulary should be pretaught to make sure the student understands all words before questioning is attempted. Using all these strategies, that student will continue to enhance factual and higher-level comprehension until decoding skills catch up to language ability.

Question 2

The answer to both problems reveals that the student is unable to visualize and make pictures and diagrams to solve math problems. He is unable to take the question and use it to draw an illustration of the situation. He has no idea that manipulatives can also be used to make a visual diagram of the problem. His difficulties with this problem arise in part because he still does not know appropriate strategies to solving word problems. He is not aware that this particular problem is not about finding the correct operation to use. The first question can be solved without doing any mathematical operation but by drawing either a circle or fraction bar and adding additional pieces and highlighting different pieces.

The second weakness that the student has is an inability to understand basic fractional concepts. He is able to turn math words into fractions, but he has little understanding of what these fractions mean. He does not understand through the use of manipulatives that two fractions have to be made equivalent in size in order to either add or subtract them. Though he understands that whole numbers can be turned into a fraction in step two, he still has not generalized that during addition and subtraction the denominators do not change because the size of the fractional pieces remains the same. He appears to understand or misunderstand fractions as a computation only.

A third weakness is the inability to use an elementary understanding of proportional reasoning to make reasonable estimations of an answer. The student does not understand that he has to find a fractional piece of a whole number and that it can be done without a computational process. He does not understand that he can find a third, half, or quarter of a number by dividing that number by its denominator, which represents a ratio of that whole number.

The first skill needed to solve Problem 1 is the use of manipulatives, such as fraction bars or circle pieces to manipulate fractions. The student first has to understand the relative size of each piece and how many of those pieces are equivalent to a whole. Next, these manipulatives are used to show, model, and relate the equivalence of two or more fractional pieces. He should understand that two one-quarter pieces are equivalent to a half piece. He should understand that two one-third pieces are equivalent to four one-sixth pieces. He can use these pieces to then determine how much of a fraction is left if pieces are either added or removed from the bar or circle. Then the student can follow similar procedures by drawing fraction bars or circles. The student should next learn to solve Problem 1 by turning manipulatives and visual illustrations into algorithms using various operational procedures. The student should learn to add fractions that contain different denominators by using manipulatives, illustrations, and bars and then use fraction bars to find equivalence in lowest terms. He can then use the manipulatives and illustrations to subtract fractions, understanding that the denominator either remains the same or reduces to lowest terms. He should conclude by turning these manipulative and visual procedures into fractional operations using addition, subtraction, and reducing.

First, the student learns to utilize the comprehension method to determine which operation to use to solve Problem 2. This KNL method determines what he knows from the problem, what he needs to find out, and what he has to learn from the problem. He uses this to create a graphic chart with the utilization of key math vocabulary words to determine which operation to use. This procedure has to be utilized in solving different types of problems involving whole numbers and then fractions containing different operations to generalize the concept. Second, he has to learn to use ratio and proportion to determine a fractional equivalent to whole numbers. In this case, he has to realize that if the whole number is nine, the third of the trip that remains is 300. The student must use different common fractions to find proportions of various whole numbers. Before computing the proportion, he should estimate the probable proportion based on manipulatives and visualization. In understanding this proportional conception, he should understand that using fractions is just another way to divide numbers and that the denominator is the key to determining the estimated proportion.

Question 3

This document-based question does not meet the standards for Level Three as outlined in the sample item. First, the student does not mention the use of any documents within his essay. Some of the documents may have been a railroad advertisement, a description of what it was like traveling on a steamship, or possibly a map of one of the canals built during the early part of the nineteenth century. The student appears to use his general knowledge of the era and does not garner any information or data from the documents.

A second problem with the essay is that some of the data is not accurate or is too broad. Furthermore, there is a lot of inaccurate data within the document-based essay. The student does not notice some of the key words in the body of the essay. Transportation before the Civil War needs to be discussed. Asian immigrants building railroads occurred after the Civil War and could not have been garnered from the documents. In addition, the conclusion that many settlers were killed on these dirt roads is probably unsubstantiated from any possible document. Also, many statements are too broad and lack details. He could mention that the government built specific roads, such as the Cumberland, and that this concept of public works was called the American System supported by Henry Clay.

Finally, the student's essay is disorganized. There is no introduction in the essay. Any introduction should state comparing and contrasting ideas. The student immediately begins to discuss details only in a sequential manner. The student's essay only contains a single body paragraph that should be divided into several paragraphs. One paragraph could be transportation in the eighteenth century, and a second paragraph could discuss nineteenth-century transportation. Lastly, there is no conclusion, which should state how the United States grew as a result of this revolution in transportation or even summarize contrasting ideas. Some summary information could be the increased Western population, resulting in new states coming into the union, as well as increased trade, resulting in more rapid industrialization of certain parts of the country.

Three specific skills should be taught to the student to help him create a satisfactory essay. The student first has to learn how to interpret and summarize various documents. Some documents may be written statements by people living at that time, newspaper articles, political speeches, lithographs, maps, and graphic organizers. Students have to learn to summarize documents, determine opinions, contrast ideas, and determine causes and effects. These concepts have to be written in coherent short sentences or statements during the scaffolding process that takes place prior to the introduction of the document-based essay.

The second step is writing a text or graphic outline of the essay. The student first must gather and summarize quickly key ideas from each document. Then the student has to use phrases to place these key ideas into an essay outline. The outline should have information to develop specific paragraphs. If two ideas are mentioned, then two detailed outlines have to be created that will each become a separate paragraph. There should be at least four Roman numerals to each outline. The first should be information for an introduction. The second and third should be information for two detail paragraphs, and the last should be information that can be turned into a concluding paragraph.

The final skill should be lessons in which the student learns to critique the answers of either scaffolding documents or essays. The student should be given criteria for the quartile scores that are given. Then the student grades the essays or documents based upon these criteria. The student writes the reasons for the grade based upon these criteria. The student can work with other students in a small group for grading specific sample essays. The group should state the quartile score and then write the justifications under the essay in full sentences or by using bullets. By working in a group, a stronger student can give insight to weaker writers based on the necessary criterion. For example, a stronger student might help the weaker student to become more aware of information that is too broad or not based upon the documents given, or whether examples are given or not given. This awareness enables a student to edit and make corrections when writing the document-based answer without outside assistance.

Question 4

In this unit, one cooperative group applies the mathematical concept of sequencing to reading by using a variety of materials to develop a time line to describe different eras of Egyptian history. Different students utilize different types of books to find the information. Students use encyclopedic, textbook, and general history books to develop an outline that is partly structured by the teacher into important events in the Old, Middle, and New Kingdoms. Different students then create several types of time lines. One is a horizontal time line, then a vertical time line, and finally a pictographic time line.

Another group compares and contrasts different eras within ancient Egypt using a Venn diagram. Different students compare different eras within the culture. One student compares the Old and Middle Kingdoms, while another compares different intermediate periods, and a third compares Egyptian culture to nomadic tribal culture, etc. Then these different Venn diagrams are put by the group onto a poster board that is used by the class to summarize different aspects of Egyptian history and culture.

A third group uses recording skills to develop charts and graphs to illustrate or determine the impact of different details about Egypt. They might use reading information from various sources to graph the propinquity of pyramids in different parts of Egypt. They use different reading from various sources to make charts concerning the number of tombs in different areas that have been excavated. Students also may chart within a group the number of cities and towns near the Nile River as opposed to other sections of Egypt. They also may chart population increases in Egypt from the Old to the New Kingdoms. The students develop different types of charts. They may create pie charts, bar graphs, pictographs, line graphs, and double line graphs, depending on the information.

A fourth group develops math problems based on a particular aspect of Egyptian culture. Students can incorporate many math concepts into the geometry and construction of a period. A group may use an Egyptian calendar to make problems concerning elapsed time in the construction of a pyramid if they have to stop and start during various seasons. Then the elapsed time as measured by the Egyptian calendar can be converted into the modern calendar. The students can make various problems deriving the area of a pyramid using different types of measures, e.g., Egyptian, metric, and English. Furthermore, rate and work problems can be developed in one or several steps concerning the construction of a pyramid. The students may be given information about how many bricks can be carried during a period day and use the information to determine how many men are needed to carry the bricks if a particular number of bricks must be used to construct a pyramid. This gives students an idea of how long it took to build a pyramid, how much work had to be done, and how many people were needed in the endeavor. All of this puts mathematics into a real-world context as determined by the NTCM standards.

Higher-level reading research skills are developed during this interdisciplinary unit. Students learn to question and seek additional information about the topic. To develop and apply the math ideas within the unit, the students must learn to use books illustrating primary sources, information from the encyclopedia, and articles about Egypt found in various journals. For example, to create bar graphs or word problems, students should look up journals containing articles from which they derive the information. Then they have to go to a microfilm machine to find the information that may have to be reported back to the cooperative group. The students utilize note-taking skills to separate important from unimportant information that is either highlighted from copies of the article or written on note cards. Finally, the gathered information is brought back to the group to either create problems or graphs.

A second reading research skill is to find data to determine and support a particular position. One group may want to decide whether flooding of the Nile was beneficial or harmful to the Egyptians. Students may have to look up ancient incidents describing floods. These primary descriptions, found in books or articles, may state the number of people killed and possibly a description of the agricultural as well as structural damage. In addition, the students may also research and find modern incidents of flooding prior to the building of dams. Then students may want to compare and contrast the number of floods and resulting damage before and after the building of the modern dams. Therefore, the students are enhancing research skills and using math data to support a particular position. Other cooperative groups use numerical data and reading research skills to justify other positions concerning Egypt.

ANSWERS AND EXPLANATIONS FOR ELEMENTARY EDUCATION: CURRICULUM, INSTRUCTION, AND ASSESSMENT

1. **The correct answer is (A).** This is the only choice that incorporates language arts into the lesson. Choices (B) and (D) incorporate mathematical concepts into the lesson, while choice (C) focuses upon scientific concepts.

2. **The correct answer is (C).** Diagnostic/prescriptive measures are most often norm reference tests in which the student is compared to other students. Portfolios, informal reading inventories, and interest inventories are all informal measures of reading ability.

3. **The correct answer is (A).** Receptive language must develop before expressive language. Then reading skills develop before written expression.

4. **The correct answer is (D).** The first three choices can create a social understanding of the ancient Greeks, while understanding the symbols within various maps attunes students to traditional geographic concepts.

5. **The correct answer is (B).** The teacher is using literature to teach social studies.

6. **The correct answer is (D).** This answer is correct because such a topic should not be taught in social studies; it is part of the theology of several religions, not comparative history.

7. **The correct answer is (B).** Maslow's needs theory would help this teacher understand the effects of poverty on learning. Dewey dealt with progressive education; Piaget, the different stages of learning; and Ravitch, with multicultural education.

8. **The correct answer is (C).** This statement cannot be turned into a scientific experiment; the two factors have no relationship to each other. The other three choices have scientific factors.

9. **The correct answer is (B).** This activity helps students identify which fractions are the same.

10. **The correct answer is (D).** The fractional symbols must be connected to the concept for them to have any meaning.

11. **The correct answer is (D).** The students are developing a number sense for decimals and how decimals and fractions are related.

12. **The correct answer is (A).** Using discussion techniques to develop moral reasoning comes from Kohlberg.

13. **The correct answer is (C).** The teacher is using the discovery approach and the constructivist view of learning, guiding students so that they discover or construct a scientific concept.

14. **The correct answer is (C).** One application of the whole language approach is being illustrated. This approach uses children's literature to develop reading skills.

15. **The correct answer is (C).** Phonics is taught on an as-needed basis in the whole language approach.

16. **The correct answer is (D).** Flavell is mostly associated with metacognition. The other three theorists widely used cooperative learning within their theories.

17. **The correct answer is (B).** A visual representation of a story can help a learning disabled student to comprehend the structure of a story.

18. **The correct answer is (B).** This taps into divergent thinking because there are many possible answers. With the other choices, only a limited number of answers exist. Therefore, their answers are convergent.

19. **The correct answer is (D).** Students who exhibit good language concepts and oral comprehension may still have problems decoding words. Research shows that the other three choices are effective in learning how to read.

20. **The correct answer is (B).** Research shows little correlation between many variables and learning how to read.

21. **The correct answer is (A).** Using problem situations, the students use math to make sense of their world. They have to understand that doing math is a common human activity that is not really separated from other activities.

22. **The correct answer is (D).** The concept of odd and even are second-grade level skills. The other skills are usually taught in fifth grade.

23. **The correct answer is (D).** Research shows that teachers should read aloud to model reading with expression and to expose children to different types of literature that the children may not read on their own.

24. **The correct answer is (B).** The teacher is engaging the students in structured comprehension; she is asking the same question in different ways. In this instance, she is asking main idea questions in different ways.

25. **The correct answer is (B).** Bruner stated that every concept need not be discovered by the student.

Part IV:

Multiple Subjects Assessment for Teachers (MSAT)

MSAT: CONTENT KNOWLEDGE TEST

The Content Knowledge test of the Multiple Subjects Assessment for Teachers is intended to measure knowledge and critical-thinking abilities for prospective elementary school teachers. The test contains 120 multiple-choice questions, and you are given 2 hours to complete this section.

The seven subtests are:

1. Literature and Language Studies

2. Mathematics

3. Visual and Performing Arts

4. Physical Education

5. Human Development

6. History/Social Sciences

7. Science

Each subtest contains multiple-choice questions with 4 choices per question. You are to select the best answer for each question, and blacken the corresponding space on the answer sheet.

MSAT Content Knowledge test scores are based on the number of questions answered correctly. Since there is no penalty for wrong answers, it is better to guess at an answer than to leave it blank.

ANSWER SHEETS

Directions: Start with number 1 for each new section. If a section has fewer than 25 questions, leave the extra answer spaces blank.

SECTION 1
SECTION 2
SECTION 3
SECTION 4
SECTION 5
SECTION 6
SECTION 7

SECTION 1: LITERATURE AND LANGUAGE STUDIES

24 Questions

> *Directions:* Each question or incomplete statement is followed by four answer choices. For each question, select the answer or completion that is best, and blacken the corresponding space on the answer sheet.

Questions 1 and 2 refer to the following quote.

> The wolf also shall dwell with the lamb, and the leopard shall lie down with the kid…
> They shall beat their swords into ploughshares, and their spears into pruning-hooks:
> nation shall not lift sword against nation, neither shall they learn war any more.

1. The lines above are taken from

   (A) a sonnet by William Wordsworth.
   (B) a poem by William Shakespeare.
   (C) the Old Testament.
   (D) a poem by Dylan Thomas.

2. The lines above describe

   (A) a mythical state.
   (B) the Messianic age.
   (C) a child's fairy tale.
   (D) the author's fervent wishes.

Questions 3–5 refer to the following choices.

(A) O Captain! my Captain! our fearful trip is done,
The ship has weathered every rack, the prize we sought is won,
The port is near, the bells I hear, the people all exulting.
While follow eyes the steady keel, the vessel grim and daring;
But O heart! heart! heart!
O the bleeding drops of red,
Where on the deck my Captain lies,
Fallen cold and dead.

(B) Hain't we got all the fools in town on our side? And Hain't that a big enough majority in any town?

(C) One catches more flies with a spoonful of honey than with twenty casks of vinegar.

(D) Is life so dear or peace so sweet as to be purchased at the price of chains and slavery? Forbid it, Almighty God! I know not what course others may take; but as for me, give me liberty, or give me death!

3. Which is a political speech?

4. Which uses colloquial speech?

5. Which upholds flattery as a means to an end?

6. *Don Giovanni, Eine kleine Nachtmusik,* and *The Magic Flute* are works by

   (A) Ludwig van Beethoven.
   (B) Gian-Carlo Menotti.
   (C) Wolfgang Amadeus Mozart.
   (D) Henry Purcell.

Questions 7–9 refer to the following choices.

(A) There was an Old Man with a beard,
    Who said, "It is just as I feared!
    Two Owls and a Hen,
    Four Larks and a Wren,
    Have all built their nests in my beard!"

(B) I hold that if the Almighty had ever made a set of men that should do all the eating and none of the work, He would have made them with mouths only and no hands; and if he had ever made another class that He intended should do all the work and no eating, He would have made them with hands only and no mouths.

(C) Her feet beneath her petticoat,
    Like little mice, stole in and out,
    As if they feared the light.

(D) Pale Death, with impartial step, knocks at the poor man's cottage and the palaces of kings.

7. Which uses a metaphor?

8. Which is an example of a limerick?

9. Which poem uses a simile?

Questions 10 and 11 refer to the following poem.

Gather ye rosebuds while ye may,
Old time is still a-flying:
  And this same flower that smiles today
Tomorrow will be dying.
  The glorious lamp of heaven, the sun,
The higher he's a-getting,
  The sooner will his race be run,
And nearer he's to setting.

10. Which of the following best describes the theme of the poem?

(A) Father Time is destructive.
(B) Time marches on.
(C) God is waiting.
(D) Races are to be won.

11. The poet uses the examples of the sun and the flowers to show

(A) love of nature.
(B) love of humanity.
(C) the fleeting nature of life.
(D) the arbitrary death of natural things.

Questions 12–14 refer to the following choices.

(A) Knowledge is the only instrument of production that is not subject to diminishing returns.

(B) All happy families resemble one another; every unhappy family is unhappy in its own way.

(C) If my theory of relativity is proven successful, Germany will claim me as a German and France will declare that I am a citizen of the world. Should my theory prove untrue, France will say that I am a German and Germany will declare that I am a Jew.

(D) Lost, yesterday, somewhere between Sunrise and Sunset, two golden hours, each set with sixty diamond minutes. No reward is offered for they are gone forever.

12. Which describes prejudice?

13. Which uses metaphor to show the value of time?

14. Which gives a sociological perspective?

Question 15 refers to the following lines.

The apparition of these faces in the crowd:
Petals on a wet, black bough.

15. Which of the following describes the lines above?

(A) Blank verse
(B) A tercet
(C) A triolet
(D) A quatrain

16. The part of the word *convivial* that means "life" is

(A) *con.*
(B) *convi.*
(C) *ial.*
(D) *viv.*

17. The literal meaning of the prefix *ab-* in the word *abnormal* is

(A) toward.
(B) away from.
(C) within.
(D) under.

18. Which *mis-* has a meaning different from the *mis-* of the three other given words?

    (A) Misanthrope
    (B) Misspell
    (C) Misguided
    (D) Misinformed

19. "I was never so humiliated in all my days!"

    This sentence is an example of

    (A) hyperbole.
    (B) hypodermic.
    (C) hypertrophy.
    (D) hypocrisy.

20. A phrase can NEVER be a

    (A) fragment of a sentence.
    (B) modifier.
    (C) complete thought.
    (D) noun.

21. If someone has *deep pockets*, she has

    (A) apparel with large pockets.
    (B) large amounts of money.
    (C) a long family tree.
    (D) a scarred face.

22. If someone is described as *fly-by-night*, he is

    (A) an evening traveler.
    (B) impermanent.
    (C) like a bat.
    (D) evil.

23. The Greek suffix *-logy* means

    (A) study of.
    (B) writing.
    (C) cylindrical.
    (D) life.

24. The following quote is from a speech by Bertrant Barere, given in 1792.

    "The tree of liberty grows only when watered by the blood of tyrants."

    This quotation is an example of

    (A) simile.
    (B) metaphor.
    (C) onomatopoeia.
    (D) redundancy.

SECTION 2: MATHEMATICS

24 Questions

> *Directions:* Each question or incomplete statement is followed by four answer choices. For each question, select the answer or completion that is best, and blacken the corresponding space on the answer sheet.

1. A nonstop flight from Atlanta to London leaves Atlanta at 8:30 p.m. Eastern Standard Time and arrives in London at 8:15 a.m. Greenwich Mean Time. There is a 5-hour difference in the time between Atlanta and London. Therefore, the amount of time spent in flight was

   (A) 3 hours 30 minutes.
   (B) 6 hours 45 minutes.
   (C) 11 hours 45 minutes.
   (D) 13 hours 30 minutes.

2. Finishing times for the last three runners in the mini-marathon are as follows:

Runner	Hours	Minutes
#1	2	10
#2	2	13
#3	1	55

   How many minutes would Runner #2 have had to take off his time in order to win the race?

   (A) 4
   (B) 6
   (C) 7
   (D) Insufficient data is given to solve the problem.

3.

   If the area of a square postage stamp is .64 inches, what is the length of one of its sides in inches?

   (A) .0008
   (B) .008
   (C) .08
   (D) .8

4.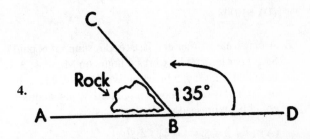

   A gate, (BC), can swing open only 135 degrees because of a rock that is wedged behind it. Without the rock, the gate could swing all the way back against the fence, (AD), to form a straight angle. Find the number of degrees that the gate is prevented from opening (angle ABC in the diagram above).

   (A) 45
   (B) 55
   (C) 60
   (D) 135

Questions 5 and 6 refer to the following information.

A family has a monthly income of $3600. Their monthly expenditures are as shown in the graph below.

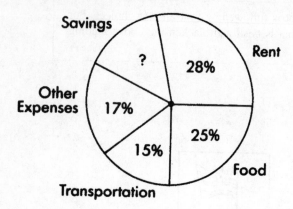

5. How much money does the family save in a year?

   (A) $6,000
   (B) $6,320
   (C) $6,480
   (D) $6,900

6. What is the cost of rent each month?

   (A) $612
   (B) $750
   (C) $1,000
   (D) $1,008

7. A part-time worker at a fast-food restaurant is paid $4.50 per hour. If he works 4 hours on Monday, 3 hours on Tuesday, 5 hours on Wednesday, 4 hours on Thursday, and 4 hours on Saturday, his income could be expressed algebraically as $x =$

   (A) $(4 + 3 + 5 + 4 + 4) + 4.50$
   (B) $(4.50)(4 \times 3 \times 5 \times 4 \times 4)$
   (C) $(4.50)(24)$
   (D) $(4 + 3 + 5 + 4 + 4)(4.50)$

Questions 8–10 are based on the following graph.

CO_2 Production by Yeast from Four Different Sugar Solutions at 40°C.

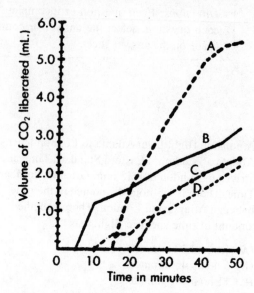

8. From which solution was CO_2 liberated first?

   (A) A
   (B) B
   (C) C
   (D) D

9. In how many minutes was the same volume of CO_2 liberated from solution A and solution B?

   (A) 1.1
   (B) 1.6
   (C) 6
   (D) 20

10. From which solution was the most CO_2 liberated at the end of 30 minutes?

    (A) A
    (B) B
    (C) C
    (D) D

11. A statement that is always true whether its premises are true or false is called a(n)

    (A) syllogism.
    (B) tautology.
    (C) equivalence.
    (D) paradox.

12. Two numbers are relatively prime if their greatest common divisor is 1. Which pair of numbers is relatively prime?

    (A) 3 and 12
    (B) 15 and 28
    (C) 25 and 30
    (D) 18 and 36

13. The sum of 2 coins of value x and 3 coins of value y is 50 cents. If the value of y is 10 cents, which of the following equations can be used to express this relationship?

    (A) $x + y = 5$
    (B) $x + 3y = 50$
    (C) $2x = 50 - 3y$
    (D) $x = 50 - y$

14. 11 to the fourth power may be expressed correctly as

    (A) $11 + 11 + 11 + 11$
    (B) 4^{11}
    (C) $4\sqrt{11}$
    (D) $11(11)(11)(11)$

15. $\dfrac{6,464}{32} =$

    (A) .2
    (B) 2
    (C) 20
    (D) 202

16. Express the integer 30 as a percent.

    (A) 3,000%
    (B) 300%
    (C) 30%
    (D) 3%

17. How many 25-passenger buses are required to transport 105 people?

    (A) 3
    (B) 4
    (C) 5
    (D) 6

18. At 30 mph, a trip from Town A to Town B takes 6 hours. If the speed were doubled, how many hours would the trip take?

    (A) 18
    (B) 12
    (C) 6
    (D) 3

19. $21(73 \times 26)$ is equivalent to all of the following EXCEPT

    (A) $21(73) \times 26$
    (B) $21 \times (73)(26)$
    (C) $(21)(73)(26)$
    (D) $21(73) + 21(26)$

20. Simplify the equation:

    $$5x + 5y + 5z = 5$$

    (A) $x + y + z = 1$
    (B) $21x = 5$
    (C) $5x + 11y + 5z = 1$
    (D) $11x + 5y + 5z = 5$

21. What is the product of all the consecutive integers from -5 to $+5$?

    (A) -120
    (B) -15
    (C) 0
    (D) $+15$

22. What is the mode of the following numbers?

    $$1,2,2,3,3,3,4,4,4,4,5,5,5,5,5$$

    (A) 1
    (B) 2
    (C) 3
    (D) 5

23. 10% of 13 is equivalent to all of the following EXCEPT

    (A) $\dfrac{10}{100}$
    (B) 2% of 5% of 13
    (C) $10\left(\dfrac{13}{100}\right)$
    (D) 13% of 10

24. The scale of a map represents 12 miles as 1 inch. If the distance between two cities on the map is $2\frac{3}{4}$ inches, what is the actual distance, in miles, between the cities?

    (A) 28
    (B) 30
    (C) 33
    (D) 35

SECTION 3: VISUAL AND PERFORMING ARTS

12 Questions

Directions: Each question or incomplete statement is followed by four answer choices. For each question, select the answer or completion that is best, and blacken the corresponding space on the answer sheet.

1. The painting *Bananas and Grapefruit*, shown above, is an example of

   (A) Cubism.
   (B) Pop Art.
   (C) Impressionism.
   (D) Op Art.

2. Which of the following is NOT true regarding the sculpture shown above?

   (A) Solid intertwined forms make up the sculpture.
   (B) Frailty of the figures is demonstrated by the medium used.
   (C) A family unit is suggested by the figures portrayed.
   (D) The texture of the sculpture appears slick.

Questions 3–5 refer to the following.

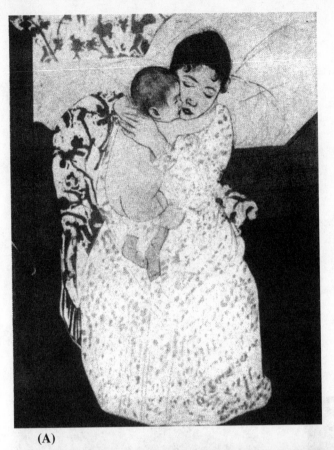

(A)

(B)

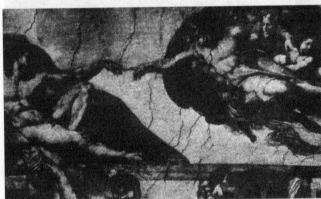

(C)

3. Which painting is by Michelangelo?

4. Which painting is by Mary Cassatt?

5. Which painting is by Rubens?

(D)

Questions 6 and 7 refer to the following.

(A)

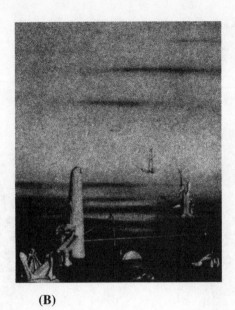

(B)

(C)

(D)

6. Which painting is by Renoir?

7. Which is a surrealist painting?

8. The novel *Don Quixote* was the inspiration for the musical

   (A) *The Wiz.*
   (B) *West Side Story.*
   (C) *Man of La Mancha.*
   (D) *Evita.*

9. Which is NOT associated with Greek theater?

   (A) Masks
   (B) Deus ex machina
   (C) Chorus
   (D) Scene changes

10. All of the following were contemporaries of Shakespeare EXCEPT

    (A) Raleigh.
    (B) Bacon.
    (C) Marlowe.
    (D) Milton.

11. Woody Allen was the major force behind all of the following films EXCEPT

    (A) *Annie Hall.*
    (B) *Sleeper.*
    (C) *All That Jazz.*
    (D) *Interiors.*

12. The "King of Ragtime Composers" was

    (A) Ferdinand "Jelly Roll" Morton.
    (B) Scott Joplin.
    (C) Edward "Duke" Ellington.
    (D) William "Count" Basie.

SECTION 4: PHYSICAL EDUCATION

8 Questions

Directions: Each question or incomplete statement is followed by four choices. Select the best answer, and blacken the corresponding space on the answer sheet.

1. Which of the following terms includes all the activities required to keep an organism alive?

   (A) Growth
   (B) Excretion
   (C) Metabolism
   (D) Nutrition

2. Humans breathe more rapidly during exercise than before because during exercise, the blood contains a(n)

   (A) increased level of oxygen.
   (B) decreased number of red blood cells.
   (C) increased level of carbon dioxide.
   (D) decreased amount of hemoglobin.

3. Smoking may damage the respiratory system because deposits from smoke can

   (A) interfere with ciliary action in the trachea.
   (B) trigger the release of antigens by the alveoli.
   (C) block the transmission of impulses that regulate breathing.
   (D) lower blood pressure in the mucous membranes of the bronchioles.

4. Which portion of the central nervous system coordinates motor activities and aids in maintaining balance?

   (A) Cerebrum
   (B) Cerebellum
   (C) Medulla
   (D) Spinal cord

5. One factor that contributes to the fatigue of a long-distance runner is the accumulation of lactic acid molecules in muscle cells. This lactic acid is produced most directly as a result of

   (A) digestion.
   (B) aerobic respiration.
   (C) photosynthesis.
   (D) anaerobic respiration.

6. In humans, food is moved down the esophagus into the stomach by means of

   (A) peristalsis.
   (B) cyclosis.
   (C) active transport.
   (D) hydrolytic enzymes.

7. Which statement concerning hormones is true?

   (A) Hormones are produced by every cell of an organism.
   (B) Hormones are produced only by the pituitary gland.
   (C) Hormones produced by endocrine glands travel through ducts to various organs.
   (D) Hormones produced in one part of the body may affect the action of another part of the body.

Question 8 refers to the following information.

Suggested Desirable Weights for Heights and Ranges for Adult Males and Females

Height (inches)	Weight (pounds) Men		Women	
58			102	(92–119)
60			107	(96–125)
62	123	(112–141)	113	(102–131)
64	130	(118–148)	120	(108–138)
66	136	(124–156)	128	(114–146)
68	145	(132–166)	136	(122–154)
70	154	(140–174)	144	(130–163)
72	162	(148–184)	152	(138–173)
74	171	(156–194)		
76	181	(164–204)		

Heights and Weights of Selected Adults

Jane	64 inches	150 pounds
Jeff	72 inches	165 pounds
Bill	68 inches	130 pounds
Sara	68 inches	130 pounds
Paul	70 inches	150 pounds

8. Based on the table of desirable weights, which of the following adults should gain some weight?

(A) Jane
(B) Jeff
(C) Bill
(D) Sara

SECTION 5: HUMAN DEVELOPMENT

8 Questions

Directions: Each question or incomplete statement is followed by four answer choices. For each question, select the answer or completion that is best, and blacken the corresponding space on the answer sheet.

1. A child with problems in spatial relations will have difficulty
   - **(A)** understanding one-to-one correspondence.
   - **(B)** visualizing geometric shapes and doing horizontal and vertical examples.
   - **(C)** counting using ordinal numbers.
   - **(D)** learning the communicative properties of multiplication and addition.

2. A child who is inattentive and distractible usually has difficulty developing
   - **(A)** expressive language concepts.
   - **(B)** spatial concepts.
   - **(C)** multiplication facts.
   - **(D)** an understanding of coin values.

3. The concept that cognitive performance is primarily determined by general ability, or "g," is based on a theory developed by
   - **(A)** Horn and Cattell.
   - **(B)** Woodcock and Mather.
   - **(C)** Salvia and Ysseldyke.
   - **(D)** Hammill and Bartell.

4. Which is NOT a component of intelligence or cognitive development?
   - **(A)** Quantitative ability
   - **(B)** Short-term memory
   - **(C)** Graphomotor skills
   - **(D)** Processing speed

5. Which of the following factors tends to inhibit cognitive development in children?
   - I. Personality style
   - II. Physical health
   - III. Anxiety
   - IV. Family structure
   - **(A)** I, II, and IV only
   - **(B)** II, III, and IV only
   - **(C)** I and III only
   - **(D)** I, II, and III only

6. This author believes in the role experience plays in intellectual development. He feels the school environment should match the individual student. He attacks the concepts of fixed intelligence, predetermined development, and the unimportance of early experience. These views primarily express the ideas of
   - **(A)** Jensen.
   - **(B)** Piaget.
   - **(C)** Bruner.
   - **(D)** Hunt.

7. A student with this problem cannot participate in a traditional academic program. This student can learn skills primarily through the use of behavior modification. These statements BEST describe a student who is
   - **(A)** learning disabled.
   - **(B)** mentally retarded.
   - **(C)** emotionally disturbed.
   - **(D)** orthopedically handicapped.

8. Peer relations become increasingly active. Communication expands to include a wide array of nonverbal and verbal responses. Identification with and imitation of models is responsible for rapid social development at this stage. Achievement-oriented behavior develops, depending upon the prompts and reinforcement received. This best describes social-emotional development occurring during which of the following age spans?
   - **(A)** Birth to one year
   - **(B)** One to three years
   - **(C)** Three to six years
   - **(D)** Six to thirteen years

SECTION 6: HISTORY/SOCIAL SCIENCES

22 Questions

> *Directions:* Each question or incomplete statement is followed by four answer choices. For each question, select the answer or completion that is best, and blacken the corresponding space on the answer sheet.

1. Social psychology is a field of study concerned with

    (A) the effect of group membership on the individual.
    (B) human behavior in crowds or mobs.
    (C) changes in values and attitudes over the individual's life span.
    (D) the process of learning the traditions of one's culture.

2. Sociological research is likely to include all of the following EXCEPT

    (A) independent variables.
    (B) dependent variables.
    (C) operational definitions.
    (D) haphazard sampling.

Questions 3–5 refer to the figure below.

3. Which of the following groups or situations does the restaurant in the cartoon represent?

    (A) The fast-food industry
    (B) Worldwide poverty and hunger
    (C) The oil crisis
    (D) The American people

4. Which of the following is a hypothesis suggested by this cartoon?

    (A) Americans eat out a great deal, especially at inexpensive fast-food restaurants.
    (B) Americans are unwilling to accept newcomers easily. As a result, immigrants tend to live in isolated groups.
    (C) Americans have become much more open to dietary innovations.
    (D) A wide variety of nationalities make up American culture.

5. Which of the following statements is best supported by evidence presented in this cartoon?

    (A) There is a wide variety of foods offered at fast-food restaurants.
    (B) The United States is made up of immigrants from many nations.
    (C) The cost of food keeps rising.
    (D) American food is imported from Europe.

6. The social scientist examining social stratification would be LEAST interested in which of the following?

    (A) The impact of education on upward mobility
    (B) The distribution of property in a given society
    (C) Which occupations are thought to be most prestigious
    (D) The impact of race on mortality and fertility

7. The Napoleonic Code was a

(A) military strategy.
(B) style of politics.
(C) style of etiquette.
(D) legal system.

8. The *Bay of Pigs* refers to which of the following events?

(A) A vote in Congress to permit the bombing of North Vietnam
(B) An anti-Castro invasion of Cuba
(C) The invasion of Cambodia by South Vietnamese troops
(D) The American refusal to permit the building of Soviet missiles in the Western Hemisphere

Questions 9–11 refer to the following statement.

"Nations sent early explorers for three reasons: gold, glory, and God. Later explorers were sent out for raw materials, trading posts, and places to colonize."

9. According to this statement, which of the following could be considered an early explorer or exploration?

(A) The Dutch East India Company trading with the Native Americans for fur
(B) Sieur de la Salle setting up trading posts
(C) James Oglethorpe settling in Savannah, Georgia
(D) Francisco Coronado searching for the Seven Cities of Cíbola in Arizona and New Mexico

10. According to this statement, which of the following could be considered a later explorer or exploration?

(A) Cortés stealing the Incas' treasures from the Yucatán
(B) Sir Francis Drake returning to England with a cargo of Spanish silver
(C) Lewis and Clark's mapping of the territory west of the Mississippi acquired in the Louisiana Purchase
(D) Ponce de León searching for the Fountain of Youth

11. According to this passage, which of the following motivated early explorers?

(A) Hopes of fame and fortune
(B) A desire for better living conditions
(C) A need for religious freedom
(D) A belief that the monarchy was always right

12. *Business cycle* refers to

(A) profits and losses of a corporation over a one-year period.
(B) fluctuations in corporate profits in a given region.
(C) upswings and downswings in the economy.
(D) the life span of a business or corporation.

Questions 13 and 14 are based on the following graph.

**Growth of Population
in the United States, 1870–1910**

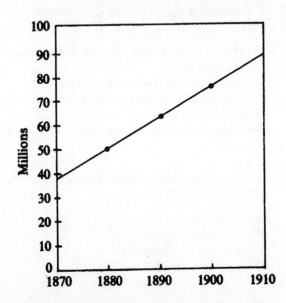

13. Between 1870 and 1910, it would be most accurate to say that the population of the United States

(A) more than doubled.
(B) almost doubled.
(C) increased by 40 percent.
(D) increased by 50 percent.

14. According to the information given above, which of the following statements is true?

(A) The rate of population increase between 1870 and 1880 was approximately the same as the rate of population increase between 1890 and 1900.
(B) The percentage of foreign-born Americans in the United States between 1900 and 1910 was greater than the percentage of foreign-born Americans in the United States from 1870 to 1880.
(C) Between 1880 and 1890, immigration accounted for approximately 10 percent of the population.
(D) The rate of population increase grew steadily from 1870 to 1910.

Questions 15–18 refer to the following information.

Each of the following statements describes an aspect of the application-review process. Choose the system in which the process would most likely occur. The categories may be used more than once in the set of items, but no one question has more than one best answer.

Throughout American history, people have been selected for positions within the government and in private companies in several ways. Some of these ways are still used today; others have fallen into disfavor. Listed below are five methods that have been used for candidate evaluation and promotion.

1. **The spoils system—**

    Candidates are selected for positions based on their membership in a political party and/or for supporting their candidate's election bid.

2. **The merit system—**

    An impartial body tests and evaluates job applicants.

3. **The "Old Boy" network—**

    People are placed in high-status jobs because they are members of the upper-middle and upper class.

4. **Nepotism—**

    Positions are awarded based on a candidate's relationship to a person within the company.

5. **Networking—**

    People look for positions through social contacts.

---

15. In 1883 Congress passed the Pendleton Act, setting up the Civil Service Commission. This impartial body was to test and rate applicants for federal jobs. Which system did this Act establish?

    (A) The spoils system
    (B) The merit system
    (C) The "Old Boy" network
    (D) Nepotism

16. Joshua Seth's father is the president of a major oil company. His mother is active in many charitable organizations. In addition, his parents are friends with many socially important people. Joshua, like his father and grandfather, attended the exclusive and expensive preparatory high school, Wooded Hills. When Joshua graduated from an Ivy League college, his father's friend told him about an excellent position in an investment banking firm. Under which system did Joshua receive his job?

    (A) The spoils system
    (B) The merit system
    (C) The "Old Boy" network
    (D) Nepotism

17. In 1939 Congress passed the Hatch Act, providing that federal employees may not be asked for political contributions and may not actively participate in political affairs. The Act was passed to lessen the influence of

    (A) the spoils system.
    (B) the merit system.
    (C) the "Old Boy" network.
    (D) nepotism.

18. Jessica Dawn was a loyal volunteer for Senator Halloway's campaign. After the senator won reelection, Jessica Dawn was given a well-paying position on the senator's staff. Which system was the senator using to justify giving Jessica Dawn a job?

    (A) The spoils system
    (B) The merit system
    (C) The "Old Boy" network
    (D) Nepotism

Questions 19–21 refer to the following paragraph and chart.

The following chart shows how the U.S. government supported scientific research and development (R&D) over an eleven-year period and how that money was distributed among the various states. The bars indicate differences during three time periods.

Federal R&D support to the 10 states leading in such support in 1986 for selected years

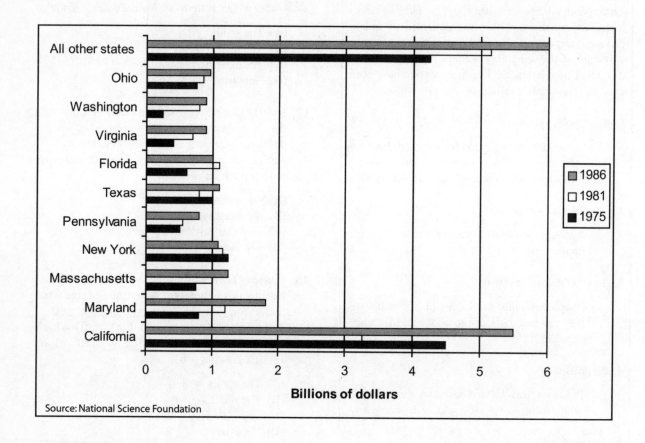

Source: National Science Foundation

19. Based on this chart, what happened to money for scientific research and development over the time period shown?

(A) It increased dramatically.
(B) It decreased dramatically.
(C) It probably just kept up with inflation.
(D) It enabled dramatic scientific breakthroughs.

20. Which combination of states had the largest share of funds in 1981?

(A) California, Pennsylvania, and Texas
(B) Maryland, Massachusetts, and New York
(C) California, Florida, and Texas
(D) Pennsylvania, Texas, and Florida

21. Which state had the largest percentage decline in funds over the time period of the chart?

(A) Florida
(B) New York
(C) California
(D) Texas

22. The caste system of social stratification connotes all of the following EXCEPT that

(A) caste membership is hereditary.
(B) caste membership is permanent.
(C) marriage within one's caste is required.
(D) an individual can change caste by gaining wealth.

SECTION 7: SCIENCE

22 Questions

Directions: Each question or incomplete statement is followed by four answer choices. For each question, select the answer or completion that is best, and blacken the corresponding space on the answer sheet.

---

1. Human interferon can be used to fight viral infections. This means that interferon may be helpful in curing

   (A) diseases that are responsible for deformities.
   (B) diseases that are genetic in origin.
   (C) problems related to psychological stress.
   (D) the common cold.

2. "Opposites attract" is the fundamental law of

   (A) momentum.
   (B) forces.
   (C) magnetism.
   (D) gravitation.

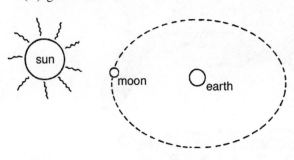

3. The illustration above is an example of

   (A) the phases of the moon.
   (B) the seasons of the year.
   (C) a lunar eclipse.
   (D) a solar eclipse.

4. All the following tend to purify water EXCEPT

   (A) bacteria.
   (B) oxidation.
   (C) sedimentation.
   (D) chlorination.

5. Cyclic changes occur at a definite rate and are repeated regularly. All of the following are examples of cyclic changes EXCEPT

   (A) the change from day to night.
   (B) the change of seasons.
   (C) the tides.
   (D) earthquakes.

6. Below is a graph describing the results of an experiment that was done by a biologist. The scientist put live bacteria and growth medium (food for bacteria to live on) into a closed container and then counted the number of live bacteria every half hour for a 16-hour period.

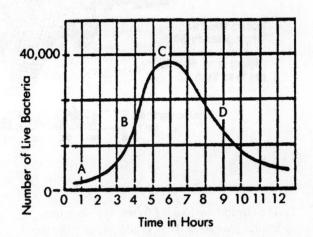

Which of the following can be inferred from the results of this experiment?

   (A) Bacteria can grow anywhere, anytime.
   (B) Bacteria can be easily eliminated with cleaners.
   (C) It takes a very long time for bacteria to grow.
   (D) It is important to store leftover food correctly.

Questions 7 and 8 are based on the information below.

Few areas in the United States are free from thunderstorms and their attendant hazards, but some areas have more storms than others. The map below shows the incidence of thunderstorm days—days on which thunderstorms are observed—for the United States.

Incidence of Thunderstorms

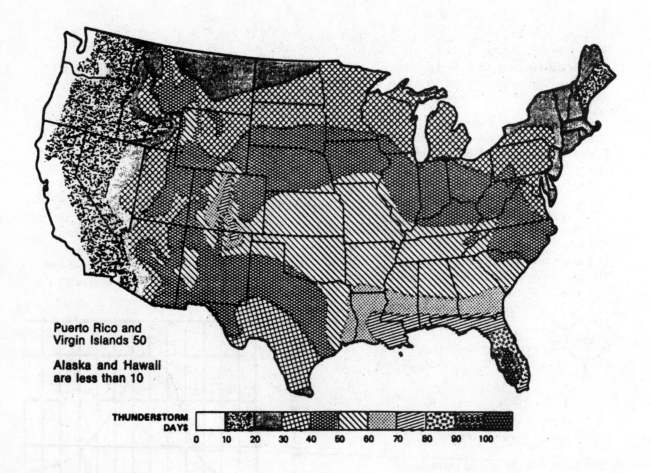

Puerto Rico and
Virgin Islands 50

Alaska and Hawaii
are less than 10

THUNDERSTORM DAYS

0 10 20 30 40 50 60 70 80 90 100

7. The Garcias are looking forward to a carefree camping vacation. They would like to avoid the frequent thunderstorms that spoiled their last camping trip. Based on the information in the map above, which region of the country would they be LEAST likely to choose for their next vacation?

(A) California, Oregon, Washington
(B) Florida, Georgia, Alabama
(C) Kentucky, Virginia, West Virginia
(D) Missouri, Iowa, Illinois

8. If they are caught in a thunderstorm despite their careful planning, they should do any of the following EXCEPT

(A) stay inside a solid building.
(B) remain in an all-metal automobile.
(C) stand under a tall tree.
(D) go to a low place such as a ravine or valley.

9. Which of the following processes is responsible for clothes drying on the line on a warm summer day?

(A) Freezing
(B) Condensation
(C) Sublimation
(D) Evaporation

10. Conductors are materials through which electrons can flow freely. Most metals make good electrical conductors, but of all, silver is the best. Next to silver, copper is a good conductor, with aluminum following closely behind.

    Which of the following best explains why copper is the metal most widely used in electrical wiring?

    (A) It is the best conductor of electricity.
    (B) It has a high resistance to electricity.
    (C) It is cheaper than aluminum.
    (D) It is a better conductor than aluminum and cheaper than silver.

11. Species that practice internal fertilization are characterized by a

    (A) fetus that develops entirely in the oceans.
    (B) wide degree of care for their young.
    (C) parental noninterest once the eggs have been laid.
    (D) diminished potency as they reach maturity.

12. As an object sinks in water, the pressure on the object

    (A) decreases.
    (B) increases.
    (C) remains the same.
    (D) first increases then decreases.

13. Which of the following offers the best summary of the Second Law of Thermodynamics?

    (A) Energy transformations are not 100 percent efficient.
    (B) The ultimate energy source in the biosphere is our sun.
    (C) Energy cannot be created or destroyed.
    (D) For each action, there exists an equal and opposite reaction.

14. Consider the following three pieces of evidence.

    I.   Identical fossil species of terrestrial plants and animals, older than Carboniferous, are found in Africa, South America, India, and Australia.

    II. The Cape Mountains of South Africa are the same type of folded mountain and made up of the same type of rocks as the mountains south of Buenos Aires in South America.

    III. The rock on the crests of the midoceanic ridges is younger than the rock on either side of the crest.

    Based upon this evidence, which of the following is the most probable conclusion?

    (A) The earth has been formed by the shrinking and cooling of an originally molten mass; this process ended prior to the Carboniferous.
    (B) Radioactive heat has caused thermal convection currents in the mantle of the earth.
    (C) Since its creation, the earth's surface has changed little.
    (D) Prior to the Carboniferous, all the land on the surface of the earth was one great continent, which subsequently began to split apart.

15. A white-cell count is helpful in determining whether a patient has

    (A) an infection.
    (B) antitoxins.
    (C) diabetes.
    (D) heart disease.

16. If a doctor describes a patient as dehydrated, the patient

    (A) has a contagious disease.
    (B) needs insulin.
    (C) cannot manufacture chlorophyll.
    (D) has lost a great deal of water.

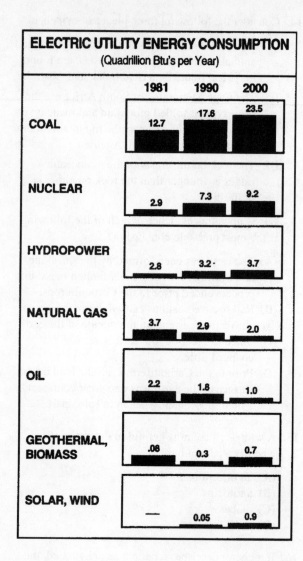

ELECTRIC UTILITY ENERGY CONSUMPTION
(Quadrillion Btu's per Year)

	1981	1990	2000
COAL	12.7	17.6	23.5
NUCLEAR	2.9	7.3	9.2
HYDROPOWER	2.8	3.2	3.7
NATURAL GAS	3.7	2.9	2.0
OIL	2.2	1.8	1.0
GEOTHERMAL, BIOMASS	.08	0.3	0.7
SOLAR, WIND	—	0.05	0.9

NORMAL TEMPERATURE DURING JANUARY FOR SELECTED CITIES

	MAXIMUM	MINIMUM
San Francisco, CA	55°	42°
Los Angeles, CA	67	48
Phoenix, AZ	65	39
Denver, CO	43	16
Miami, FL	75	59
Atlanta, GA	51	33
Chicago, IL	29	14
New Orleans, LA	62	43
Boston, MA	36	23
St. Paul, MN	20	2
New York City, NY	37	26
Portland, OR	44	34
Philadelphia, PA	39	24
Houston, TX	62	41

19. A travel agent uses the chart above to advise clients about weather conditions in the cities they plan to visit. Based on this temperature chart and the travel plans that follow, which of the travel agent's clients can expect to experience the widest range of temperatures on the trip scheduled?

(A) Pat, who will spend the week of January 12 in New York, Chicago, and Denver
(B) Julie, who will spend the first two weeks of January in Miami, Atlanta, and New Orleans
(C) Joe, who will tour New Orleans, Phoenix, and Houston the last week of January
(D) Mike, whose travel plans include visits to Phoenix, Los Angeles, and San Francisco in mid-January

17. Based on the chart above, the fuel that supplies the greatest amount of energy is

(A) nuclear.
(B) natural gas.
(C) coal.
(D) hydropower.

18. This planet revolves around the sun in an orbit between that of Venus and Mars. It is known to be covered by oceans and some land; it has but a single moon. Name the planet.

(A) Jupiter
(B) Saturn
(C) Earth
(D) Mercury

20. Which of the following common electrical devices contains an electromagnet?

(A) Iron
(B) Telephone
(C) Water heater
(D) Toaster

21. When all the colors of the spectrum are fused, the resulting light is

(A) red.
(B) white.
(C) blue.
(D) yellow.

22. The moon rotates once while going around the earth once. As a result,

(A) the moon follows an elliptical path.
(B) the sun is eclipsed by the moon every seven years.
(C) only one side of the moon faces the earth.
(D) every fourth year is a leap year.

MSAT: CONTENT AREA EXERCISES

The Multiple Subjects Assessment for Teachers Content Area Exercises consist of 3 hours of short essay questions. There are 18 essays. A nonprogrammable calculator is allowed.

Content areas include:

1. Literature and Language Studies

2. Mathematics

3. Visual and Performing Arts

4. Physical Education

5. Human Development

6. History/Social Sciences

7. Science

These essays are scored from 0 (totally incorrect) to 3 (best possible score).

1. LITERATURE AND LANGUAGE STUDIES

Question 1 refers to the following paragraph.

Professor William J. Requin is presently developing a new theory about gene mutation. He was born in Elmsford, Maryland, on January 24, 1953. He graduated from the University of Maryland in 1975. He received a medical degree in 1980. He helped map the structure of DNA molecules from 1983 to 1987. The experience greatly enhanced his present research in gene mutation.

1. Describe three ways in which the author can edit this paragraph so as to have fewer choppy and monotonous sentences.

2. Using any fictional literary work, describe how the author used contemporary sources to develop three themes within his or her written work.

Question 3 refers to the following poem.

First, Nature builds the body.

A house with doors of sense.

Wherein a strange child, the Spirit is born.

Tools he finds and uses at his pleasure.

Leaving the house, it crumbles,

But the architect always builds anew

And beckons the heavenly guest again to earthly accommodation.

—Friedrich Ruckert

3. Describe the basic theme of this poem in terms of its view of death. Focus on the author's philosophical view of death.

2. MATHEMATICS

1. If the diagonals of a two-dimensional parallelogram are perpendicular and congruent, then how can we describe the shape of this geometric form?

Question 2 refers to the following equation.

$$c(a \times b) = ca \times cb$$

2. Describe what is wrong with this equation in terms of the mathematical property or properties being used.

3. When rolling a die, the probability of getting a six is $\frac{1}{6}$, while the probability of rolling another number is $\frac{5}{6}$. If you roll the die twenty times, how can we determine the probability of rolling a six exactly eight times?

3. VISUAL AND PERFORMING ARTS

Question 1 refers to the following painting.

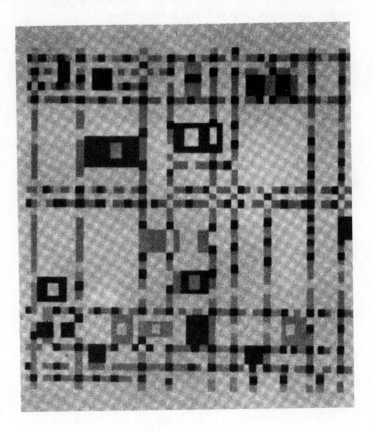

1. Briefly discuss the stylistic elements and principles of design used in the painting above.

2. Discuss the importance and uses of flying buttresses. Include structural and aesthetic purposes.

4. PHYSICAL EDUCATION

1. Define and give two examples of open skills.

2. Describe two different goals of a physical education program on the elementary level and how to reach them.

5. HUMAN DEVELOPMENT

1. Discuss, describe, and analyze two differences between the Freudian and behavioral approaches to child development.

2. Even though a child has the ability to do well in school, he or she may fail because of the concept of the "self-fulfilling prophecy." Describe this concept and how it affects a student's behavior and achievement.

6. HISTORY/SOCIAL SCIENCES

Question 1 refers to the following quotation.

A well regulated Militia, being necessary to the security of a free state, the right of the people to keep and bear arms shall not be infringed.

—Second Amendment, U.S. Constitution

1. Use this amendment to create arguments to justify and oppose gun-control legislation. Give specific historical or legal precedents to justify each argument.

2. Describe how geography affected Japan and China historically. Discuss geographic influences upon social, economic, and religious developments.

Question 3 refers to the following graph.

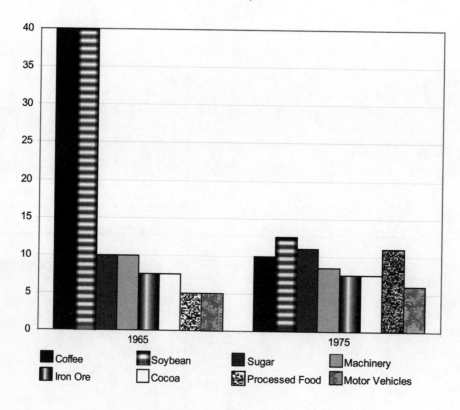

Brazil's Exports

3. Describe three possible reasons for the change in Brazil's exports from 1965 to 1975. Discuss geographic, social, and economic factors.

7. SCIENCE

1. Describe how scientists use radioactive isotopes to determine the age of various geographic forms. Identify and discuss two practical applications of radiometric dating.

2. Using the concepts of nuclear fusion and gravity, describe the formation and life cycle of a sun-like star.

3. Describe how effort and resistance turn energy into work in the simple machines listed below:

>   lever
>   pulley
>   inclined plane

Illustrate practical applications for one of these machines.

ANSWER KEY

Section 1: Literature and Language Studies	Section 2: Mathematics	Section 3: Visual and Performing Arts	Section 4: Physical Education
1. C	1. B	1. B	1. C
2. B	2. D	2. B	2. C
3. D	3. D	3. C	3. A
4. B	4. A	4. A	4. B
5. C	5. C	5. D	5. D
6. C	6. D	6. D	6. A
7. D	7. D	7. B	7. D
8. A	8. B	8. C	8. C
9. C	9. D	9. D	
10. B	10. A	10. D	
11. C	11. B	11. C	
12. C	12. B	12. B	
13. D	13. C		
14. B	14. D		
15. A	15. D		
16. D	16. A		
17. B	17. C		
18. A	18. D		
19. A	19. D		
20. C	20. A		
21. B	21. C		
22. B	22. D		
23. A	23. B		
24. B	24. C		

Section 5: Human Development	Section 6: History/Social Sciences	Section 7: Science
1. B	1. A	1. D
2. C	2. D	2. C
3. A	3. D	3. D
4. C	4. D	4. A
5. D	5. B	5. D
6. D	6. D	6. D
7. B	7. D	7. B
8. C	8. B	8. C
	9. D	9. D
	10. C	10. D
	11. A	11. B
	12. C	12. B
	13. A	13. A
	14. A	14. D
	15. B	15. A
	16. C	16. D
	17. A	17. C
	18. A	18. C
	19. C	19. B
	20. C	20. B
	21. B	21. B
	22. D	22. C

ANSWERS AND EXPLANATIONS

Section 1: Literature and Language Studies

1. **The correct answer is (C).** These lines come from the prophet Isaiah in the Old Testament.

2. **The correct answer is (B).** The lines describe a total peace that will exist when the Messiah comes.

3. **The correct answer is (D).** Patrick Henry's famous oration is a political speech from Revolutionary War times.

4. **The correct answer is (B).** Mark Twain's use of "hain't we got . . ." is an example of colloquial speech.

5. **The correct answer is (C).** Catching more flies with honey (flattery) than vinegar (punishment) is using flattery as a means to an end.

6. **The correct answer is (C).** Mozart (1756–91) was an Austrian whom many consider to be the greatest composer of all time. He began composing at the age of 5 and wrote his first symphony at 9. In all, he wrote more than 600 works, and his mastery of all classical forms makes his work the epitome of classical music.

7. **The correct answer is (D).** A metaphor is a figure of speech that compares one thing to another without the use of "like" or "as." Death is portrayed as knocking upon the door of the poor and the rich alike.

8. **The correct answer is (A).** A limerick is a light or humorous poem of five lines.

9. **The correct answer is (C).** A simile is a figure of speech that compares one thing to another using the terms "like" or "as."

10. **The correct answer is (B).** The poet is telling readers to appreciate things while they last, because time moves quickly and nothing lasts forever.

11. **The correct answer is (C).** The fact that flowers die and the sun sets shows that life's pleasures do not last.

12. **The correct answer is (C).** Einstein states that if he is proved wrong, each nationality will disavow him and claim he belonged elsewhere.

13. **The correct answer is (D).** "Two golden hours, each set with sixty diamond minutes . . ." is used to show how valuable time is. It can never be recaptured.

14. **The correct answer is (B).** Tolstoy, in the first sentence of his classic work *Anna Karenina*, discusses the sociology of families.

15. **The correct answer is (A).** The lines are blank verse, unrhymed iambic pentameter.

16. **The correct answer is (D).** The Latin root *viv* means "life."

17. **The correct answer is (B).** The prefix *ab-* means "away from." *Abnormal* is literally "away from the norm."

18. **The correct answer is (A).** The *mis* in *misanthrope* means "hated." The *mis* in the remaining choices means "wrong."

19. **The correct answer is (A).** Hyperbole is an exaggeration.

20. **The correct answer is (C).** A phrase cannot be a complete thought. A clause, on the other hand, can be a complete thought.

21. **The correct answer is (B).** *Deep pockets* refers to large amounts of available money.

22. **The correct answer is (B).** *Fly-by-night* means "impermanent."

23. **The correct answer is (A).** *Logy* means "study of something." Thus, biology is the study of life.

24. **The correct answer is (B).** A metaphor is a comparison between two things without the use of "like" or "as."

Section 2: Mathematics

1. **The correct answer is (B).** Add the time difference (5 hours) to the starting time:

   8:30 p.m. EST + 5 hours = 1:30 a.m. GMT
   1:30 a.m. to 8:15 a.m. = 6 hours 45 minutes

2. **The correct answer is (D).** To find out how much faster Runner #2 must run, we need to know the time of the winner. Without this, there is insufficient information to solve the problem.

3. **The correct answer is (D).** Know the squares of the numbers from 1 to 10. Here, 8 squared is 64. Reversing this, the square root of 64 is 8. And the square root of .64 is .8.

4. **The correct answer is (A).** Angle ABC and Angle DBC (135°) are supplementary angles. That means the sum of these two angles is 180°.

   Angle ABC + 135° = 180°
   Angle ABC = 180° − 135° = 45°

5. **The correct answer is (C).** First calculate the amount spent on known items: 28 + 25 + 15 + 17 = 85%. Subtract this figure from 100% to find out how much was saved: 100 − 85 = 15%. Multiply by total income, $3,600: .15 × 3,600 = $540 in 1 month, and 12 × 540 = $6,480 in 1 year.

6. **The correct answer is (D).** Since 28% is spent on rent, the cost of rent each month is .28 × $3,600 = $1,008.

7. **The correct answer is (D).** Hourly Wage × Hours Worked = Total Income ($4.50)(4 + 3 + 5 + 4 + 4) = Total Income. The actual numerical solution is not asked for, just the equation you would use to solve the problem, which is choice (D).

8. **The correct answer is (B).** The curve for solution B (the solid line) shows that CO_2 was liberated after about 5 minutes, well before any of the other solutions showed CO_2 production.

9. **The correct answer is (D).** The curves for solution A and solution B intersect at a point before 20 minutes. At this point, 1.6 mL of CO_2 was liberated by both solutions. This can be determined by drawing a line horizontally from the point of intersection to the scale at the left.

10. **The correct answer is (A).** At the end of 30 minutes, the most CO_2 was liberated from solution A. Draw a horizontal line from this point to the scale at the left. The volume of liberated CO_2 is 3.4 mL.

11. **The correct answer is (B).** A statement that is true independently of the truth of its premises is a tautology.

12. **The correct answer is (B).** The greatest common divisor (GCD) of 3 and 12 is 3, the GCD of 25 and 30 is 5, the GCD of 18 and 36 is 18, and the GCD of 35 and 60 is 5. Because 15 and 28 have no common divisors other than 1, their GCD is 1 and they are relatively prime.

13. **The correct answer is (C).** Write the equation for the information given:

   2 coins of value x = 2x
   3 coins of value x = 3y
   2x + 3y = 50 cents
   Therefore, 2x = 50 − 3y

14. **The correct answer is (D).** $11^4 = 11(11)(11)(11)$

15. **The correct answer is (D).** $\dfrac{6{,}464}{32} = 202$

16. **The correct answer is (A).** To get the percent, multiply by 100.

   $$30(100) = 3{,}000\%$$

17. **The correct answer is (C).** $\dfrac{105}{25} = 4.2$. Therefore, 5 buses are required.

18. **The correct answer is (D).** Doubling the speed makes the trip take half the time.

19. **The correct answer is (D).** Multiplication does NOT distribute over multiplication.

20. **The correct answer is (A).** Divide both sides of the equation by 5:

   $$\frac{5x + 5y + 5z}{5} = \frac{5}{5}$$
   $$x + y + z = 1$$

21. **The correct answer is (C).**
   $$-5(-4)(-3)(-2)(-1)(0)(1)(2)(3)(4)(5) = 0$$

22. **The correct answer is (D).** The mode is the most frequent number.

23. **The correct answer is (B).**

   $$2\% \text{ of } 5\% = \frac{2}{100} \cdot \frac{5}{100} = \frac{10}{10{,}000} = .1\%, \text{ not } 10\%$$

24. **The correct answer is (C).** $2\frac{3}{4} \times 12 = 33$

Section 3: Visual and Performing Arts

1. **The correct answer is (B).** Lichtenstein's *Bananas and Grapefruit* (1972) is an example of Pop Art.

2. **The correct answer is (B).** All the answers are applicable to the sculpture pictured except choice (B). In this sculpture by Henry Moore, titled *Family Group*, the medium is bronze, and its use suggests anything but frailty.

3. **The correct answer is (C).** Michelangelo: *Creation of Man*, Sistine Chapel (1508–12).

4. **The correct answer is (A).** Mary Cassatt: *Maternal Caress* (1891).

5. **The correct answer is (D).** Peter Paul Rubens: *An Allegory of Peace and War* (1629). The other work shown is choice (B), Leonardo Da Vinci: *Mona Lisa* (c. 1503–05).

6. **The correct answer is (D).** Pierre-Auguste Renoir: *On the Terrace* (1881).

7. **The correct answer is (B).** Yves Tanguy: *The Sun in its Casket* (1937). The other works shown are:

   Choice (A), James Abbott McNeill Whistler: *Carlyle* (1872).

   Choice (C), Claude Monet: *The Cliff at Fécamp* (1881).

8. **The correct answer is (C).** *Don Quixote*, Miguel de Cervantes's (1547–1616) masterpiece, contains the characters Don Quixote, Sancho Panza, and Dulcinea, as well as the broken-down horse, Rocinante.

9. **The correct answer is (D).** The Greek dramatists observed the unity of place and therefore did not employ changes of scene.

10. **The correct answer is (D).** The English poet John Milton, author of *Paradise Lost*, lived from 1608–74; Shakespeare lived from 1564–1616.

11. **The correct answer is (C).** *All That Jazz* is associated with Bob Fosse, as are *Sweet Charity* and *Cabaret*.

12. **The correct answer is (B).** Scott Joplin (1868–1917), the pianist-songwriter who composed *Maple Leaf Rag*, *Wall Street Rag*, and *Sugar Cane Rag*, was the major ragtime composer of his time.

Section 4: Physical Education

1. **The correct answer is (C).** Metabolism is the term used to incorporate all processes designed to keep an organism alive.

2. **The correct answer is (C).** During exercise, the rate of respiration increases. Carbon dioxide is a waste product produced during cellular respiration.

3. **The correct answer is (A).** Cilia move mucus with foreign material out of the trachea. Smoking incapacitates the cilia.

4. **The correct answer is (B).** The cerebellum is that part of the brain that coordinates motor activities and helps maintain balance.

5. **The correct answer is (D).** Anaerobic respiration produces the lactic acid in the muscles of a long-distance runner.

6. **The correct answer is (A).** Peristalsis is the name for the muscular contractions by which food moves down the esophagus into the stomach.

7. **The correct answer is (D).** The endocrine glands produce hormones, which then travel through the bloodstream to particular organs.

8. **The correct answer is (C).** The desirable weight for a man 68 inches tall is 145. At 130, Bill is underweight.

Section 5: Human Development

1. **The correct answer is (B).** Choice (A) is wrong because this concept has to do with the ability to learn how to count in a meaningful fashion. Choice (C) is related to one-to-one correspondence and not spatial relations. Choice (D) is wrong because this skill is related to the concept of reversibility.

2. **The correct answer is (C).** A child who is inattentive and distractible usually will have difficulty developing multiplication facts. This skill requires concentration and memory. Choice (B) is obviously incorrect because students with attention deficit disorders may have no difficulty with perception and fine-motor ability. Understanding coin value, choice (D), does not necessitate a high degree of concentration and attention. Choice (A) has nothing to do with the problem at hand.

3. **The correct answer is (A).** The concept of "g" theory comes from the work of Horn and Cattell. Woodcock and Mather do utilize "g" theory in the development of their achievement and cognitive batteries, but they did not develop the theory per se. Choice (C) is wrong because these two authors are closely associated with their critical research pertaining to educational and psychological testing. Hammill and Bartell, choice (D), are best known for describing remedial techniques for students who have learning problems.

4. **The correct answer is (C).** Most intelligence tests do not consider handwriting to be a measurable component of intelligence. The other choices are usually assessed when given a standardized intelligence test.

5. **The correct answer is (D).** Personality style (Item I) is known to inhibit cognitive development—especially if the child tends to respond impulsively rather than carefully. It is obvious that Item II also inhibits cognitive development. A child in poor health would have a great deal of difficulty in learning. It is also obvious that a child with high levels of anxiety may become blocked and do poorly on a standardized test (Item III). Item IV is not a correct response because research demonstrates that family structure has very little to do with the development of cognitive skills.

6. **The correct answer is (D).** The views described are most closely associated with Hunt. Using twin and animal studies, Hunt concluded that experience plays a critical role in the development of cognitive ability. On the other hand, both Piaget, choice (B), and Bruner, choice (C), believed in fixed biological stages of cognitive development. Choice (A) is wrong because Jensen believed that genetics played a major role in determining intelligence.

7. **The correct answer is (B).** A severely mentally retarded student is being described. Such a student cannot do traditional academic work and is usually taught through the use of task analysis and behavior modification. Students with the other three handicapping conditions can usually be taught a traditional academic program with modifications.

8. **The correct answer is (C).** The passage best describes social-emotional development from 3 to 6 years old. Choice (A) is obviously wrong because at this stage, a child is helpless and dependent. Choice (B) is incorrect because language is simple at this stage and socially aggressive behaviors are often manifested. Choice (D) is also wrong because at this latter stage, moral development continues and a child begins to identify with ethnic, racial, and religious groups.

Section 6: History/Social Sciences

1. **The correct answer is (A).** Choice (D) describes the process of socialization. The other answers are inappropriate.

2. **The correct answer is (D).** Haphazard sampling is unlikely to yield useful results. In the sample survey, sociologists select a sample that is representative of a larger population.

3. **The correct answer is (D).** The restaurant represents the American population with its many different kinds of people.

4. **The correct answer is (D).** The cartoon suggests America is made up of a number of different nationalities, as indicated by foods representative of each culture.

5. **The correct answer is (B).** The different foods indicate the United States has been settled by people from many other countries.

6. **The correct answer is (D).** The researcher examining social stratification is interested in the distribution of power, property, and prestige within a society. These factors are mentioned in all answer options except choice (D).

7. **The correct answer is (D).** The Napoleonic Code, derived from Roman law, went into effect in 1805 and remained a lasting monument to Napoleonic rule. Its five sections covered all areas of civil law, from domestic relations to property rights and commercial life.

8. **The correct answer is (B).** In 1961, about 1,000 Cuban exiles, who had left Cuba during its revolution, staged a brief, unsuccessful invasion of Cuba with the assistance of the Central Intelligence Agency. The Bay of Pigs was the site of the invasion. The exiles had been led to believe that the Cuban people would welcome them as liberators, but this never occurred. Instead, the Bay of Pigs fiasco increased Castro's animosity toward the United States and caused further tensions between the two nations.

9. **The correct answer is (D).** Francisco Coronado was looking for gold in the American Southwest. The Seven Cities of Cíbola were reported by Native Americans to be rich in gold, a precious metal sought by explorers.

10. **The correct answer is (C).** Mapping land already acquired implies Lewis and Clark were seeking raw materials and places to colonize. Choices (A) and (B) sought treasure; choice (D) sought fame.

11. **The correct answer is (A).** "Glory" is fame and fortune.

12. **The correct answer is (C).** *Business cycle* refers to fluctuations in the economy as a whole.

13. **The correct answer is (A).** Between 1870 and 1910, the population of the United States rose from almost 40 million to approximately 90 million, or more than doubled.

14. **The correct answer is (A).** From 1870 to 1880, the population rose from about 40 million to about 50 million, for about a 25 percent rate of population increase. From 1890 to 1900, the population rose from about 60 million to about 75 million, with again approximately a 25 percent rate of population increase. The rate of population increase did not grow steadily, as suggested in choice (D). Choices (B) and (C) cannot be supported by the information provided in the graph.

15. **The correct answer is (B).** The Pendleton Act established the merit system.

16. **The correct answer is (C).** Awarding a job to a candidate because of social standing is an example of the "Old Boy" network in action.

17. **The correct answer is (A).** The Hatch Act greatly decreased the effects of the spoils system.

18. **The correct answer is (A).** Jessica Dawn got her job as a result of the spoils system.

19. **The correct answer is (C).** By observation, we can see that there was probably less than a 50 percent increase in available funds over the eleven years. The only possible option among all the answers is choice (C).

20. **The correct answer is (C).** The 1981 bar shows that Florida and Texas combined had more funding than Pennsylvania and Texas combined. Add California, and you have the largest combination.

21. **The correct answer is (B).** Only New York showed a consistent decline over the eleven-year period.

22. **The correct answer is (D).** A caste system is a hierarchy of endogamous divisions, which means that people are required to choose marriage partners from the same division or caste. Caste membership is hereditary and permanent. It is "ascribed" in that it is determined by forces that an individual is unable to change.

Section 7: Science

1. **The correct answer is (D).** Since the common cold is a virus infection, interferon might be helpful in curing it.

2. **The correct answer is (C).** The like poles of different magnets repel each other, and the unlike poles attract each other.

3. **The correct answer is (D).** During a solar eclipse, the moon travels between the sun and the earth, blocking out the view of the sun totally or partially on at least some part of the earth.

4. **The correct answer is (A).** The more bacteria in the water, the less pure it is.

5. **The correct answer is (D).** Earthquakes are changes that occur suddenly after long periods of inactivity. All of the other changes are examples of regular or cyclic change.

6. **The correct answer is (D).** The bacteria flourished in a growth medium (food). In the same way, we can infer that incorrectly stored food provides a breeding ground for bacteria.

7. **The correct answer is (B).** Based on the map, Florida shows the highest incidence of thunderstorm activity, up to 100 thunderstorm days per year.

8. **The correct answer is (C).** Standing under a tall tree or telephone pole or on the top of a hill creates a natural lightning rod. In a forest, seek shelter under a thick growth of small trees. In open areas, go to a low place such as a ravine or valley.

9. **The correct answer is (D).** Evaporation is described by the following:

   Water (liquid) → Water (gas)

10. **The correct answer is (D).** Copper is the metal most widely used in electrical wiring because it is almost as good a conductor of electricity as silver and considerably less expensive.

11. **The correct answer is (B).** Internal fertilization is important in terrestrial forms, many of which provide no care for their young, while others provide extensive care for their young.

12. **The correct answer is (B).** Water pressure increases with depth. For every foot of depth in fresh water, the pressure increases 62.5 pounds, while in salt water, it increases 64 pounds for each foot of depth.

13. **The correct answer is (A).** According to the First Law of Thermodynamics, energy is neither created nor destroyed but is transformed from one type to another. When energy changes form, according to the Second Law of Thermodynamics, some energy is always dispersed or lost. Thus, the transformation is not 100 percent efficient.

14. **The correct answer is (D).** From the evidence given, it is most probable that all the land on the surface of the earth was once connected.

15. **The correct answer is (A).** The function of white cells is to remove unwanted organisms from the bloodstream and surrounding tissue. Of the choices given, only an infection indicates the presence of unwanted organisms. The white-cell count in this case would go up.

16. **The correct answer is (D).** To dehydrate something is to deprive it of water.

17. **The correct answer is (C).** Coal shows the highest bar for each year.

18. **The correct answer is (C).** Earth is the planet between Venus and Mars.

19. **The correct answer is (B).** Find the difference between the lowest and highest temperatures expected for the cities named for each traveler. Julie will experience temperatures ranging from a low of 33° in Atlanta to a high of 75° in Miami. This is a range of 42°, which is the widest range of the four scheduled trips.

20. **The correct answer is (B).** The telephone is the only one of the four electrical devices that uses an electromagnet, which produces a force field.

21. **The correct answer is (B).** White is the result of the fusion of many colors of the spectrum.

22. **The correct answer is (C).** The moon revolves around the earth over the same amount of time as it rotates. This means that the same side of the moon faces the earth at all times. The side away from us is referred to as the dark side of the moon.

ABOUT THE AUTHORS

Joan U. Levy, Ph.D.

B.A., City College of New York; M.S. in Guidance and Counseling, Fordham University; Ph.D. in Behavioral Science. Director of NJL College Preparation and Learning Center. Guidance Counselor and Educational Evaluator for the New York City Board of Education with more than twenty years of teaching and guidance experience.

Norman Levy, Ph.D.

B.E., City College of New York; M.S. in Operations Research, New York University; Ph.D. in Educational Administration. Executive Director of NJL College Preparation and Learning Center, a private tutoring, test preparation, and college guidance service; Coordinator of Mathematics, Hebrew Academy of Nassau County.

NOTES

NOTES

NOTES

NOTES

NOTES

NOTES

NOTES